Contents

4

Early model 4-door Peugeot 104

10 12   7,50   T28670

Peugeot 104 Owners Workshop Manual

R G O Hawes

Models covered

Peugeot 104, GL, ZL, SL, ZS and S;
954 cc and 1124 cc

Does not cover Rallye, ZR, GR or SR

ISBN 0 85696 401 8

Printed in England

HAYNES PUBLISHING GROUP
SPARKFORD YEOVIL SOMERSET ENGLAND
distributed in the USA by
HAYNES PUBLICATIONS INC
861 LAWRENCE DRIVE
NEWBURY PARK
CALIFORNIA 91320
USA

Acknowledgements

Thanks are due to Peugeot Automobiles UK Ltd for their ready assistance in the supply of technical information and for the use of certain illustrations. We are also indebted to Gliddons Garage, Williton, Somerset, for their help which was freely given. The Champion Sparking Plug Company supplied the illustrations showing the various spark plug conditions. The bodywork repair photographs used in this manual were provided by Holt Lloyd Ltd who supply 'Turtle Wax', 'Dupli-Color Holts' and other Holts range products. Castrol Limited supplied the lubrication data.

Thanks are also due to the hard working staff at Sparkford who have helped in the production of this manual. In particular, these are Alan Jackson and Tony Stedman who did the mechanical work and produces the photographs respectively; Stanley Randolph who planned the layout of each page and Matthew Minter the editor.

About this manual

Its aim

The aim of this manual is to help you get the best value from your car. It can do so in several ways. It can help you decide what work must be done (even should you choose to get it done by a garage), provide information on routine maintenance and servicing and give a logical course of action and diagnosis when random faults occur. However, it is hoped that you will use the manual by tackling the work yourself. On simpler jobs it may even be quicker than booking the car into a garage, and going there twice to leave and collect it. Perhaps most important, a lot of money can be saved by avoiding the costs the garage must charge to cover its labour and overheads.

The manual has drawings and descriptions to show the function of the various components so that their layout can be understood. Then the tasks are described and photographed in a step-by-step sequence so that even a novice can do the work.

Its arrangements

The manual is divided into eleven Chapters, each covering a logical sub-division of the vehicle. The Chapters are each divided into Sections, numbered with single figures, eg 5; and the Sections into paragraphs (or sub-sections), with decimal numbers following on from the Section they are in, eg 1, 5.2, 5.3 etc.

It is freely illustrated, especially in those parts where there is a detailed sequence of operations to be carried out. There are two forms of illustration; figures and photographs. The figures are numbered in sequence with decimal numbers, according to their position in the Chapter; eg Fig. 6.4 is the 4th drawing/illustration in Chapter 6. Photographs are numbered (either individually or in related groups) the same as the Section or sub-section of the text where the operation they show is described.

There is an alphabetical index at the back of the manual as well as a contents list at the front.

References to the 'left' or 'right' of the vehicle are in the sense of a person in the driver's seat facing forwards.

Unless otherwise stated, nuts and bolts are removed by turning anti-clockwise, and tightened by turning clockwise.

Whilst every care is taken to ensure that the information in this manual is correct, no liability can be accepted by the authors or publishers for loss, damage or injury caused by any errors in, or omissions from, the information given.

Introduction to the Peugeot 104

First produced in 1973, the Peugeot 104 is the baby of the Peugeot family, and the high manufacturing standards associated with the parent are evident in the car.

In its original form the 104 was a four-door, 954 cc engined saloon with a small boot. A folding rear seat was introduced to extend the scope of the boot, but eventually a tailgate version of the car set the pattern for all subsequent models. The range was extended in due course to include a larger engine of 1124 cc capacity, with an additional high performance version and a 2-door (plus tailgate) so-called 'Shortcut' body form.

The engine, which can also be found in the Renault 14, is mounted transversely to drive the front wheels through driveshafts. In addition to the usual complications this layout provides for the DIY man, other features exist which introduce further problems.

The engine has been inclined to the rear with the cylinder head adjacent to the bulkhead. Whilst this reduces the height of the the power unit, it also means that the normally simple process of renewing a cylinder head gasket requires the engine to be removed! The transmission assembly is mounted directly underneath the crankcase and incorporates the differential housing. The gearbox also serves as the sump, since the engine and transmission share the same lubricant. Both the engine and transmission housings are manufactured from an aluminium alloy.

In typical continental fashion removable wet cylinder liners are used. The aluminium cylinder head is located by dowels and is secured by through-bolts which also secure the overhead camshaft bearing pedestals. The bolts pass through the head and the top half of the cylinder block; the securing nuts are located in channels formed in the side of the cylinder block. The camshaft is chain-driven whereas the oil pump is gear-driven; both drives are taken from the nose of the crankshaft.

The distributor is mounted onto the cylinder head at the flywheel end of the engine, driven directly from the camshaft.

Drive from the engine is via a diaphragm clutch and transfer gears which are encased separately on the outside of the clutch housing.

The gearbox has synchromesh on all four forward gears and drive to the differential is direct, the crownwheel being a helical spur gear which is driven by the mainshaft pinion gear. The differential unit runs in shell bearings with thrust washers taking up the end play as opposed to the more conventional ball or roller bearing system.

The suspension is fully independent with MacPherson struts at the front, and trailing arms and coil springs at the rear. Double-acting hydraulic shock absorbers are employed front and rear to soak up the road shocks, and this they do in an efficient fashion.

The Peugeot 104 has proved to be a popular member of the Peugeot family, and given the right treatment it will undoubtedly prove as reliable and practical as its relatives. However it must be said that it does not readily endear itself to the DIY mechanic, due to its previously mentioned unconventional layout. Although most of the basic routine maintenance tasks can be easily undertaken, more serious problems will require careful thought and in some cases special tools. For this reason it is advisable to read through the Sections concerning the job at hand before starting to dismantle in order to assess the special requirements and points to watch out for.

Peugeot 104 ZS 'Shortcut'

General dimensions and weights

Overall length
GL . . . . 141 in (3.58 m)
S, SL . . . . 142 in (3.61 m)
ZS, ZL . . . . 132.5 in (3.37 m)

Overall width
All models . . . . 60 in (1.52 m)

Overall height (unladen)
GL, S, SL . . . . 55 in (1.4 m)
ZS, ZL . . . . 53.5 in (1.34 m)

Wheelbase
GL, S, SL . . . . 95 in (2.42 m)
ZS, ZL . . . . 88 in (2.23 m)

Kerb weight (unladen)
GL . . . . 1720 lb (780 kg)
S . . . . 1760 lb (800 kg)
SL . . . . 1764 lb (800 kg)
ZS . . . . 1719 lb (780 kg)
ZL . . . . 1631 lb (740 kg)

Turning circle
GL, S, SL . . . . 399.2 in (10.14 m)
ZS, ZL . . . . 370.1 in (9.4 m)

Maximum towing capacity
GL, ZS, ZL . . . . 1764 lb (800 kg)
S, SL . . . . 1989 lb (900 kg)

Maximum roof rack load
All models . . . . 110 lb (50 kg)

Buying spare parts and vehicle identification numbers

Buying spare parts

Spare parts are available from many sources, for example: Peugeot garages, other garages and accessory shops and motor factors. Our advice regarding spare parts is as follows:

Officially appointed Peugeot garage – This is the best source of parts which are peculiar to your car and otherwise not generally available (eg complete cylinder heads, internal gearbox components, badges, interior trim etc). It is also the only place at which you should buy parts if your car is still under warranty; non-Peugeot components may invalidate the warranty. To be sure of obtaining the correct parts it will always be necessary to give the storeman your car's engine and chassis number, and if possible, to take the old part along for positive identification. Remember that many parts are available on a factory exchange scheme – any parts returned should always be clean. It obviously makes good sense to go straight to the specialist on your car for this type of part for they are best equipped to supply you.

Other garages and accessory shops – These are often very good places to buy material and components needed for the maintenance of your car (eg oil filters, spark plugs, bulbs, fan belts, oils and grease, touch-up paint, filler paste etc). They also sell general accessories, usually have convenient opening hours, charge lower prices and can often be found not far from home.

Motor factors – Good factors will stock all of the more important components which wear out relatively quickly (eg clutch components, pistons, valves, exhaust systems, brake cylinders/pipes/hoses/seals/shoes and pads, etc). Motor factors will often provide new or reconditioned components on a part exchange basis – this can save a considerable amount of money.

Vehicle identification numbers

Modifications are a continuing and unpublished process in vehicle manufacture, quite apart from major model changes. Spare parts manuals and lists are compiled upon a numerical basis, the individual vehicle numbers being essential for correct identification of the component required.

Although many individual parts, and in some cases, sub-assemblies, fit a number of different models it is dangerous to assume that, just because they look the same, they are the same. Differences are not always easy to detect except by serial, part or identity numbers. Make sure, therefore, that the appropriate numerical details for the model or sub-assembly are known and quoted when a spare part is ordered.

The vehicle type and serial number are stamped on the maker's plate which is located just behind the right front suspension mounting in the engine compartment (photo).

The bodyshell number is stamped on the right front suspension mounting in the engine compartment.

The engine serial number is stamped on the block flange adjacent to the timing window (photo).

Individual components such as the starter motor, alternator, carburettor and so on also have numerical identities and these details will be found stamped on the components themselves.

The vehicle type and serial number are stamped on this plate

The engine serial number

Tools and working facilities

Introduction

A selection of good tools is a fundamental requirement for anyone contemplating the maintenance and repair of a motor vehicle. For the owner who does not possess any, their purchase will prove a considerable expense, offsetting some of the savings made by doing-it-yourself. However, provided that the tools purchased are of good quality, they will last for many years and prove an extremely worthwhile investment.

To help the average owner to decide which tools are needed to carry out the various tasks detailed in this manual, we have compiled three lists of tools under the following headings: *Maintenance and minor repair*, *Repair and overhaul*, and *Special*. The newcomer to practical mechanics should start off with the *Maintenance and minor repair* tool kit and confine himself to the simpler jobs around the vehicle. Then, as his confidence and experience grows, he can undertake more difficult tasks, buying extra tools as, and when, they are needed. In this way, a *Maintenance and minor repair* tool kit can be built-up into a *Repair and overhaul* tool kit over a considerable period of time without any major cash outlays. The experienced do-it-yourselfer will have a tool kit good enough for most repair and overhaul procedures and will add tools from the *Special* category when he feels the expense is justified by the amount of use to which these tools will be put.

It is obviously not possible to cover the subject of tools fully here. For those who wish to learn more about tools and their use there is a book entitled *How to Choose and Use Car Tools* available from the publishers of this manual.

Maintenance and minor repair tool kit

The tools given in this list should be considered as a minimum requirement if routine maintenance, servicing and minor repair operations are to be undertaken. We recommend the purchase of combination spanners (ring one end, open-ended the other); although more expensive than open-ended ones, they do give the advantages of both types of spanner.

Combination spanners – 10, 11, 12, 13, 14, 17 mm
Adjustable spanner – 9 inch
Engine sump/gearbox/rear axle drain plug key
Spark plug spanner (with rubber insert)
Spark plug gap adjustment tool
Set of feeler gauges
Brake adjuster spanner
Brake bleed nipple spanner
Screwdriver – 4 in long x $\frac{1}{4}$ in dia (flat blade)
Screwdriver – 4 in long x $\frac{1}{4}$ in dia (cross blade)
Combination pliers – 6 inch
Hacksaw (junior)
Tyre pump
Tyre pressure gauge
Grease gun
Oil can
Fine emery cloth (1 sheet)
Wire brush (small)
Funnel (medium size)

Repair and overhaul tool kit

These tools are virtually essential for anyone undertaking any major repairs to a motor vehicle, and are additional to those given in the *Maintenance and minor repair* list. Included in this list is a comprehensive set of sockets. Although these are expensive they will be found invaluable as they are so versatile – particularly if various drives are included in the set. We recommend the $\frac{1}{2}$ in square-drive type, as this can be used with most proprietary torque wrenches. If you cannot afford a socket set, even bought piecemeal, then inexpensive tubular box spanners are a useful alternative.

The tools in this list will occasionally need to be supplemented by tools from the *Special* list.

Sockets (or box spanners) to cover range in previous list
Reversible ratchet drive (for use with sockets)
Extension piece, 10 inch (for use with sockets)
Universal joint (for use with sockets)
Torque wrench (for use with sockets)
'Mole' wrench – 8 inch
Ball pein hammer
Soft-faced hammer, plastic or rubber
Screwdriver – 6 in long x $\frac{5}{16}$ in dia (flat blade)
Screwdriver – 2 in long x $\frac{5}{16}$ in square (flat blade)
Screwdriver – 1$\frac{1}{2}$ in long x $\frac{1}{4}$ in dia (cross blade)
Screwdriver – 3 in long x $\frac{1}{8}$ in dia (electricians)
Pliers – electricians side cutters
Pliers – needle nosed
Pliers – circlip (internal and external)
Cold chisel – $\frac{1}{2}$ inch
Scriber
Scraper
Centre punch
Pin punch
Hacksaw
Valve grinding tool
Steel rule/straight-edge
Allen keys
Selection of files
Wire brush (large)
Axle-stands
Jack (strong scissor or hydraulic type)

Special tools

The tools in this list are those which are not used regularly, are expensive to buy, or which need to be used in accordance with their manufacturers' instructions. Unless relatively difficult mechanical jobs are undertaken frequently, it will not be economical to buy many of these tools. Where this is the case, you could consider clubbing together with friends (or joining a motorists' club) to make a joint purchase, or borrowing the tools against a deposit from a local garage or tool hire specialist.

The following list contains only those tools and instruments freely available to the public, and not those special tools produced by the vehicle manufacturer specifically for its dealer network. You will find occasional references to these manufacturers' special tools in the text of this manual. Generally, an alternative method of doing the job without the vehicle manufacturer's special tool is given. However, sometimes, there is no alternative to using them. Where this is the case and the relevant tool cannot be bought or borrowed, you will have to entrust the work to a franchised garage.

Valve spring compressor
Piston ring compressor
Balljoint separator
Universal hub/bearing puller
Impact screwdriver
Micrometer and/or vernier gauge
Dial gauge
Stroboscopic timing light
Dwell angle meter/tachometer
Universal electrical multi-meter
Cylinder compression gauge
Lifting tackle (photo)
Trolley jack
Light with extension lead

Buying tools

For practically all tools, a tool factor is the best source since he will have a very comprehensive range compared with the average garage or accessory shop. Having said that, accessory shops often offer excellent quality tools at discount prices, so it pays to shop around.

Remember, you don't have to buy the most expensive items on the shelf, but it is always advisable to steer clear of the very cheap tools. There are plenty of good tools around at reasonable prices, so ask the proprietor or manager of the shop for advice before making a purchase.

Care and maintenance of tools

Having purchased a reasonable tool kit, it is necessary to keep the tools in a clean serviceable condition. After use, always wipe off any dirt, grease and metal particles using a clean, dry cloth, before putting the tools away. Never leave them lying around after they have been used. A simple tool rack on the garage or workshop wall, for items such as screwdrivers and pliers is a good idea. Store all normal spanners and sockets in a metal box. Any measuring instruments, gauges, meters, etc, must be carefully stored where they cannot be damaged or become rusty.

Take a little care when tools are used. Hammer heads inevitably become marked and screwdrivers lose the keen edge on their blades from time to time. A little timely attention with emery cloth or a file will soon restore items like this to a good serviceable finish.

Working facilities

Not to be forgotten when discussing tools, is the workshop itself. If anything more than routine maintenance is to be carried out, some form of suitable working area becomes essential.

It is appreciated that many an owner mechanic is forced by circumstances to remove an engine or similar item, without the benefit of a garage or workshop. Having done this, any repairs should always be done under the cover of a roof.

Wherever possible, any dismantling should be done on a clean, flat workbench or table at a suitable working height.

Any workbench needs a vice: one with a jaw opening of 4 in (100 mm) is suitable for most jobs. As mentioned previously, some clean dry storage space is also required for tools, as well as for lubricants, cleaning fluids, touch-up paints and so on which become necessary.

Another item which may be required, and which has a much more general usage, is an electric drill with a chuck capacity of at least $\frac{5}{16}$ in (8 mm). This, together with a good range of twist drills, is virtually essential for fitting accessories such as mirrors and reversing lights.

Last, but not least, always keep a supply of old newspapers and clean, lint-free rags available, and try to keep any working area as clean as possible.

Spanner jaw gap comparison table

Jaw gap (in)	Spanner size
0·250	$\frac{1}{4}$ in AF
0·276	7 mm
0·313	$\frac{5}{16}$ in AF
0·315	8 mm
0·344	$\frac{11}{32}$ in AF; $\frac{1}{8}$ in Whitworth
0·354	9 mm
0·375	$\frac{3}{8}$ in AF
0·394	10 mm
0·433	11 mm
0·438	$\frac{7}{16}$ in AF
0·445	$\frac{3}{16}$ in Whitworth; $\frac{1}{4}$ in BSF
0·472	12 mm
0·500	$\frac{1}{2}$ in AF
0·512	13 mm
0·525	$\frac{1}{4}$ in Whitworth; $\frac{5}{16}$ in BSF
0·551	14 mm
0·563	$\frac{9}{16}$ in AF
0·591	15 mm
0·600	$\frac{5}{16}$ in Whitworth; $\frac{3}{8}$ in BSF
0·625	$\frac{5}{8}$ in AF
0·630	16 mm
0·669	17 mm
0·686	$\frac{11}{16}$ in AF
0·709	18 mm
0·710	$\frac{3}{8}$ in Whitworth; $\frac{7}{16}$ in BSF
0·748	19 mm
0·750	$\frac{3}{4}$ in AF
0·813	$\frac{13}{16}$ in AF
0·820	$\frac{7}{16}$ in Whitworth; $\frac{1}{2}$ in BSF
0·866	22 mm
0·875	$\frac{7}{8}$ in AF
0·920	$\frac{1}{2}$ in Whitworth; $\frac{9}{16}$ in BSF
0·938	$\frac{15}{16}$ in AF
0·945	24 mm
1·000	1 in AF
1·010	$\frac{9}{16}$ in Whitworth; $\frac{5}{8}$ in BSF
1·024	26 mm
1·063	$1\frac{1}{16}$ in AF; 27 mm
1·100	$\frac{5}{8}$ in Whitworth; $\frac{11}{16}$ in BSF
1·125	$1\frac{1}{8}$ in AF
1·181	30 mm
1·200	$\frac{11}{16}$ in Whitworth; $\frac{3}{4}$ in BSF
1·250	$1\frac{1}{4}$ in AF
1·260	32 mm
1·300	$\frac{3}{4}$ in Whitworth; $\frac{7}{8}$ in BSF
1·313	$1\frac{5}{16}$ in AF
1·390	$\frac{13}{16}$ in Whitworth; $\frac{15}{16}$ in BSF
1·417	36 mm
1·438	$1\frac{7}{16}$ in AF
1·480	$\frac{7}{8}$ in Whitworth; 1 in BSF
1·500	$1\frac{1}{2}$ in AF
1·575	40 mm; $\frac{15}{16}$ in Whitworth
1·614	41 mm
1·625	$1\frac{5}{8}$ in AF
1·670	1 in Whitworth; $1\frac{1}{8}$ in BSF
1·688	$1\frac{11}{16}$ in AF
1·811	46 mm
1·813	$1\frac{13}{16}$ in AF
1·860	$1\frac{1}{8}$ in Whitworth; $1\frac{1}{4}$ in BSF
1·875	$1\frac{7}{8}$ in AF
1·969	50 mm
2·000	2 in AF
2·050	$1\frac{1}{4}$ in Whitworth; $1\frac{3}{8}$ in BSF
2·165	55 mm
2·362	60 mm

A Haltrac hoist and gantry in use during a typical engine removal sequence

Jacking and towing

Jacking points

Four jacking points are provided for use with the jack supplied with the car, one in front of each rear wheel and one behind each front wheel. The jack and its handle are located in stowages in the luggage area.

To change a wheel in an emergency, park the vehicle on a firm level surface (if possible), apply the handbrake, engage first or reverse gear and chock the wheel diagonally opposite the one being changed. Switch on the hazard warning lights if necessary.

Remove the hub cap from the wheel to be changed and slacken the three hub nuts. Insert the jack spigot into the jacking point and open up the jack, ensuring that it is sitting squarely on the ground. Raise the car until the wheel is clear of the ground. Remove the hub nuts and the wheel. Fit the spare wheel and nuts but do not tighten them completely. Lower the car to the ground, then tighten the hub nuts, refit the hubcap and remove the jack. Check the tyre pressure and adjust if required.

Never get under the car when it is supported only by the jack.

Support it on blocks, axle stands or a ramp if you want to work underneath.

Towing and being towed

Front and rear anchorage points are provided for securing the car during transportation on a car transporter, boat, train and so on. These points can also be used for towing the car or for towing another in an emergency. For permanent towing requirements a tow-bar is necessary, properly attached to the vehicle.

If your car is being towed with the front wheels on the ground *caution is necessary* due to the transmission lubrication problem. The gearbox and final drive are pressure lubricated by the engine oil system and *if the engine is not running, no oil will be fed to the transmission.* Arrange for a front suspended tow, if possible, to prevent damage to the final drive. In exceptional circumstances the car may be towed with the front wheels on the ground provided that a speed of 30 mph (50 kph) and a distance of 18 miles (30 km) are not exceeded.

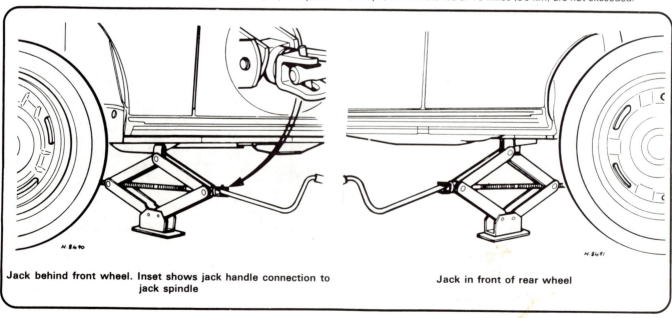

Jack behind front wheel. Inset shows jack handle connection to jack spindle

Jack in front of rear wheel

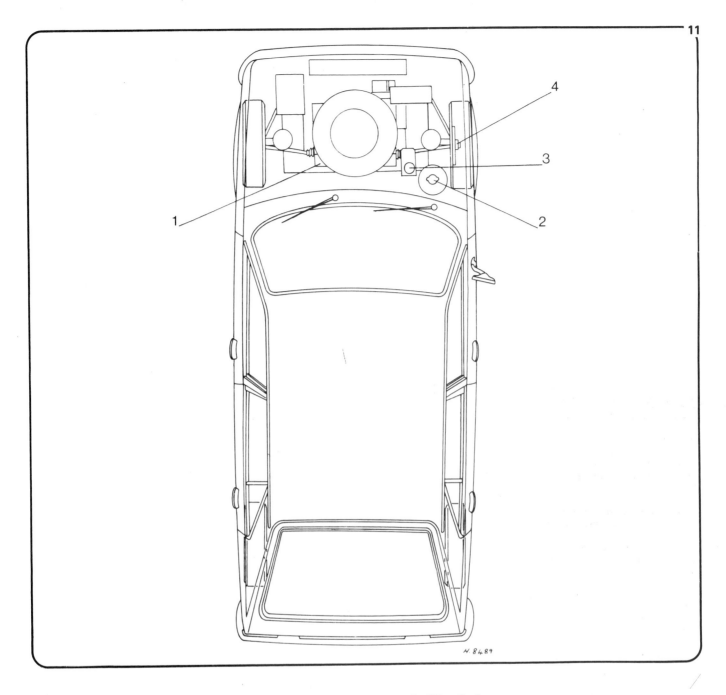

H.8489

Recommended lubricants and fluids

Component or system	Lubricant type or specification	Castrol product
Engine/transmission (1)	Multigrade engine oil 10W/40	Castrol GTX
Cooling system (2)	Peugeot antifreeze PN 9730 43 or 9730 70 (see Chapter 2)	Castrol Antifreeze
Hydraulic system (3)	Hydraulic fluid to SAE J1703	Castrol Girling Universal Brake and Clutch Fluid
Wheel bearings (4)	General purpose grease	Castrol LM Grease
Chassis – general	General purpose grease	Castrol LM Grease
Hinges, locks, pivots etc	Engine oil	Castrol GTX

With regard to lubrication the above are general recommendations. Lubrication requirements vary from territory to territory and also with vehicle usage – consult the operator's handbook supplied with your car.

Safety First!

Professional motor mechanics are trained in safe working procedures. However enthusiastic you may be about getting on with the job in hand, do take the time to ensure that your safety is not put at risk. A moment's lack of attention can result in an accident, as can failure to observe certain elementary precautions.

There will always be new ways of having accidents, and the following points do not pretend to be a comprehensive list of all dangers; they are intended rather to make you aware of the risks and to encourage a safety-conscious approach to all work you carry out on your vehicle.

Essential DO's and DON'Ts

DON'T rely on a single jack when working underneath the vehicle. Always use reliable additional means of support, such as axle stands, securely placed under a part of the vehicle that you know will not give way.

DON'T attempt to loosen or tighten high-torque nuts (e.g. wheel hub nuts) while the vehicle is on a jack; it may be pulled off.

DON'T start the engine without first ascertaining that the transmission is in neutral (or 'Park' where applicable) and the parking brake applied.

DON'T suddenly remove the filler cap from a hot cooling system — cover it with a cloth and release the pressure gradually first, or you may get scalded by escaping coolant.

DON'T attempt to drain oil until you are sure it has cooled sufficiently to avoid scalding you.

DON'T grasp any part of the engine, exhaust or catalytic converter without first ascertaining that it is sufficiently cool to avoid burning you.

DON'T syphon toxic liquids such as fuel, brake fluid or antifreeze by mouth, or allow them to remain on your skin.

DON'T inhale brake lining dust — it is injurious to health.

DON'T allow any spilt oil or grease to remain on the floor — wipe it up straight away, before someone slips on it.

DON'T use ill-fitting spanners or other tools which may slip and cause injury.

DON'T attempt to lift a heavy component which may be beyond your capability — get assistance.

DON'T rush to finish a job, or take unverified short cuts.

DON'T allow children or animals in or around an unattended vehicle.

DO wear eye protection when using power tools such as drill, sander, bench grinder etc, and when working under the vehicle.

DO use a barrier cream on your hands prior to undertaking dirty jobs — it will protect your skin from infection as well as making the dirt easier to remove afterwards; but make sure your hands aren't left slippery.

DO keep loose clothing (cuffs, tie etc) and long hair well out of the way of moving mechanical parts.

DO remove rings, wristwatch etc, before working on the vehicle — especially the electrical system.

DO ensure that any lifting tackle used has a safe working load rating adequate for the job.

DO keep your work area tidy — it is only too easy to fall over articles left lying around.

DO get someone to check periodically that all is well, when working alone on the vehicle.

DO carry out work in a logical sequence and check that everything is correctly assembled and tightened afterwards.

DO remember that your vehicle's safety affects that of yourself and others. If in doubt on any point, get specialist advice.

IF, in spite of following these precautions, you are unfortunate enough to injure yourself, seek medical attention as soon as possible.

Fire

Remember at all times that petrol (gasoline) is highly flammable. Never smoke, or have any kind of naked flame around, when working on the vehicle. But the risk does not end there — a spark caused by an electrical short-circuit, by two metal surfaces contacting each other, or even by static electricity built up in your body under certain conditions, can ignite petrol vapour, which in a confined space is highly explosive.

Always disconnect the battery earth (ground) terminal before working on any part of the fuel system, and never risk spilling fuel on to a hot engine or exhaust.

It is recommended that a fire extinguisher of a type suitable for fuel and electrical fires is kept handy in the garage or workplace at all times. Never try to extinguish a fuel or electrical fire with water.

Fumes

Certain fumes are highly toxic and can quickly cause unconsciousness and even death if inhaled to any extent. Petrol (gasoline) vapour comes into this category, as do the vapours from certain solvents such as trichloroethylene. Any draining or pouring of such volatile fluids should be done in a well ventilated area.

When using cleaning fluids and solvents, read the instructions carefully. Never use materials from unmarked containers — they may give off poisonous vapours.

Never run the engine of a motor vehicle in an enclosed space such as a garage. Exhaust fumes contain carbon monoxide which is extremely poisonous; if you need to run the engine, always do so in the open air or at least have the rear of the vehicle outside the workplace.

If you are fortunate enough to have the use of an inspection pit, never drain or pour petrol, and never run the engine, while the vehicle is standing over it; the fumes, being heavier than air, will concentrate in the pit with possibly lethal results.

The battery

Never cause a spark, or allow a naked light, near the vehicle's battery. It will normally be giving off a certain amount of hydrogen gas, which is highly explosive.

Always disconnect the battery earth (ground) terminal before working on the fuel or electrical systems.

If possible, loosen the filler plugs or cover when charging the battery from an external source. Do not charge at an excessive rate or the battery may burst.

Take care when topping up and when carrying the battery. The acid electrolyte, even when diluted, is very corrosive and should not be allowed to contact the eyes or skin.

If you ever need to prepare electrolyte yourself, always add the acid slowly to the water, and never the other way round. Protect against splashes by wearing rubber gloves and goggles.

Mains electricity

When using an electric power tool, inspection light etc which works from the mains, always ensure that the appliance is correctly connected to its plug and that, where necessary, it is properly earthed (grounded). Do not use such appliances in damp conditions and, again, beware of creating a spark or applying excessive heat in the vicinity of fuel or fuel vapour.

Ignition HT voltage

A severe electric shock can result from touching certain parts of the ignition system, such as the HT leads, when the engine is running or being cranked, particularly if components are damp or the insulation is defective. Where an electronic ignition system is fitted, the HT voltage is much higher and could prove fatal.

Routine maintenance

Maintenance is essential for ensuring safety and desirable for the purpose of getting the best in terms of performance and economy from the car. Over the years the need for periodic lubrication – oiling and greasing – has been drastically reduced if not totally eliminated. This has unfortunately tended to lead some owners to think that because no such action is required the components either no longer exist or will last for ever. This is a serious delusion. If anything, there are now more places, particularly in the steering and suspension, where joints and pivots are fitted. Although you do not grease them any more you still have to look at them – and look at them just as often as you may previously have had to grease them. It follows therefore that the largest initial element of maintenance is visual examination. This may lead to repairs or renewal.

Every 250 miles (400 km), or weekly, whichever comes first

Check coolant level
Check engine oil level (photos)
Check battery electrolyte level
Check tyre pressures and examine for minimum tread depth of one mm over three quarters of the tread width. Look for damage and blisters
Check operation of all lights, with the help of an assistant if necessary
Check windscreen washer fluid level
Check brake reservoir fluid level, even where a low level warning

Removing the oil dipstick

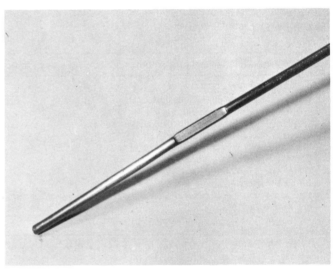

The high and low levels are indicated by the extremities of the flat on the dipstick. Some models have notches instead of the flat

Topping up engine oil

Checking a tyre pressure

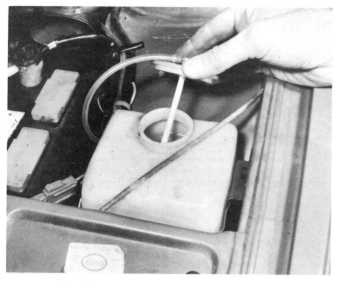

Checking the windscreen washer fluid level

Checking the brake fluid level

switch is fitted – the switch might not be working!
Check roadwheel nuts for tightness and visually check shock absorbers for signs of fluid leakage

Every 5000 miles (7500 km) or six months, whichever comes first

Carry out the 250 miles (400 km) or weekly servicing, and in addition:
   Change the engine oil (includes gearbox and differential)
   Grease the steering rack plunger (early models)
   Check operation of brakes. Inspect all pipes and unions for leaks
   Check thickness of the front brake pads
   Lubricate bodywork hinges and locks with oil
   Clean and reset spark plugs
   Check operation of horn and windscreen wipers
   Check the specific gravity of the battery electrolyte
   Check that the electric cooling fan and the rear window demister are working correctly

Every 10 000 miles (15 000 km) or twelve months, whichever comes first

Carry out the 5000 mile (7500 km) or six-monthly servicing, except for cleaning the spark plugs, and in addition:
   Renew the engine oil filter cartridge
   Renew the spark plugs
   Clean and reset the contact breaker gap. Check the dwell angle and static advance
   Check the tension and condition of the alternator drivebelt

Check the clutch control free play
Examine the condition of all rubber gaiters on the driveshafts and the steering system
Check the condition of the steering column flexible joint
Examine all hoses and housings for signs of fluid leaks
Check seat belt retaining bolts for tightness and belts for fraying
Check the rear brake shoes for wear and contamination, and clean out the brake dust

Every 20 000 miles (30 000 km) or two years, whichever comes first

Carry out the 10 000 miles (15 000 km) or twelve-monthly servicing, and in addition:
   Renew the air filter element
   Check, and if necessary adjust, the handbrake
   Clean out the carburettor float chamber and inlet filter
   Clean out the fuel pump and filter
   Lubricate the distributor

Every 30 000 miles (45 000 km) or three years, whichever comes first

Carry out the 10 000 miles (15 000 km) or twelve-monthly servicing, and in addition:
   Examine the driveshafts, track rods and all balljoints for play
   Drain the brake hydraulic system and replenish with new fluid

Chapter 1 Engine

Contents

Specifications

General

Engine type	Four-cylinder, in-line, ohc, water cooled, transverse mounting		
Engine type reference	**XV3** **(108)**	**XW3** **(109)**	**XW3S** **(121)**
Cubic capacity	954 cc	1124 cc	1124 cc
Bore	70 mm	72 mm	72 mm
Stroke	62 mm	69 mm	69 mm
Compression ratio	8.8:1	9.2:1	9.2:1
Oil capacity:			
Maximum	7 pints (4 litres)	8 pints (4.5 litres)	8 pints (4.5 litres)
Minimum	5.3 pints (3 litres)	6.2 pints (3.5 litres)	6.2 pints (3.5 litres)
Oil pressure (minimum), new engine with oil at 90°C (194°F)	1 bar (14.5 lbf/in^2) at 1000 rpm		
	2.5 bars (36.25 lbf/in^2) at 2500 rpm		
	3 bars (43.5 lbf/in^2) at 4000 rpm		
Firing order	1 – 3 – 4 – 2 (No 1 cylinder at flywheel end)		

Valves and valve gear

Clearance (cold):	
Inlet	0.004 in (0.10 mm)
Exhaust	0.010 in (0.25 mm)
Seat angle (inclusive):	
Inlet	120°
Exhaust	90°
Stem diameter	0.315 in (8 mm)
Head diameter:	
Inlet	1.370 in (34.8 mm)
Exhaust	1.094 in (27.8 mm)
Valve spring height (36 lbf (16 kgf) load)	1.57 in (39.8 mm)
Camshaft	Overhead, running in five bearings

Pistons
Type . . . . Aluminium alloy, bulged skirt and oval cross-section. Two compression rings and one oil control ring. Gudgeon pin free in piston, interference fit in connecting rod
Running clearance . . . . 0.003 to 0.004 in (0.07 to 0.09 mm)

Liners
Type . . . . Cast iron, wet liners, classified in three categories according to mean bore diameter

Crankshaft
Number of bearings . . . . Five
Endfloat . . . . 0.003 in (0.07 mm) to 0.011 in (0.27 mm)
Thrust washer thicknesses available . . . . 0.091 in (2.3 mm)
0.094 in (2.4 mm)
0.096 in (2.45 mm)
0.098 in (2.5 mm)

Intermediate gear case and clutch housing
Flatness of mating faces . . . . 0.002 in (0.05 mm) maximum distortion between any two points 3.937 in (100 mm) apart; 0.004 in (0.10 mm) maximum between any two points more than 3.937 in (100 mm) apart

Torque wrench settings

	lbf ft	kgf m
Cylinder head bolts (threads oiled):		
Pre 10/9 grade bolts		
Stage 1	29	4
Stage 2	43	6
10/9 grade bolts		
Stage 1	29	4
Stage 2	49	6.75
Oil drain plug (new washer)	20	2.75
Cylinder block coolant drain plug (new washer)	25	3.5
Engine mounting to cylinder block nuts	25	3.5
Lower limiter stop bolt	25	3.5
Big-end cap nuts	27	3.75
Main bearing bolts:		
Stage 1	27	3.75
Stage 2	38	5.25
Crankcase flange bolts (11)	10	1.4
Timing chain tensioner bolts (2)	4.3	0.6
Oil pump Allen screws (4)	4.3	0.8
Camshaft sprocket bolt	54	7.5
Sump oil strainer bolts (4)	7.25	1
Sump cover bolts (12)	7.25	1
Sump protector bolts (3)	13	1.75
Engine/gearbox bolts (13) and nuts (3)	10	1.4
Engine mounting crossbar bolts (4)	13	1.75
Timing chain cover bolts (18)	4.3	0.6
Crankshaft pulley nut	65	9
Water pump bolts (3)	10	1.4
Carburettor nuts (2)	10	1.4
Flywheel bolts (6) (with thread locking compound)	50	6.8
Clutch assembly to flywheel Allen screws (6)	7.25	1
Clutch housing bolts	13	1.75
Starter motor bolts (except those in clutch housing)	9	1.25
Rocker cover bolts (2) and nut	4.3	0.6
Alternator, bolts in bracket (2)	13	1.75
Alternator pivot bolt (1)	33	4.5
Transfer gear housing cover plate bolts (12)	8	1.1

1 General description

The Peugeot 104 has either a 954 cc or a 1124 cc engine fitted, the two engines being almost identical except for different bore and stroke dimensions with correspondingly different carburettors, distributors and so on. The engine, which has four cylinders and an overhead camshaft, is mounted transversely driving the front wheels and it is inclined to the rear at an angle of 72°.

The manual gearbox is also mounted transversely in line with the engine, and the final drive to the roadwheels is via the differential unit which is integral with the gearbox. Drive from the engine to the transmission is by means of transfer gears which are separately encased in the clutch housing.

The crankcase, cylinder head, gearcase and clutch housing are all

manufactured from aluminium alloy. Removable wet cylinder liners are fitted; the aluminium pistons each have two compression rings and one oil control ring. The valves are operated by the single overhead camshaft and rocker arms. The camshaft drives the distributor at the flywheel end, and the timing sprocket, located at the other end of the camshaft, incorporates a separate eccentric lobe which actuates the fuel pump. The timing chain is driven from the crankshaft sprocket. Next to the timing chain sprocket is the gear wheel which drives the oil pump. This is mounted low down against the crankcase face and is enclosed in the timing chain cover.

The crankshaft runs in five shell main bearings and the endfloat is adjustable via a pair of semi-circular thrust washers. Somewhat inconveniently, the lower half crankcase interconnects the engine with the transmission unit.

The engine and transmission units share the same mountings. On early models there are two on each side, one at the front and one at the rear, but later models have two mountings on the left and only one on the right side on the timing case.

Special notes

Because of the unconventional layout of the engine and transmission systems, extra care and attention must be taken during the maintenance and overhaul procedures which, in many instances, differ considerably from the more conventional systems.

Read through the various Sections concerned to analyse the instructions so that any snags or possible difficulties can be noted in advance. Because the sub-assembly casings are manufactured from aluminium alloy, it is of utmost importance that all fastenings are tightened to the specified torque settings, which are contained in Specifications.

Very few jobs can be undertaken without removal of the engine and transmission unit; but in addition when they are extracted the design in many instances demands that other sub-assemblies, not directly associated with the offending item, will have to be removed to gain access to the part concerned.

In most instances, special tools will not be required and the majority of procedures are not particularly difficult, but extra care and attention must be exercised to ensure a successful conclusion to the particular task at hand.

2 Major operations possible with engine installed

Very little work of a major nature can be done on this engine with it installed in the car. Even adjusting the valve clearances requires the exhaust valves to be set from underneath the car. It might be possible to remove the timing chain cover on the right side of the engine but even then the working space is so limited it would probably justify removing the engine – especially on later engines which have one engine mounting on the timing cover. To remove the cover it would need the engine to be lifted off its mounting that side.

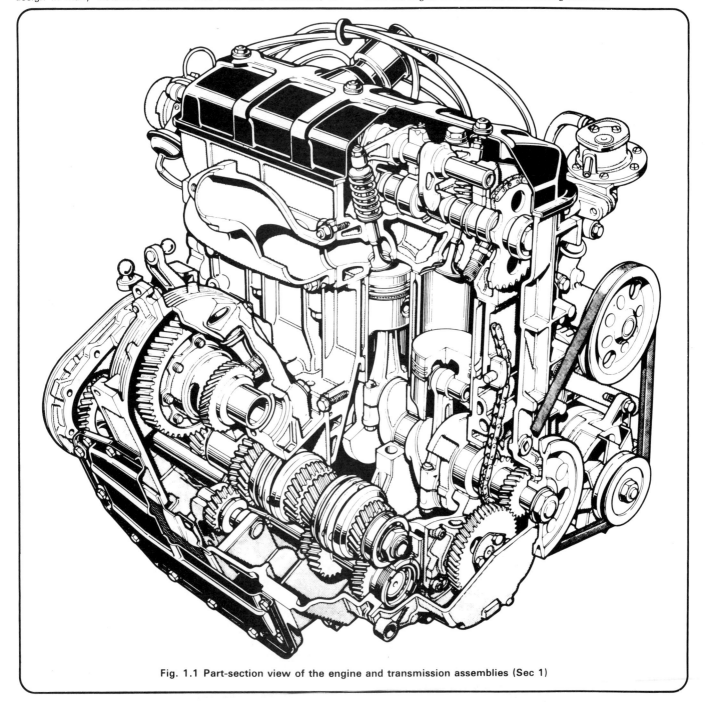

Fig. 1.1 Part-section view of the engine and transmission assemblies (Sec 1)

3 Major operations requiring engine removal

1   It follows from the previous Section that the engine must be removed for all major work to be done including the following:

(a) *Removal and refitting of the transfer gears*
(b) *Removal and refitting of the clutch unit*
(c) *Removal and refitting of the camshaft assembly*
(d) *Removal and refitting of the cylinder head*
(e) *Removal and refitting of pistons, connecting rods and bearing shells*
(f) *Removal and refitting of crankshaft and bearing shells*
(g) *Removal and refitting of the transmission and differential unit*

4 Engine removal

1   The engine and transmission units must be removed as a complete assembly and cannot be separated until removed. Although the combined weight of the two components is not great, certain operations are awkward and care must be taken not to damage surrounding components in the engine compartment, particularly during removal. It therefore pays to have an assistant on hand whenever possible. On average, removal may be expected to take $1\frac{1}{2}$ to 2 hours.
2   Position the car with the engine under the lifting tackle location and check that there is sufficient room around the car to work, particularly at the rear where space should be allowed for the body to be wheeled back, after raising the engine.
3   Chock the rear wheels.
4   Raise and support the bonnet. Mark the position of the bonnet hinge on the panel. Support the bonnet and unscrew the retaining bolts. Lift it clear and remove to a safe place.
5   Disconnect the battery leads; lift the battery clear and place safely aside.
6   Remove the spare wheel and its support bracket.
7   Remove the battery drip tray and undo and remove the battery support extension. Remove the horn.
8   Disconnect the air cleaner unit from the carburettor and detach the connecting hoses from the engine. Remove the air cleaner unit and hoses. The hose retaining clips can be used again if in good condition, otherwise renew them on reassembly.
9   Detach the HT leads, remove the distributor cap, and withdraw the plastic cover and rotor arm.
10 Disconnect the fuel pump inlet hose from the pump.
11 Drain the cooling system (see Chapter 2).
12 Drain the engine/transmission oil.
13 Disconnect the brake servo unit vacuum pipe from the cylinder head, if your car has servo-assisted brakes.
14 Disconnect the radiator coolant hoses from the cylinder head at the water pump and at the cylinder head outlet.
15 Disconnect the heater hoses from the water pump and the cylinder head outlet; also the preheat hose from the cowling.
16 Take careful note of their respective positions and disconnect the following wire connectors:

(a) *Alternator*
(b) *Coolant temperature sender unit*
(c) *Oil pressure switch*
(d) *Coil*
(e) *Radiator temperature sender unit (to electric fan)*
(f) *Starter solenoid wires*
(g) *Battery earth wire from clutch housing stud*

17 Disconnect the expansion tank hoses (keeping the hoses connected to the tank) and remove the expansion tank.
18 Remove the radiator fan assembly. If it is not intended to remove the radiator, position a piece of hardboard to protect the radiator when removing the engine (photo).
19 Disconnect the accelerator and choke cables from the carburettor.
20 Disconnect the clutch cable.
21 Working underneath the car, unscrew the retaining nuts from the flange and detach the exhaust downpipe from the manifold (photo).
22 Disconnect the exhaust pipe stay bracket and remove it (photo).
23 Remove the preheat cowling from the exhaust manifold.
24 Unscrew the speedometer outer cable connector just to the rear and above the steering rack, and separate the cable connection.

25 Unscrew the selector quadrant retaining bolt from the steering box.
26 Disconnect the gearchange links. The lower one, with two ball-joints, is disconnected by levering a balljoint off its ball. The other is disconnected by removing the nut, washer and spring washer (photos).
27 Unscrew and remove the engine mounting retaining nuts and washers, and the lower limiting stop bolt (photos).
28 Check that all engine or transmission attachments are disconnected, and raise the front of the car so that the wheels hang free.
29 Connect the lifting tackle to the engine hoist brackets and raise the unit two or three inches. When lifting, take great care not to damage any component, especially when the assembly swings free.
30 Push the assembly hard over to the right-hand side of the engine bay and, at the same time, disengage the left-hand driveshaft from the differential. Be careful not to damage the seal in the gearcase. When the driveshaft is free, lower it onto the sub-frame, taking care that the seal bearing face is not damaged (photo).
31 Carefully push the engine assembly hard over to the left-hand side, again taking care not to damage anything and, in a similar fashion, disengage the right-hand driveshaft (photo).
32 Raise the engine assembly clear of the car (photo) and remove the cylinder block coolant drain plug (under the block near the timing chain cover) to drain any residual coolant. Park the engine assembly where it can be thoroughly cleaned before doing any further work on it, as described in the next Section.

5 Engine dismantling – general

1   A good size clean work area will be required, preferably on a bench. Before moving the engine/transmission unit to the area reserved for dismantling, clean the outside of the various components as detailed below.
2   During the dismantling process, the greatest care should be taken to keep the exposed parts free from dirt. As an aid to achieving this thoroughly clean down the outside of the engine/transmission unit, first removing all traces of oil and congealed dirt.
3   A good grease solvent will make the job much easier, for, after the solvent has been applied and allowed to stand for a time, a vigorous jet of water will wash off the solvent and grease with it. If the dirt is thick and deeply embedded, work the solvent into it with a strong stiff brush.
4   Finally, wipe down the exterior of the engine/transmission unit with a rag and only then, when it is quite clean, should the dismantling process begin. As the engine is stripped, clean each part in a bath of paraffin.
5   Never immerse parts with oilways in paraffin (eg crankshaft and rocker shaft). To clean these parts, wipe down carefully with a petrol dampened rag. Oilways can be cleaned out with wire. If an air-line is available, all parts can be blown dry and the oilways blown through as an added precaution.
6   Re-use of old gaskets or oil seals is false economy. To avoid the possibility of trouble after the engine has been reassembled always use new items throughout.
7   Do not throw away the old gaskets, for sometimes it happens that an immediate replacement cannot be found and the old gasket is then very useful as a template. Hang up the gaskets as they are removed.
8   If this is the first time that you have dismantled your Peugeot 104 engine/transmission unit then special attention should be given to the location of the various components and sub-assemblies. This is especially necessary due to the slightly unconventional layout of the model.
9   Many of the component casings are manufactured in aluminium alloy and special care must therefore be taken not to knock, drop or put any unnecessary pressure on these components.
10 Whenever possible, refit nuts, bolts and washers from where they were removed in order not to mix them up. If they cannot be reinstalled lay them out in such a way that it is clear where they came from.
11 Do not remove or disturb the TDC plate on the clutch housing.

6 Engine dismantling – ancillary items

1   Irrespective of whether you are going to dismantle the engine completely and rebuild it, or are simply going to exchange it for a reconditioned unit, the ancillary components will have to be removed.

4.18 Use a piece of hardboard to protect the radiator

4.21 Unscrewing the exhaust pipe manifold nuts

4.22 The exhaust pipe stay bracket

4.26a The lower of the two gear change links and ...

4.26b ... the upper

4.27a One of the front engine mounting bolts and ...

4.27b ... one of the rear bolts

4.30 Disengaging the left-hand driveshaft and ...

4.31 ... the right-hand driveshaft

4.32 Raising the engine and transmission assembly out of the car

20

Fig. 1.2 Turn the screw anti-clockwise to lock the tensioner before removing the timing chain assembly (Sec 7)

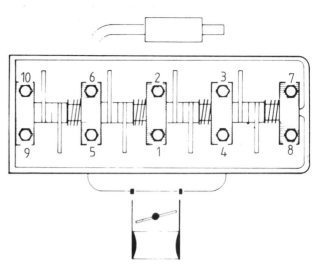

Fig. 1.3 The sequence for loosening or tightening the cylinder head bolts (Sec 7)

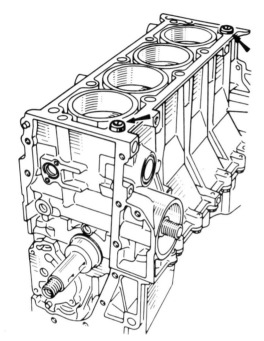

Fig. 1.4 The cylinder head locating dowels (arrowed) (Sec 7)

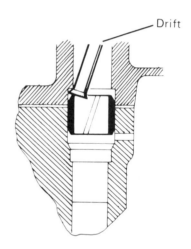

Fig. 1.5 Tap the dowel down with a drift until it is flush with the block face (Sec 7)

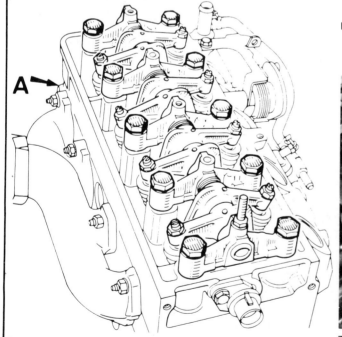

Fig. 1.6 Tap the cylinder head sideways at point A (Sec 7)

7.16 Unscrewing the camshaft location plate bolt

2   The only possible method of discovering the exact condition of the engine, and determining the extent of reconditioning required, is to dismantle it completely. If, having done this, it is decided that a reconditioned short block unit is needed then the block must be loosely reassembled, but check for replacement availability first.
3   Refer to the relevant Chapter and remove the following units:

  (a) Generator – Chapter 9
  (b) Distributor – Chapter 4
  (c) Carburettor – Chapter 3
  (d) Thermostat – Chapter 2
  (e) Water pump – Chapter 2
  (f) Starter motor – Chapter 9
  (g) Fuel pump – Chapter 3

4   Remove the exhaust manifold rear engine crossmember, and front mounting brackets.
5   If the block is to be stripped or exchanged, remove the oil pressure switch, and the coolant temperature sender unit.
6   If the engine is to be exchanged check what ancillary items are included in an exchange unit. Make sure that the engine is cleaned before being exchanged.

7 Cylinder head – removal

1   It is necessary to remove the engine/transmission unit in order to remove the cylinder head. To do this refer to Sections 4, 5 and 6.
2   If not already removed, detach the alternator drivebelt.
3   Unscrew the crankshaft pulley nut. To prevent the crankshaft from turning when undoing the nut, wedge a suitable bar through the timing aperture in the clutch housing into the teeth of the starter ring on the flywheel. Align the flywheel timing mark with the O mark on the fixed plate. Lever the pulley from the crankshaft.
4   Remove the rocker cover which is retained by two bolts and a nut, each with flat and nylon washers.
5   Unscrew the timing cover bolts and withdraw the cover (complete with fuel pump and plunger, if still fitted).
6   Before removing the timing chain assembly, the chain tensioner must be locked in position to prevent it from springing open when released. To lock it use a suitable screwdriver to rotate the ratchet anti-clockwise as shown (Fig. 1.2).
7   Unscrew the bolt from the camshaft sprocket, and remove the bolt and fuel pump drive eccentric.
8   Withdraw the camshaft sprocket and release the chain.
9   Progressively unscrew the cylinder head bolts in the sequence shown (Fig. 1.3).
10 Withdraw the through-bolts and recover the nuts from their channels in the crankcase. Remove the rocker shaft assembly.
11 Before removing the cylinder head the following must be noted. The cylinder head is positioned during assembly by means of two dowels, located as shown in Fig. 1.4. When removing the cylinder head it is most important not to lift it directly from the cylinder block; it must be twisted slightly. This action prevents the cylinder liners from sticking to the cylinder head face and being lifted with it, thus breaking their bottom seals.
12 Before the cylinder head can be twisted, the dowel at the flywheel end must be tapped down flush with the top of the cylinder block, using a drift as shown in Fig. 1.5.
13 When the dowel is flush with the top of the cylinder block, twist the cylinder head by tapping at the point indicated in Fig. 1.6 using a block of wood or a soft hammer.
14 When the seal between the top of the liners and the cylinder head face has been broken lift the head clear and remove the gasket.
15 If the cylinder head is to be removed for a prolonged period fit a pair of liner retaining plates to prevent any possibility of the liner bottom seals being disturbed.
16 To remove the camshaft, unscrew the location plate retaining bolt (photo). Remove the plate and extract the camshaft taking care not to score or damage the bearing surfaces in the cylinder head with the edges of the cam lobes.

8 Clutch housing and transfer gears – removal

1   The clutch and transfer gear housings are combined and, because of the lengths of the transfer driveshafts together with the limited

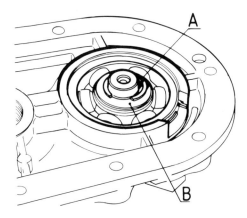

Fig. 1.7 Prise the circlip A out of its groove and remove the dished spring washer B (Sec 8)

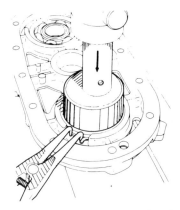

Fig. 1.8 Spread the circlip and press the bearing out (Sec 8)

space in the engine compartment, the engine assembly must be removed from the car before the clutch housing and transfer gears can be removed. Refer to Sections 4 and 5 for engine removal and preparation for dismantling, then proceed as follows.
2   Unscrew and remove the main housing retaining bolts, noting their respective positions (one is located beneath the oil gallery). Also note the engine lifting bracket location. Detach the clutch lever spring and remove the actuating rod.
3   Carefully tap and prise the housing free and remove with gasket.
4   Mark the position of the clutch unit in relation to the flywheel, progressively unscrew the clutch unit retaining bolts and remove from the flywheel.
5   Unscrew the retaining bolts and remove the flywheel (if required).
6   Unscrew the retaining bolts and separate the transfer pinion and cover assembly from the clutch housing. Remove the intermediate pinion to prevent it falling out, and separate the cover.
7   To dismantle the transfer gear assembly proceed as follows.
8   Support the intermediate plate and press or drive out the needle roller bearing.
9   Prise the circlips from their grooves in the engine output and gearbox input shafts. Remove the dished spring washers.
10 Support the intermediate plate to prevent any distortion, and press or drive the shafts out of the bearings using a piece of suitable diameter tube.
11 The ball bearings can be removed in the same manner having spread the locating circlips so that they no longer engage the outer race grooves. You will probably have to apply a little pressure to the bearing initially to free the circlip, spreading it as much as possible with a suitable pair of pliers while pressing the bearing through. Do not apply too much pressure initially as the circlip may not be free of the bearing groove, and damage or distortion may occur.

9 Timing cover – removal and refitting

1   The timing cover is removed for access to the timing chain,

tensioner and sprockets, also to the oil pump and its drive pinions.

2   Although the crankshaft oil seal is retained in the timing cover, directly behind the crankshaft pulley, special tools are necessary to extract the old seal and accurately insert the new replacement with the timing cover in-situ. Therefore, unless the cover is to be removed, it is generally recommended that this operation be left to your Peugeot dealer.

3   To remove the timing cover, it is recommended that the engine unit is first removed owing to the limited space available between the timing cover and the bodywork. Refer to Sections 4 and 5 for engine removal and preparation for dismantling, then proceed as follows.

4   Loosen the alternator bolts, disconnect the drivebelt and remove the alternator.

5   Remove the plastic cover from the timing aperture in the clutch housing. If the timing chain or sprockets are to be removed, position the flywheel at TDC. Jam the starter ring gear on the flywheel with a large screwdriver or similar implement, and unscrew the crankshaft pulley nut. Remove the nut with the flat washer.

6   Withdraw the pulley. If levering is necessary, do not apply excessive pressure against the timing cover; being aluminium, it is easily damaged.

7   Remove the rocker cover.

8   Unscrew and remove the eighteen timing cover bolts. When all are removed, carefully tap the timing cover away from the crankcase assembly and remove.

9   Details of dismantling and inspection of the timing chain and associated components are given in Sections 7, 11 and 21.

10   When reassembling ensure that all the old timing cover gasket is removed and of course use a new gasket when replacing the cover. When the cover is refitted and bolted in position, carefully trim the protruding section of gasket away flush with the rocker cover face.

11   Lubricate the crankshaft oilseal lips to ease assembly, and tighten all bolts to the specified torque.

12   Readjust the alternator drivebelt tension on assembly.

13   After refitting, run the engine and check for oil or water leaks.

10 Engine and gearbox – separation

1   With the engine assembly removed from the car remove the timing cover and flywheel as described in Sections 8 and 9, then unscrew and remove the crankcase-to-gearbox securing bolts and nuts. As the bolt lengths vary, take careful note of their locations on removal. Do not disturb or remove the TDC plate on the clutch housing.

2   In addition to the nuts and bolts on the top and bottom flanges of the casings there are two bolts and a nut to be removed from the flywheel end flange (Fig. 1.9).

3   Support the engine and gearbox as the last bolts are removed, and carefully separate the two units. Should they be stuck together prise them apart using a piece of wood as a lever between the differential housing and the exhaust manifold (if still fitted). If the manifold has been removed use a wooden block in its place.

11 Crankcase – dismantling

Timing components and oil pump

1   Remove the timing case as described in Section 9, paragraphs 5, 6 and 8; then proceed as follows.

2   Use the correct size Allen key and remove the oil pump unit complete with drivegear and gasket. Access to the retaining screws can be gained through the holes in the gear.

3   Use a suitable puller and remove the oil pump drive pinion from the crankshaft. Also remove the spacer. Note that the gear has a recessed flange and this faces inwards. (On some models the spacer is integral with the gear). Remove the Woodruff key.

4   Lock the chain tensioner (see Section 7, paragraph 6) and unscrew the retaining bolts. Remove the tensioner and filter.

5   Remove the timing chain and drive sprocket from the crankshaft, together with the camshaft sprocket (see Section 7).

Main bearing housing

6   Invert the engine, then unscrew the combined main bearing cap and housing bolts and remove the housing (Fig. 1.12).

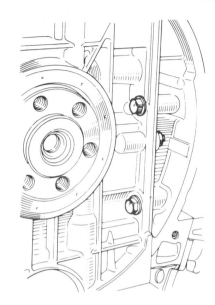

Fig. 1.9 The two bolts and nut at the flywheel end flange (Sec 10)

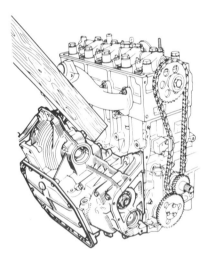

Fig. 1.10 Use a piece of wood as a lever to separate the engine and gearbox (Sec 10)

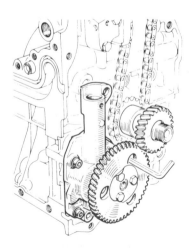

Fig. 1.11 Unscrew the oil pump securing screws using an Allen key through the holes in the gear (Sec 11)

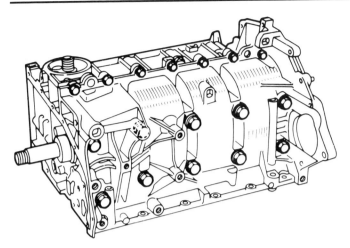

Fig. 1.12 The main bearing housing bolts (Sec 11)

7   Note its location and remove the crankshaft oil seal.

Pistons and connecting rods

8   Inspect the big-end assemblies and ensure that the connecting rods and caps are marked with a file or dot punch to identify their location and orientation. They should be marked on the oil filter side with No 1 at the flywheel end.

9   Unscrew the big-end nuts and remove the caps. The caps and rods may have to be prised apart but take care not to damage the bearing shells in any way in case they are to be used again. Keep the shell bearings with their respective rods and caps.

10   Assuming that liner retaining plates have been fitted (see Section 7, paragraph 15), the pistons can be withdrawn from the top of each liner complete with their connecting rods, although to prevent damage, it is better to remove the pistons with the liners.

11   If the liners are to be removed, matching marks should be made on the piston crowns and on the liners (on the oil pump side of the engine) before they are withdrawn. In this way the respective liners, pistons, and rods will be kept together and may be set aside for inspection or refitting. Under no circumstances allow the liners to interchange positions if they are to be reinstalled. Mark them numerically on the outer surface to avoid confusion.

Crankshaft

12   Lift the crankshaft clear of the crankcase and remove the main bearing shells and thrust half washers, noting their locations and keeping them in order.

13   The crankcase is now dismantled and ready for cleaning and inspection.

12 Engine components – examination and renovation – general

1   With the engine dismantled, all components must be thoroughly cleaned and examined for wear as described in the following Sections.

2   If a high mileage has been covered since new or the last engine rebuild, and general wear is evident, consideration should be given to renewing the engine assembly.

3   If a single component has malfunctioned and the rest of the engine is in good condition endeavour to find out the cause of its failure if not readily apparent. For example, if a bearing has failed, check that the adjoining oilways are clear; the new bearing will not last long if it is not being lubricated!

4   If uncertain about the condition of any components, seek a second opinion, preferably from a Peugeot dealer/mechanic who will obviously have an expert knowledge of your model and be able to advise on the best course of action.

5   Check on the availability of replacement parts before discarding the old ones. Check the new part against the old to ensure that you have the correct replacement.

6   Some of the measurements required will need the use of feeler blades or a micrometer, but in many instances wear will be visually evident or the old component can be compared with a new one.

13 Lubrication system – general description

1   A forced feed lubrication system is employed and is shown in Fig. 1.13. The oil pump is attached to the crankcase in the lower section of the timing chest and it incorporates the pressure relief valve. The pump is driven by gears from the crankshaft.

2   Oil from the pump passes via an oilway to the oil filter, and thence to the crankshaft main bearings, connecting rod bearings and transmission components. Another oilway from the filter delivers oil to the overhead camshaft and rocker components. Oil from the cylinder head passes to the transfer gear housing and then back to the sump contained within the transmission housing.

3   Apart from the standard replaceable canister filter located on the outside of the crankcase there is a gauze filter incorporated in the oil pump suction intake.

4   The oil level must be correctly maintained by reference to the dipstick. The oil filler cap is in the rocker cover. An oil pressure warning switch is fitted which illuminates a warning light in the instrument panel should a drop in pressure occur.

5   At the intervals specified in Routine Maintenance, drain the engine oil, refit the drain plug and refill with new oil of the specified grade. The oil is best drained immediately after a run when any sludge or sediment will be in suspension. Renew the oil filter also at alternate oil changes (see Section 14).

6   Under adverse operating conditions, for example if the car is used for towing or mainly for short journeys, it may be advisable to change the oil more frequently. Consult your dealer if in doubt.

14 Oil filter – removal and refitting

1   The oil filter is contained in a canister mounted just above the alternator and is renewed as a complete assembly when a filter change is due. To remove the filter canister a strap or chain wrench is necessary, but if one of these is not available, pierce the side of the canister with a long pointed tool and use this as a lever to unscrew the canister from its mounting. Be prepared for oil spillage.

2   The new filter will be supplied with a new oil seal mounted in it. Before fitting the filter, carefully remove the seal and apply a little clean engine oil between the seal and canister, then refit the seal.

3   Clean the outer face of the seal and its contact face on the engine and screw the canister down by hand only, until the seal contacts the face. Then tighten it a further $\frac{3}{4}$ of a turn. Two rows of numbers on the canister are provided to measure this amount. Identify any number which is conveniently in sight on the upper row and tighten the canister until the same number in the bottom row is in the position of the original (photo).

4   Note that new or service exchange engines are supplied with a red-identified 5 to 8 micron filter. This type of filter is also provided with a cylinder liner replacement kit. It must be removed after the engine has run for 600 miles (1000 km) and a standard 10 to 15 micron filter fitted instead.

5   After renewing a filter always check for oil leaks when the engine is next run and top up the engine oil.

15 Cylinder head – dismantling, inspection and renovation

1   Having removed the cylinder head, place it onto a clean workbench where it can be dismantled and examined. Note that there is no separate inlet manifold; the inlet tracts are cast into the cylinder head.

2   Remove each valve and spring assembly using a valve spring compressor. Extract the split collets from between the spring retaining cup washer and valve stem (photo).

3   Progressively release the tension of the compressor until it can be removed, the spring and retainer withdrawn, and the valve extracted from the guide.

4   As the valves are removed, keep them in order by inserting them in a card having suitable holes punched in it, numbered from 1 to 8.

5   Wash the cylinder head clean and carefully scrape away the carbon build-up in the combustion chambers and exhaust ports, using a scraper which will not damage the surfaces to be cleaned. If a rotary wire brush and drill is available this may be used for removing the carbon. Take care to prevent foreign matter entering the inlet manifold;

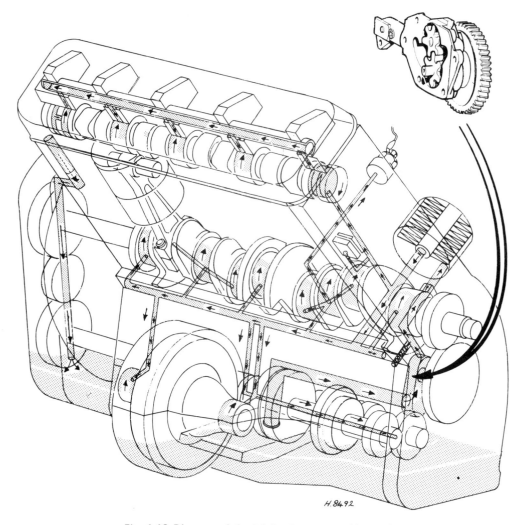

Fig. 1.13 Diagram of the lubrication system (Sec 13)

14.3 Fitting a new oil filter

15.2 Extracting the collets using a magnet

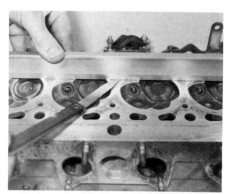

15.7 Using a straight-edge and feeler gauges to check the head mating surface flatness

since it is cast into the cylinder head, cleaning is difficult.

6   The valves may also be scraped and wire-brushed clean in a similar manner.

7   With the cylinder head cleaned and dry, examine it for cracks or damage. In particular inspect the valve seat areas for signs of hairline cracks, pitting or burning. Check the head mating surfaces for distortion, the maximum permissible amount being 0·002 in (0·05 mm) (photo).

8   Minor surface wear and pitting of the valve seats can probably be removed when the valves are reground. More serious wear or damage

should be shown to your Peugeot dealer or a competent automotive engineer who will advise you on the action necessary.

9   Carefully inspect the valves, in particular the exhaust valves. Check the stems for distortion and signs of wear. The valve seat faces must be in reasonable condition and if they have covered a high mileage they will probably need to be refaced on a valve grinding machine; again, this is a job for your Peugeot dealer or local garage/automotive machine shop.

10   Insert each valve into its respective guide and check for excessive wear (photo). Worn valve guides allow oil to be drawn past the inlet

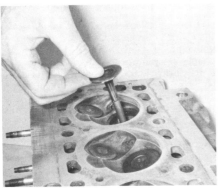

15.10 Inserting a valve in its guide to check for wear

15.15 Renewing a valve spring seat washer

15.16a Reassembling the valve spring and ...

15.16b ... spring retainer

15.16c Lubricate the camshaft bearings before ...

15.16d ... inserting the camshaft

valve stem causing a smoky exhaust, while exhaust leakage through the exhaust valve guide can overheat the valve guide and cause sticking valves.

11 If the valve guides are to be renewed this is a job best left to your Peugeot agent who will have the required specialist equipment.

12 Assuming the valves and seats are in reasonable condition they should be reseated by grinding them using valve grinding carborundum paste. The grinding process must also be carried out when new valves are fitted.

13 The carborundum paste used for this job is normally supplied in a double-ended tin with coarse paste at one end and fine at the other. In addition, a suction tool for holding the valve head so that it may be rotated is also required. To grind in a valve, first smear a trace of the coarse paste onto the seat face and fit the suction grinder to the valve head. Then with a semi-rotary motion grind the valve head into its seat, lifting the valve occasionally to redistribute the grinding paste. When a dull matt continuous line is produced on both the valve seat and the valve then the paste can be wiped off. Apply a little fine paste and finish off the grinding process, then remove all traces of the paste. If a light spring is placed over the valve stem behind the head this can often be of assistance in raising the valve from time to time against the pressure of the grinding tool so as to redistribute the paste evenly round the job. The width of the line which is produced after grinding indicates the seat width, and this width should not exceed about 0·08 in (2 mm). If, after a moderate amount of grinding, it is apparent that the seating line is too wide, it probably means that the seat has already been cut back one or more times previously, or else the valve has been ground several times. Here again, specialist advice is best sought.

14 Examine all the valve springs to make sure that they are in good condition and not distorted. It will have been noticed when they were being removed whether any were broken, and if they are then they must be renewed. It is a good idea to renew all the valve springs anyway. If you have reached this stage it is false economy not to do so. They are relatively cheap.

15 At the same time renew the valve spring seating washers which sit directly on the cylinder head. These wear reasonably quickly (photo).

16 Before reassembling the valve and springs to the cylinder head

make a final check that everything is thoroughly clean and free from grit, then lightly smear all the valve stems with engine oil prior to reassembly. The camshaft can now be refitted in the cylinder head and located with the retaining plate. This is then secured with its bolt and a new shakeproof washer (photos).

16 Crankshaft – examination and renovation

1 Carefully examine the crankpin and main journal surfaces for signs of scoring or scratches, and check the ovality and taper of each journal in turn. Use a dial gauge and V-blocks and check the main bearing journals for ovality. If any journals are found to be more than 0·001 in (0·02 mm) out of round then they will have to be reground. If the crankpins are scored or scratched, don't bother measuring them as they will have to be reground.

2 If a bearing has failed after a short period of operation look for the cause and rectify before reassembly.

3 If the crankshaft is to be reground this will have to be done by your Peugeot dealer or a competent automotive engineer. The regrinder will also be able to supply the new shell bearings to suit the undersize requirement.

17 Big-end and main bearings – examination and renovation

1 The main bearing shells themselves are normally a matt grey in colour all over and should have no signs of pitting or ridging or discolouration as this usually indicates that the surface bearing metal has worn away and the backing material is showing through. It is worthwhile renewing the main bearing shells anyway if you have gone to the trouble of removing the crankshaft, but they must, of course, be renewed if there is any sign of damage to them or if the crankshaft has been reground.

2 If the crankshaft is not being reground, yet bearing shells are being renewed, make sure that you check whether or not the crankshaft has been reground before. This will be indicated by looking at the back of

the bearing shell and this will indicate whether it is undersize or not. The same type of shell bearing must be used when they are renewed.

3   The big-end bearings are subject to wear at a greater rate than the crankshaft journals. A sign that one or more big-end bearings are getting badly worn is a pronounced knocking noise from the engine, accompanied by a significant drop in oil pressure due to the increased clearance between the bearing and the journal permitting oil to flow more freely through the resultantly larger space. If this should happen quite suddenly and action is taken immediately, and by immediately is meant within a few miles, then it is possible that the bearing shell may be renewed without any further work needing to be done.

4   If this happens in an engine which has been neglected, and oil changes and oil filter changes have not been carried out as they should have been, it is most likely that the rest of the engine is in a pretty terrible state anyway. If it occurs in an engine which has been recently overhauled, then it is almost certainly due to a piece of grit or swarf which has got into the oil circulation system and finally come to rest in the bearing shell and scored it. In these instances renewal of the shell alone accompanied by a thorough flush through of the lubrication system may be all that is required.

18 Cylinder liner bores – examination and renovation

1   The liner bores may be examined for wear either in or out of the engine block; the cylinder head must, of course, be removed in each case. If the liners are still in the block (and it is hoped that they will not need renovation) the liner retainers must be left in place so that relocation does not become necessary. However, if you have got to the stage where the pistons are out it is probably better to remove the liners for inspection even if they do not require renovation. Refer to Section 30 to see what is involved in refitting them.

2   First of all examine the top of the cylinder about a quarter of an inch below the top of the liner and with the finger feel if there is any ridge running round the circumference of the bore. In a worn cylinder bore a ridge will develop at the point where the top ring on the piston comes to the uppermost limit of its stroke. An excessive ridge indicates that the bore below the ridge is worn. If there is no ridge, it is reasonable to assume that the cylinder is not badly worn. Measurement of the diameter of the cylinder bore both in line and with the piston gudgeon pin and at right angles to it, at the top and bottom of the cylinder, is another check to be made. A cylinder is expected to wear at the sides where the thrust of the piston presses against it. In time this causes the cylinder to assume an oval shape. Furthermore, the top of the cylinder is likely to wear more than the bottom of the cylinder. It will be necessary to use a proper bore measuring instrument in order to measure the differences in bore diameter across the cylinder, and variations between the top and bottom ends of the cylinder. As a general guide it may be assumed that any variation more than 0·010 inch (0·25 mm) indicates that the liners should be renewed. Provided all variations are less than 0·010 inch (0·25 mm) it is probable that the fitting of new piston rings will cure the problem of piston-to-cylinder bore clearances. Once again it is difficult to give a firm ruling on this as so much depends on the amount of time, effort and money which the individual owner is prepared, or wishes to spend, on the task. Certainly if the cylinder bores are obviously deeply grooved or scored, the liners must be renewed regardless of any measurement differences in the cylinder diameter.

3   If new liners are to be fitted, new pistons will be required also.

19 Connecting rods, pistons and piston rings – examination and renovation

1   With the pistons removed from the liners, carefully clean them and remove the old rings, keeping them in order and the correct way up. The ring grooves will have to be cleaned out, esepcially the top, which will contain a burnt carbon coating that may prevent the ring from seating correctly. A blunt hacksaw blade and a strip of fine emery cloth or a broken piston ring will assist in groove cleaning. Take care not to scratch the ring lands or piston surface in any way.

2   The top ring groove is likely to have worn the most. After the groove has been cleaned out, refit the top ring and any excessive wear

will be obvious by a sloppy fit. The degree of wear may be checked by using a feeler gauge.

3   Examine the piston surface and look for signs of any hairline cracks especially round the gudgeon pin area. Check that the oil relief holes below the oil control ring groove are clear, and, if not, carefully clean them out using a suitable size drill, but don't mark the piston.

4   If any of the pistons are obviously badly worn or defective they must be renewed. A badly worn top ring land may be machined to accept a wider, stepped ring, the step on the outer face of this type of ring being necessary to avoid fouling the unworn ridge at the top of the cylinder bore.

5   Providing the engine has not seized up or suffered any other severe damage, the connecting rods should not require any attention other than cleaning. If damage has occurred or the piston/s show signs of irregular wear it is advisable to have the connecting rod alignment checked. This requires the use of specialised tools and should therefore be entrusted to a Peugeot agent or a competent automotive engineer, who will be able to check and realign any defective rods.

6   New Peugeot rings are supplied with their gaps already preset, but if you intend to use other makes the gaps should be checked and adjusted if necessary. Before fitting the new rings on the pistons, each should be inserted approximately 3 in (75 mm) down the cylinder bore and the gap measured with a feeler gauge. This should be between 0·015 in (0·38 mm) and 0·038 in (0·97 mm). It is essential that the gap should be measured at the bottom of the ring travel, as if it is measured at the top of a worn bore and gives a perfect fit, it could easily seize at the bottom. If the ring gap is too small, rub down the ends of the ring with a very fine file until the gap, when fitted, is correct. To keep the rings square in the bore for measurement, line each up in turn by inserting an old piston in the bore upside down, and use the piston to push the ring down. Remove the piston and measure the piston ring gap.

7   When fitting new pistons and rings to a rebored engine the piston ring gap can be measured at the top of the bore as the bore will not now taper. It is not necessary to measure the side clearance in the piston ring grooves with the rings fitted as the groove dimensions are accurately machined during manufacture.

20 Gudgeon pins – removal

The gudgeon pins float in the piston and are an interference fit in the connecting rods. This interference fit between gudgeon pin and connecting rod means that heat is required (230–260°C/450–500°F) before a pin can be satisfactorily fitted in the connecting rod. If it is necessary to renew either the piston or connecting rod, we strongly recommend that the separation and assembly of the two be entrusted to someone with experience. Misapplied heat can ruin one, or all, of the components very easily.

21 Timing chain and sprockets – examination and renovation

1   Examine the teeth of both sprockets for wear. Each tooth on a sprocket is an inverted V-shape and wear is apparent when one side of the tooth becomes more concave in shape than the other. When badly worn, the teeth become hook-shaped and the sprockets must be renewed.

2   If the sprockets need to be renewed then the chain will have worn also and should also be renewed. If the sprockets are satisfactory, examine the chain and look for play between the links. When the chain is held out horizontally, it should not bend appreciably. Remember, a chain is only as strong as its weakest link, and being a relatively cheap item it is worthwhile fitting a replacement anyway.

3   Check the condition of the tensioner shoe for wear. It is not recommended that the tensioner be dismantled as it too is a relatively cheap item and normally replaced as a unit.

4   Inspect the oil pump drive gears for wear or damage and renew if necessary.

22 Transfer gear unit – inspection and renovation

1   The condition of the transfer gears, their bearings and the input and output shafts, is obviously critical as they transmit the power of the engine to the transmission unit, and are liable to be a source of

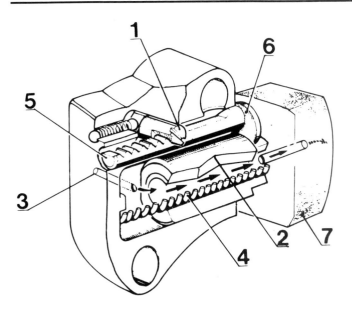

Fig. 1.14 Part section view of the timing chain tensioner (Sec 21)

1 Ratchet screw	5 Rack
2 Piston	6 Washer
3 Oil supply	7 Shoe
4 Spring	

noise on this model.

2   Clean the input and output shaft ball bearings and check them for excessive play and/or signs of damage. Inspect the intermediate shaft needle roller bearings. Renew any suspect or worn bearings. If a bearing has collapsed due to general wear and fatigue, then the chances are that the other bearings are close to failure and it is therefore advisable to renew all the bearings.

3   Carefully inspect the transfer gears. If excessive transmission noise has been experienced it may be reduced by changing the transfer gears. If the teeth are worn or damaged, then the gears should be renewed. Renew the gear set rather than a single gear; it is not good practice to mesh new gears with old as the wear rate of both is increased and they will be noisy in operation.

4   Check the input and output shafts, and inspect their splines for wear or damage. Renew them if necessary.

5   Note that if the intermediate gear or clutch housings are damaged, they must be renewed as a unit and not individually. Check that the flatness of the mating faces is within the specified limits (photo).

23 Camshaft and rocker arms – examination and renovation

1   The camshaft lobes should be examined for signs of flats or scoring or any other form of wear and damage. At the same time the rocker arms should also be examined, particularly on the faces where they bear against the camshaft, for signs of wear. If the case-hardened surfaces of the cam lobes or rocker arm faces have been penetrated it will be quite obvious as there will be a darker, rougher pitted appearance to the surface in question. In such cases, the rocker arm or the camshaft will need renewal. Where the camshaft or rocker arm surface is still bright and clean, showing slight signs of wear, it is best left alone. Any attempt to reface either will only result in the case-hardened surface being reduced in thickness with the possibility of extreme and rapid wear later on.

2   The camshaft bearing journals should be in good condition and show no signs of pitting or scoring as they are relatively free from stress.

3   If the bearing surfaces are scored or discoloured it is possible that the shaft is not running true, and in this case it will have to be renewed. For an accurate check get your Peugeot agent to inspect both the camshaft and cylinder head.

4   The rocker arm assembly can be dismantled on removing the circlip from the end of the rocker shaft (photos).

5   When removing the various rocker components from the shaft take careful note of the sequence in which they are removed. In particular note that the No 2 and 4 rocker bearings are identical. Keep the components in order as they are removed from the shaft for inspection.

6   Check the rocker shaft for signs of wear. Check it for straightness by rolling it on a flat surface. It is unlikely to be bent but if this is the case it must either be straightened or renewed. The shaft surface should be free of wear ridges caused by the rocker arms. Check the oil feed holes and clear them out if blocked or sludged-up.

7   Check each rocker arm for wear on an unworn part of the shaft. Check the end of the adjuster screw and the face of the rocker arm where it bears on the camshaft. Any signs of cracks or serious wear that may have penetrated the case-hardening will necessitate renewal of the rocker arm.

24 Flywheel – examination and renovation

1   There are two areas in which the flywheel may have been worn or damaged. The first is on the driving face where the clutch friction plate bears against it. Should the clutch plate have been permitted to wear down beyond the level of the rivets, it is possible that the flywheel will have been scored. If this scoring is severe it may be necessary to have it refaced or even renewed.

2   The other part to examine is the teeth of the starter ring gear around the periphery of the flywheel. If several of the teeth are broken or missing, or the front edges of all teeth are obviously very badly chewed up, then it would be advisable to fit a new ring gear.

3   The old ring gear can be removed by cutting a slot with a hacksaw down between two of the teeth as far as possible, without cutting into the flywheel itself. Once the cut is made a chisel will split the ring gear which can then be drawn off. To fit a new ring gear requires it to be heated first to a temperature of 220°C (435°F), no more. This is best done in a bath of oil or an oven, but not, preferably, with a naked flame. It is much more difficult to heat evenly and to the required temperature with a naked flame. Once the ring gear has attained the correct temperature it can be placed onto the flywheel making sure that it beds down properly onto the register. It should then be allowed to cool

22.5 Checking the clutch housing mating face for flatness

23.4a Remove the rocker shaft circlip ...

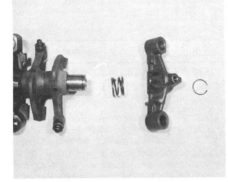

23.4b ... to dismantle the rocker assembly

down naturally. If by mischance, the ring gear is overheated, it should not be used. The temper will have been lost, therefore softening it, and it will wear out in a very short space of time.

4   Although not actually fitted into the flywheel itself, there is a bush in the centre of the crankshaft flange onto which the flywheel fits. Whilst more associated with gearbox and clutch it should always be inspected when the clutch is removed. The main bearing oil seal is revealed when the flywheel is removed. This can be prised out with a screwdriver but must always be renewed once removed. The spigot bush is best removed using a suitable extractor. Another method is to fill the recess with grease and then drive in a piece of close fitting steel bar. This should force the bush out. A new bush may be pressed in, together with a new seal. Make sure that the chamfered end of the bush abuts the seal. The bush is self-lubricating.

25 Oil pump – examination and renovation

1   The oil pump will have to be removed from the crankcase before any inspection can be made, and therefore the timing case will have to be removed.

2   The pump unit is retained by four Allen screws and these can be unscrewed using a suitable Allen key inserted through the holes in the pump drivegear where necessary.

3   The drivegear can be removed after bending flat the ears of the washer and unscrewing the retaining bolts.

4   Remove the retaining pin from the relief valve housing and withdraw the cup, spring, guide and piston (photos).

5   Clean and examine all components. Any damaged, scored or badly worn parts must be renewed. If the oil pump gears are obviously worn and the car has covered a high mileage, consideration should be given to renewing the complete pump unit, as the body will have worn with the other components.

26 Inlet and exhaust manifolds – inspection

1   The inlet manifold is integral with the cylinder head casting. Check that the mating face to which the carburettor is attached is smooth and undamaged. Check the exhaust manifold for cracks or other damage.

2   Use a straight-edge to check the faces of the exhaust manifold for distortion. If there should be any sign of pitting or warping of the faces, they must be refaced by a competent machinist, or renewed.

3   Any accumulations of carbon within the exhaust manifold ports can be removed using a flexible wire brush and/or scraper.

27 Engine mountings – inspection

The engine mounting rubbers are often ignored simply because they do not normally present any problems. However their work rate is probably equal to any other engine component and therefore if the engine is removed at any time, it is worthwhile checking the condition of the mounting rubbers. If they show signs of deterioration due to oil impregnation, heat or simply age, they should be renewed. Mountings that have lost their resistance to shocks will cause engine/transmission vibrations and increase the fatigue rate of other associated engine/transmission connections, as well as for the driver and occupants of the car.

28 Engine reassembly – general

It is during the process of engine reassembly that the job is either made a success or a failure. From the word go there are certain basic rules which it is folly to ignore, namely:

(a) *Absolute cleanliness. The working area, the components of the engine and the hands of those working on the engine must be completely free of grime and grit. One small piece of carborundum dust or swarf can ruin a big-end in no time, and nullify all the time and effort you have spent. No matter what the pundits say this engine and its other components can be reconditioned and rebuilt very successfully and continue working efficiently.*

(b) *Always, no-matter what the circumstances may be, use new gaskets, locking tabs, seats, nyloc nuts and any other parts mentioned in the Sections in this Chapter. It is pointless to dismantle an engine, spend considerable money and time on it and then to waste all this for the sake of something as small as a failed oil seal. Delay the rebuilding if necessary*

(c) *Don't rush it. The most skilled and experienced mechanic can easily make a mistake if he is rushed*

(d) *Check that all nuts and bolts are clean and in good condition and ideally renew all spring washers, lockwasher and tab washers as a matter of course. A supply of clean engine oil and clean cloths (to wipe excess oil off your hands only!) and a torque spanner are the only things which should be required in addition to all the tools used in dismantling the engine*

(e) *The torque wrench is an essential requirement when reassembling the engine (and transmission) components, especially with the Peugeot 104. This is because the various housings are manufactured from aluminium alloy and whilst this gives the advantage of less weight, it also means that the various fastenings must be accurately tightened as specified to avoid distortion and/or damage to the components. Cracked or distorted housings are not cheap to renew so beware.*

29 Engine – preparation for reassembly

1   Assuming that the engine has been completely stripped for reconditioning and that the block is now bare, before any reassembly takes place it must be thoroughly cleaned both inside and out.

2   The ideal situation is to dip the block in a garage's cleaning tank usually filled with a mixture of paraffin and cleaning fluid, and then to leave it submerged for an hour or so. Then get to work on it with a wire brush and screwdriver. Clean out all the crevices, do not scratch any machined surfaces, and scrub both inside and out. A great deal of sediment often collects around the liner seatings. Chip this away if necessary.

3   Hose down the block with a garden hose and if possible dry it off with an air jet. Dry and thoroughly clean out the block with a lint-free cloth until it is spotless. Check the cylinder block mating face for flatness using a straight-edge and feeler gauges (photo).

4   Clean out the oilways using a bottle brush, pipe cleaner or other suitable implement, and blow through with compressed air. Squirt some clean engine oil through to check that the oilways are clear.

5   If the core plugs are defective and show signs of weeping, they must be renewed at this stage. To remove, carefully drive a punch through the centre of the plug and use the punch to lever the plug out. Clean the aperture thoroughly and prior to fitting the new plug, smear the orifice with sealant. Use a small-headed hammer and carefully drive the new core plug into position with the convex side outwards. Check that it is correctly seated on completion.

6   As the components are assembled, lubricate them with clean engine oil and use a suitable sealant as and where applicable.

30 Cylinder liners – refitting

1   Each liner is marked with 1, 2 or 3 lines on the top flange and these lines correspond to the three grades of piston A, B or C marked on the piston heads. A liner with 2 lines must be used with a B-piston in it and so on. All four piston/liner assemblies should be of the same category. When reassembling parts that have already been used in the engine, make sure that they go back in their original positions and that they are fitted the same way round as before.

2   It is of prime importance that the liners are accurately assembled otherwise serious troubles with coolant leaks, cylinder head gasket leaks, and possibly mechanical problems could arise. The liners have to be assembled in the block so that they fit squarely within an overall height tolerance and a tolerance relative to each other. Peugeot provide special tools with which to measure liner height and squareness in the block and, if possible, these should be borrowed or hired. Alternatively your Peugeot garage will fit the liners for you. For those who have the ability and facilities to do precision work the procedure is as follows.

3   Make doubly sure that the liners and their beds in the block are meticulously clean and insert the liners, dry, into their correct locations. Used liners should have the marks which were made on

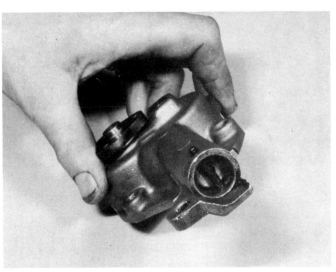

25.4a Depress the spring retainer and remove the retaining pin ...

25.4b ... to dismantle the oil pump relief valve

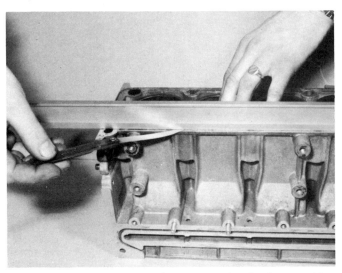

29.3 Checking the cylinder head/block mating face for flatness with a straight-edge and feeler gauge

30.6 A paper gasket assembled on a liner. Note the inner tabs fitting in the liner groove

dismantling lined up in their original positions. The liner protrusion above the top face of the block must be between 0·11 mm (0·004 in) and 0·18 mm (0·007 in), as near to the latter as possible without exceeding it. The difference in protrusion between any two adjacent liners must not exceed 0·04 mm (0·0016 in). Height adjustment is achieved by selecting a paper gasket of appropriate thickness which is then located between the liner bottom flange and the block.

4   First check the liners, one at a time, for squareness by gauging the top flange at four equally spaced points on the top surface with a dial test indicator gauge (clock gauge). The difference between the highest and lowest must not exceed 0·02 mm (0·0008 in). If out of limit, check for dust between the liner and block or in the measuring equipment or, if necessary, check the liner on a surface plate for distortion.

5   When all the liners are square within tolerance, measure the height of each top flange from the block top face, that is, the liner protrusion. Take three readings on each flange upper face; the difference must not exceed 0·05 mm (0·002 in). Subtract the highest reading from 0·18 mm (0·007 in) to obtain the theoretical thickness of gasket required. Four thicknesses of gaskets, identified by a coloured tab, are available as follows:

Colour	Mean thickness
Blue	0·087 mm (0·00343 in)
White	0·102 mm (0·004 in)
Red	0·122 mm (0·0048 in)
Yellow	0·147 mm (0·0058 in)

Select the gasket which is equal to or immediately below the theoretical thickness required. For example, assume that the three readings on a liner were 0·03, 0·04 and 0·02 mm. These are within the permitted variation of 0·05 mm. By subtracting the highest, 0·04 mm, from 0·18 mm, the gasket thickness required is shown to be 0·14 mm. A gasket with a red tab (0·122 mm) is selected, since the one with a yellow tab (0·147 mm), although it is nearer to the required 0·14 mm, exceeds it, and would give a protrusion greater than 0·18 mm (0·007 in).

6   Fit a gasket with the same colour tab on all four liners, working the internal tabs into the groove beneath the bottom flange. Fit the liners in the block with the coloured tabs visible and not overlapping (photo).

7   Repeat the squareness and protrusion checks on all four liners, pressing each liner down to compress the gasket during each check.

31.3 Inserting a piston, with a ring compressor fitted, into a liner

31.4a Fitting a liner/piston assembly into the block

31.4b Liner retaining clamps fitted with temporary bolts and nuts

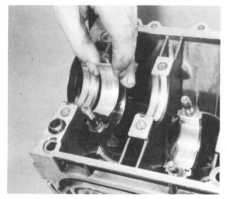

32.2 Fitting a big-end bearing upper shell

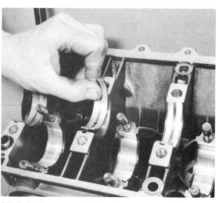

32.3 Fitting a main bearing upper shell

32.4 A new seal fitted to the flywheel end of the crankshaft

32.5 Lowering the crankshaft into the main bearings

32.6 Inserting one of the thrust washers (crankshaft removed for clarity)

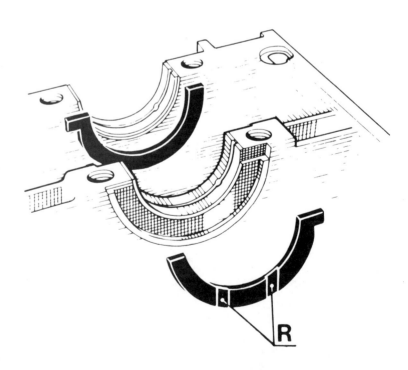

Fig. 1.15 Fit the crankshaft thrust washers with the oil grooves(R) towards the crankshaft (Sec 32)

The difference in protrusion between adjacent liners measured at their nearest points must not exceed 0·04 mm (0·0018 in). If it does, change the gasket for one immediately below it in thickness on the liner or liners whose protrusion reading is the highest.

8   Use a felt tip pen to mark each liner, and the block adjacent to each, so that each liner can be replaced in its own location and precise orientation on reassembly.

31 Pistons, connecting rods and liners – refitting

1   As explained previously, the pistons and connecting rods are best separated and reassembled by your Peugeot agent, due to the difficulty of removing and refitting the gudgeon pin. Check that the pistons have been correctly fitted to the connecting rod so that the arrow mark on the piston crown will face the timing gear when the connecting rods and caps are assembled to the crankshaft with their identifying numbers on the oil filter side.

2   It is assumed that new piston rings will have been checked in their respective bores to ensure that the ring gap is sufficient as described in Section 19. Fit the piston rings to each piston using a ring expander if available, or by carefully spreading the ends and lowering over the piston ring lands using a feeler gauge as a guide. Do not fit them from the bottom upwards as you may score the piston skirt. Keep the ring square to the piston as it is lowered. Do not distort or over-expand it. When the rings are fitted, making sure that the marked faces are fitted uppermost, position the ring gaps as follows. The slot in the oil scraper expander should be in line with the gudgeon pin axis and the gaps in the upper and lower parts at 20 to 50 mm (1 to 2 in) on either side of the expander slot. The gap in the next ring above, with a tapered face, should be 120° from the expander slot. The gap in the top compression ring, with a domed face, should also be 120° from the expander slot, but on the other side to that in the tapered face ring. If oversize rings are fitted follow the manufacturer's instructions carefully.

3   Lubricate the pistons and rings, and each liner bore in turn. Compress the rings with a suitable ring clamp and insert the piston and connecting rod assembly upwards into the liner. Make sure that, when the assembly mark on the liner is in its relative assembled position, *the arrow on the piston head with the marking DIST points towards the timing chain end of the cylinder block,* and **not** to the distributor end. Repeat the process until all piston assemblies are in their respective liners. Remove the four big-end caps and their retaining nuts (photo).

4   Lightly smear the liner beds in the block with a good quality non-setting sealing compound, and fit the liners into their respective locations and in their correct orientation relative to the block. Fit the liner retaining clamps, which can be made up from suitable scrap bar if required. These will prevent the liners from moving when the connecting rods and caps are fitted to the crankshaft (photos).

32 Crankcase, main bearings and crankshaft – reassembly

1   Invert the cylinder block, with the liner and piston assemblies fitted and retained with clamps and make sure that the bearing shell housings are perfectly clean in the connecting rod big-ends and the crankcase.

2   Fit the four connecting rod big-end bearing upper shells to their

housings in the rods. Ensure that each location tab engages with its slot and lubricate with clean engine oil (photo).

3   Fit the five main bearing upper shells, each of which has an oil groove, to their housings in the block. Ensure that each location tongue is engaged and lubricate with clean engine oil (photo).

4   It is easier to fit a new seal to the crankshaft flywheel end with the shaft out of the engine. Clean the seal bearing surface on the crankshaft and lubricate it with clean engine oil. Carefully fit a new seal, with the lip facing into the crankcase, and clean the seal housings in the crankcase upper and lower halves (photo).

5   Lubricate the crankshaft pins and journals and carefully lower the shaft into position in the crankcase (photo).

6   Insert the two crankshaft thrust washers, with the oil grooves towards the shaft, and lubricate with clean engine oil (photo).

7   Measure the crankshaft endfloat with feeler gauges or a dial test indicator (clock) gauge. If the endfloat is not within the specified tolerance, select a pair of thrust washers of equal thickness which will provide the correct endfloat and fit them instead of the originals (photo).

8   Clean the big-end bearing caps and fit the bearing shells, making sure that each is properly located and adequately lubricated. Check that the connecting rod identification marks are towards the oil filter side of the block. Fit a big-end to its crankshaft pin and place the bearing cap and bearing shell in position, making sure that the rod and cap identification numbers align. Fit the retaining nuts and tighten to the specified torque. Repeat until all big-end caps are fitted (photos).

9   Check that the two locating dowels are in place in the face of the joint flange of the crankcase and fit a new O-ring seal to the oil transfer sleeve (photos).

10 Insert the five lower bearing shells in the cleaned housings in the lower crankcase half, the grooved bearings being fitted to Nos 2 and 4 housings. Lubricate the shells with clean engine oil (photos).

11 Smear the mating joint faces of the crankcase with a suitable sealant and carefully fit the lower crankcase into position, taking care that the bearing shells do not move from their housings (photo).

12 Fit the ten bolts and washers securing the main bearings, making sure that they are located in their original positions. Tighten the bolts, in the order shown in Fig. 1.16, first to the initial torque all round, and then, repeating the cycle, to the final torque; see Specifications (photo).

13 Fit the seven bolts with spring washers in the joint flange on the oil filter side of the block and tighten them to their specified torque. Tap the crankshaft seal in so that it is flush with the case (photo).

14 If it has not already been done, renew the output shaft oil seal and the bearing bush located in the crankshaft at the flywheel end. Prise out the old seal and remove the bush with an extractor. Carefully tap a new bush into position using a socket spanner as a drift and position the new seal afterwards.

15 Providing the liners are retained by plates, if the cylinder head is not fitted, the crankshaft should now be tested for freedom of movement. Temporarily fit two bolts in the flywheel flange and, with a suitable lever in the bolts, turn the shaft. Although some resistance to rotation is inevitable, the shaft should turn smoothly in its bearings.

33 Cylinder head – refitting

1   Since March 1979 Peugeot have recommended that new cylinder

32.7 Measuring crankshaft endfloat

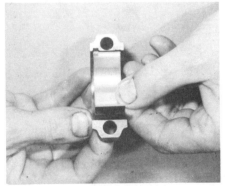
32.8a Fitting a big-end bearing shell to a cap and ...

32.8b ... fitting the cap to a connecting rod

32.8c Tightening the big-end bearing nuts

32.9a Ensure that the two locating dowels (arrowed) are fitted ...

32.9b ... and fit a new O-ring seal to the oil transfer sleeve

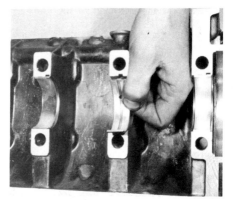

32.10a Fitting a lower main bearing shell in the lower crankcase half and ...

32.10b ... lubricating thoroughly before assembly

32.11 Fitting the lower crankcase half before ...

32.12 ... tightening the main bearing bolts with a torque wrench

32.13 Tightening the seven bolts in the flange joint

33.3 Check that the two locating dowels are fitted in the block to the correct height

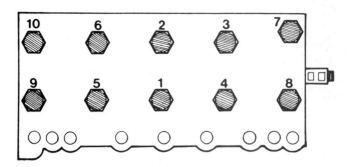

Fig. 1.16 The sequence for tightening or loosening the main bearing bolts
(Sec 32)

head bolts (grade 10/9) should be fitted on rebuild. These bolts are tightened to a slightly higher torque (see Specifications). Originally the bolts had flat washers under the heads, but these have been discontinued since January 1977; on models manufactured prior to this date, if the same bolts are re-used, they must retain their washers.

2　If checks have not been made on the cylinder liner protrusions since the head was removed, refer to Section 30 and ensure that the protrusions are within limits. Note that, if new liner gaskets have not been fitted, the old ones being still in place, the protrusion limits are 0·07 mm (0·003 in) minimum to 0·18 mm (0·007 in) maximum.

3　Having checked that the mating surfaces of the cylinder head and crankcase are perfectly clean, ensure also that they protrude by 7 mm (0·276 in) above the surface of the crankcase (photo).

4　Rotate the crankshaft and position it so that the pulley keyway is in alignment with the crankcase to main bearing housing joint as shown in Fig. 1.17. This is necessary to position the pistons at the halfway position in the bores to prevent the possibility of the pistons and valves touching, and to enable the correct valve timing to be set.

5　Place a new cylinder head gasket into position on the crankcase (photo). Do not apply any form of sealant.

6　Lower the cylinder head into position and locate over the protruding dowels. The dowels must not be pushed down into the crankcase when fitting the cylinder head (photo).

7　Rotate the camshaft so that the sprocket keyway is aligned as shown in Fig. 1.18.

8　Refit the rocker shaft assembly to the cylinder head and check that the alignment dowels are properly located. The rocker finger wear faces should be lubricated with multi-purpose grease.

9　Install the cylinder head bolts, with their washers if applicable (paragraph 1), and with their threads and the contact surfaces under the bolt heads oiled. Fit the retaining nuts to the bolts and tighten the

33.5 Fit a new cylinder head gasket using no sealant

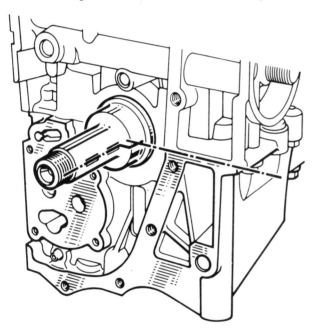

Fig. 1.17 Align the crankshaft key with the case flange joint (Sec 33)

33.6 Lowering the cylinder head onto the block

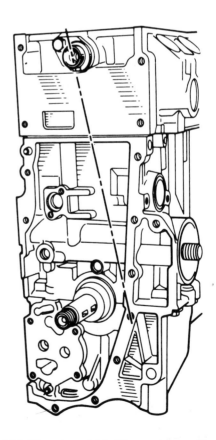

Fig. 1.18 Align the camshaft key as shown (Sec 33)

bolts in two stages to the specified torque in the sequence shown in Fig. 1.3. Initially tighten all bolts to the first stage load and then repeat the sequence to the full tightening load.
10 See Section 42 for the retightening procedure that is necessary after the first engine run.

34 Timing sprockets and chain – refitting

1   Check that the keyways of the crankshaft and the camshaft are positioned as shown in Figs. 1.17 and 1.18, and insert the keys.
2   Fit the respective camshaft and crankshaft sprockets into the timing chain so that the timing marks on the chain and sprockets correspond, see Fig. 1.19. If the marks on the chain are not visible, lay the chain out as shown in the photo and mark the three links as indicated (photo).
3   Supporting the sprockets in position in the chain, assemble them onto their respective shafts and tap evenly into position over the keys.
4   Refit the chain tensioner filter into its recess in the end of the cylinder block (photo).
5   Refit the chain tensioner unit, retaining with two bolts which must be tightened to the torque figure specified.
6   Using a screwdriver, release the tensioner lock ratchet by screwing in a clockwise direction and allow the tensioner spring to automatically take up the chain tension (photo).
7   Check that the sprockets are in alignment, then refit the fuel pump operating cam and bolt (photo). Tighten the bolt to the specified torque.
8   The oil pump unit is fitted next and should be lubricated with clean engine oil prior to installation. Make sure that the locating dowel is in place. Fit the pump together with its spacer plate and secure with the four Allen screws and spring washers, which must be progressively tightened to the specified torque (photo).
9   When tightened, check that the pump spindle is free to rotate. If it is stiff or binds, loosen the retaining bolts and relocate the pump unit. Retighten the bolts and recheck the pump spindle action. It is essential that the pump rotates freely.
10 If not already fitted to the pump unit, refit the driven gear to the spindle flange, and retain with the special tab washer and three bolts. Tighten the bolts and then bend over the tab washer to lock the bolt heads (photos).
11 Fit the key into the crankshaft and slide the oil pump drive gear into position (or spacer and drive gear – dependent on the type fitted).

35 Engine and gearbox – reassembly

1   Before assembling the two units, check that the respective mating faces are perfectly clean.
2   If the transmission unit has not been dismantled it is advisable to remove the bottom cover plate and extract the gauze oil pump suction filter, retained by four bolts. Clean the filter thoroughly using petrol, and dry with compressed air. Refit the suction filter unit and sump cover in the reverse sequence using a new gasket. Tighten the bolts to the specified torque. This additional chore is well worthwhile, ensuring

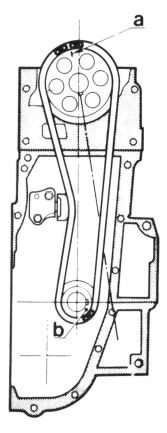

Fig. 1.19 Fit the timing chain to the sprockets so that the bright links (a and b) align with the sprocket marks (Sec 34)

that any sludge or particles trapped in the sump tray or suction filter will not be circulated around the rebuilt engine.
3   Install a new O-ring into position where the oil pump suction pipe passes through the engine/transmission joint face (photo).
4   Check that the two locating dowels are in position on the joint face of the engine (Fig. 1.20) and then smear a layer of sealer over the joint face. Be careful not to get carried away applying the sealer as it must not be allowed to enter the oil supply channel (photo).
5   Fit the gearbox to the engine taking care not to press the location dowels inwards (photo). Insert four convenient bolts to hold the casings together and do them up finger tight. Do not fully tighten until all the fastenings are in position. These consist of four top bolts and one nut at the timing end, one top bolt and one nut at the flywheel end, six bottom bolts, and two bolts and one nut on the flywheel face (Fig. 1.9). When all the fastenings are installed and finger tight use a torque wrench to tighten to the specified torque. **Do not overtighten.**

34.2 To identify the timing chain marked links, place the chain as shown. A indicates two adjacent marked links (camshaft sprocket) and B one marked link (crankshaft sprocket)

34.4 Refitting the tensioner filter

34.6 Releasing the tensioner lock ratchet

34.7 Tightening the camshaft bolt

34.8 Fitting the oil pump spacer plate. Note the spacer fitted to the crankshaft

34.10a The oil pump drive wheels installed

34.10b Tighten the retaining bolts and then ...

34.10c ... bend up the locking washer

35.3 Fitting a new O-ring to the oil pipe

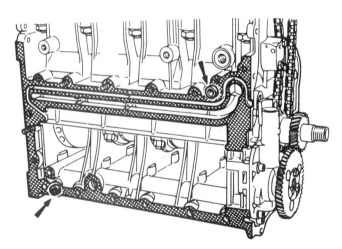

Fig. 1.20 Ensure that the two locating dowels (arrowed) are in position (Sec 35)

36 Timing cover – refitting on rebuild

1   Check that the mating surfaces of the timing cover and gearbox crankcase are clean.

2   If it has been removed, fit a new oil seal into the timing cover with the cavity side inwards. Use a tube drift or socket spanner to tap it squarely into position until the inner face is flush with the housing. Ensure that the seal is fitted correctly and do not distort or damage it during assembly. Lubricate the seal lips (photo).

3   Position the timing cover gasket on the cylinder block but do not use any sealant. Fit the timing cover and install the retaining bolts, but do not tighten (photo).

4   Fit the key and pulley to the crankshaft and centralise the cover

before tightening the timing cover bolts fully to the specified torque (photos).

5   Carefully trim off the portion of gasket protruding above the cylinder head flush with the rocker cover face using a sharp knife (photo).

6   Fit the pulley retaining nut and new a tab washer and then tighten the nut to the specified torque load. Restrain the crankshaft from turning with two bolts and a lever. Bend up the tab washer to lock the nut when tight (photo).

7   Lubricate the fuel pump actuating rod and insert it in the housing. Refit the fuel pump using a new gasket (photos).

37 Valve rocker clearances – checking and adjustment

1   This operation is the same whether carried out with the engine installed or removed. When performed as a maintenance task with the engine installed, the work must only be undertaken when the engine is cold.

2   The engine can be turned by using a spanner on the crankshaft pulley bolt – rotation is made easier if the spark plugs are removed.

3   Remove the rocker cover and then turn the engine until the valves on No 1 cylinder are rocking (ie inlet valve opening and exhaust valve closing). The rocker arm clearances of both valves of No 4 cylinder can now be checked and if necessary adjusted. Remember that No 1 cylinder is at the flywheel end of the engine.

4   The feeler gauge of the correct thickness is inserted between the valve stem and rocker arm. When the clearance is correctly set the feeler gauge should be a smooth sliding fit between the valve stem and rocker arm.

5   If the feeler gauge is a tight or loose fit then the clearance must be adjusted. To do this, loosen the locknut of the adjustment stud and screw the adjuster stud in or out until the feeler gauge blade can be felt to drag slightly when drawn from the gap.

6   Hold the adjuster firmly in this position and tighten the locknut. Recheck the gap on completion to ensure that it has not altered when locking the nut and stud.

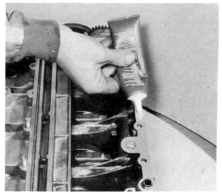
35.4 Take care not to contaminate oilways with sealant

35.5 Fitting the gearbox to the engine

36.2 Using a socket spanner to fit a new oil seal in the timing cover

36.3 Use a new gasket and fit the timing cover

36.4a Before tightening the bolts, use the crankshaft pulley to centralise the seal and cover ...

36.4b ... then tighten the retaining bolts

36.5 Trim off the surplus gasket

36.6 Tighten the pulley retaining nut to the specified torque

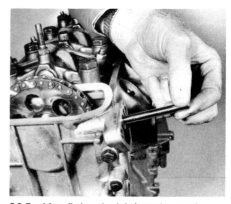
36.7a After fitting the lubricated actuating rod ...

36.7b ... fit a new gasket ...

36.7c ... and then fit the fuel pump

37.7 Adjusting No 1 cylinder exhaust valve clearance

7   Check each valve clearance in turn in the following sequence (photo):

Valves rocking on cylinder	Adjust clearances on cylinder
1	4
3	2
4	1
2	3

8   Refit the rocker cover using a new gasket (photo).

38 Flywheel – refitting

1   Prior to refitting the flywheel to the crankshaft flange the mating faces must be examined for any signs of dents or burrs and if necessary these must be carefully removed using a fine file. Any oil or dirt must also be wiped away before the flywheel is fitted.
2   Fit the flywheel to the flange and align the bolt holes. These are asymmetrically spaced to ensure correct alignment of the two components (photo).
3   Insert the bolts, which must be smeared with thread locking compound to prevent them working loose, and tighten them to the specified torque (photos).
4   Refit the clutch unit as described in Chapter 5.

39 Transfer gear unit and clutch housing – reassembly

1   Fit the snap-rings to the grooves in the bearing housing apertures.
2   Ensure that the bearing housings are perfectly clean before inserting the bearings.
3   Lubricate the bearings and press or drift them into their apertures in the housing. As the bearings are inserted the snap-rings will have to be expanded to allow the bearing entry. Check that the bearings are inserted with the snap-ring groove in the outer race offset to the top.
4   Use a suitable diameter tube to press or drive the bearing home. If a press is used take care not to use too much pressure as the bearing

aperture may be damaged or crack if the bearing is not in correct alignment with the housing. Press the bearing in until the snap-ring locates in both the bearing and housing grooves.
5   The input and output shafts are fitted to their respective bearings so that the gears are located on the opposite side of the bearing to the snap-ring.
6   The gearbox input shaft is located at the widest end of the housing. Each shaft should be pressed or drifted in until it butts against its respective bearing (photo).
7   Each shaft is retained by a dished spring washer and a snap-ring. The washer is fitted with its concave side towards the bearing.
8   Press or drift a snap-ring into position on each shaft so that it locates in the shaft groove against the pressure of the spring washer.
9   Lubricate the needle roller bearings and insert one into the clutch housing and the other into the transfer gear housing using the intermediate gear as an aid to installation. Tape the input shaft splines. Align the intermediate gear to mesh with the input and output gears and fit it into the transfer gear housing (photos).
10   When the intermediate gear is in position the teeth of the gear must be in exact alignment with those of the output and input gears. Place a straight-edge along the side of the three gears to check that their heights are the same. Also check that the gears rotate freely.
11   Check that the dowels are in position in the clutch housing, apply sealant to the joint faces and locate the transfer gear housing over the dowels (photos).
12   Before refitting the cover plate apply sealant to both joint faces. Refit the cover using a new gasket. Tighten the retaining bolts to the specified torque. Remove the tape from the input shaft splines (photos).
13   Make sure the locating dowels are positioned in the crankcase and fit a new gasket over them. Do not use sealant. Offer up the clutch housing and transfer gear housing assembly to the engine – turn the flywheel and input shaft alternately to enable the splines to mesh. When correctly positioned retain with the bolts. Do not forget that the engine bracket and the clutch cable sleeve stop are attached to the engine by these bolts. Tighten the bolts to the specified torque. See Chapter 5 for further details.

37.8 Fitting the rocker cover

38.2 Fit the flywheel to the crankshaft

38.3a Use a gag to prevent rotation and ...

38.3b ... tighten the retaining bolts

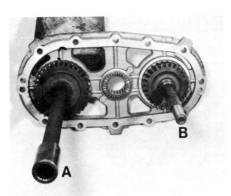
39.6 The input shaft (A) and the output shaft (B) positioned in the housing

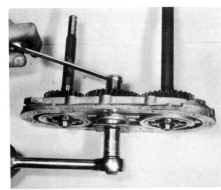
39.9a Fitting a new needle roller bearing in the housing

39.9b Bind the input shaft splines to protect the clutch housing seal on assembly

39.9c Lubricate the needle roller bearing in the housing and ...

39.9d ... fit the intermediate gear

39.11a Check that the two locating dowels (arrowed) are fitted in the clutch housing

39.11b Apply sealant to the mating faces then ...

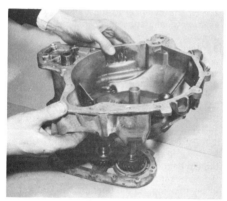
39.11c ... assemble the clutch housing to the transfer gear housing

39.12a Using a new gasket and sealant, refit the transfer gear cover plate and ...

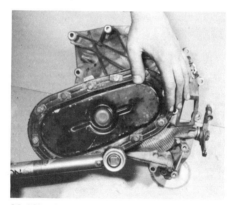
39.12b ... tighten the retaining bolts to the specificied torque

39.12c Make sure that the protective binding is removed after assembly!

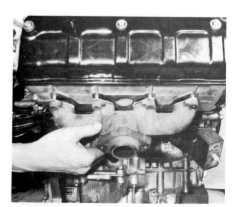
40.3 Refitting the exhaust manifold using new gaskets

40.4 Fit a new O-ring seal to the distributor before refitting

41.3 Grease the driveshaft seal bearing faces before refitting the engine

40 Engine reassembly – final stages

1 Having reassembled the major engine components, the various ancillary components can now be refitted. We chose to reassemble most of those components prior to engine installation. However you may for some reason prefer to delay fitting some of the items mentioned below until the engine is reinstalled. In this case ensure that it will be possible to refit the component once the engine is in position.

2 Refit the rear engine mounting crossmember.

3 Refit the exhaust manifold using new gaskets and tighten the retaining nuts to the specified torque (photo).

4 Refit the distributor making sure its offset drive pegs engage into the corresponding slots in the end of the camshaft. Use a new O-ring seal (photo) and secure with three bolts and washers. Refer to Chapter 4 and adjust the ignition timing, then tighten the bolts.

5 Bolt the carburettor directly onto the cylinder head, using a new gasket.

6 Place the starter motor into position and retain with the three bolts at the clutch housing and two bolts in the bracket at the tail end.

7 Refit the water pump, alternator, and adjusting bracket. Fit the drivebelt and adjust the tension, see Chapter 2.

8 Refit the forward engine mounting brackets and tighten the retaining bolts to the specified torque. Temporarily secure the limiters with elastic bands.

9 Reconnect the gearbox end of the speedometer cable and tighten the retaining bolt.

10 The engine is now ready for refitting

41 Engine/transmission unit – refitting

1 Generally speaking the installation of the engine is a reversal of the removal procedure and is as follows.

2 Check that the lifting sling is securely located and is adequate for the job. Raise the front of the car and support it on stands so that the front wheels hang free.

3 Before lowering the engine into the car check that the surrounding components in the engine compartment are out of the way, and grease the driveshafts (photo).

4 Lower the engine slowly and guide it carefully into a position, offset to the left-hand side of the car, at a suitable height to allow the right-hand driveshaft to enter the differential housing. Guide the driveshaft carefully into position and take care not to damage the oil seal in the differential housing. This may prove fiddly and patience will be necessary. Do not force the shaft home.

5 When the right-hand side driveshaft has slid into position, slowly swing the engine over to the right-hand side of the car taking care not to damage any components or fittings.

6 Guide the left-hand driveshaft into place in a similar manner.

7 When both driveshafts are re-engaged, slowly centralize the engine over its mountings. Refit any washers that have been removed before lowering the engine. Refit the mounting nuts and tighten to the specified torque.

8 Refit the gear control linkage, inserting the retaining bolt into the steering rack housing (just to the right of centre).

9 Reconnect the exhaust pipe to the manifold.

10 Reconnect the gear change control rods and clamp, aligning the reference marks. Assuming that the gearbox is in neutral, restrain the gear lever in the corresponding position and tighten the clamp. Check the gear lever engagement positions, and if necessary adjust accordingly until all gears can be selected satisfactorily. (See Chapter 6 for further details). Alternatively, engage 1st gear, move the gear lever into the corresponding position and tighten the rod connecting clamp. Recheck for satisfactory gear engagement.

11 Refit the preheat duct which is attached to the exhaust manifold and the crossmember.

12 Reconnect the speedometer cable.

13 Attach the exhaust pipe stay bracket to the differential housing and retain with spacers and bolts.

14 Refit the clutch actuating rod and connect the spring over the lever – see Chapter 5 for further information and adjustment procedure.

15 Reconnect the fuel supply line to the fuel pump inlet pipe and connect the carburettor fuel line to the pump outlet.

16 Refit the distributor rotor arm, plastic cover and cap. Reconnect the HT leads to the spark plugs and coil.

17 Reconnect the coolant system hoses to their relevant connections. Check that the thermostat is located in the cylinder block outlet hose before connecting the hose to the block.

18 If your car is equipped with servo assisted brakes, reconnect the brake servo hose to the cylinder head connection.

19 Connect the choke cable to the carburettor and attach the outer cable (in rubber protector sleeve) to the vertical bracket on the cylinder head, adjacent to the temperature sender unit.

20 Attach the accelerator cable and the throttle connector rod to the throttle return spring bracket. Check the operation of the choke and accelerator controls on assembly.

21 Reconnect the hose from the cowling to the preheat ducting.

22 Connect the battery earth cable to the clutch housing stud and retain with nut, and reconnect the yellow earth cable to the inner wing panel.

23 Remove the hardboard protector from the radiator or, if the radiator was removed, refit it, locating the bottom pins into their holes in the car structure, and secure the retaining bolt. Refit the fan unit and reconnnect the coolant hoses.

24 Refit the battery support extension and locate the plastic drip tray on it. Refit the battery but do not connect it yet, and secure the retaining clamp plate (photo). Refit the horn.

25 Replace the lower limiting stop bolt.

26 Reconnect the following electrical components:

(a) Alternator
(b) Coolant temperature sender switch (photo)
(c) Oil pressure switch (photo)
(d) Coil
(e) Radiator temperature sender unit and fan
(f) Starter solenoid
(g) Engine earth strap

27 Refit the air filter unit and connect up the ducting.

28 Refit the coolant expansion tank and reconnect the hoses. Refill the cooling system after checking that all hose joints are made secure, with their clips tight, and drain plugs fitted. See Chapter 2 for filling procedure.

29 Refit the spare wheel support bracket, but leave the wheel out

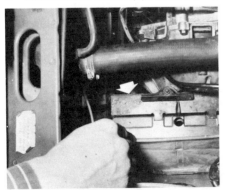
41.24 With the battery support extension (arrowed) fitted, refit the plastic drip tray

41.26a The coolant temperature sender switch

41.26b The oil pressure switch

until the engine runs and adjustments have been completed.
30 Refill the engine/transmission unit with the correct grade and quantity of engine oil. Wipe up any spillages to avoid confusion with possible oil leaks.
31 Go round the engine and check that all refitting operations have been completed. When satisfied, reconnect the battery terminals, earth terminal last, and then test the operation of the electrical circuits. If all is well the engine is ready for starting. Make sure that all tools and rags are removed from the engine compartment. Refit the bonnet.

42 Engine – initial start-up after overhaul

1 Make sure that the battery is fully charged and that all lubricants, coolant and fuel are replenished.
2 It will require several revolutions of the engine on the starter motor to pump the petrol up to the carburettor.
3 As soon as the engine fires and runs, keep it going at a fast tickover only (no faster), and bring it up to the normal working temperature.
4 As the engine warms up there will be odd smells and some smoke from parts getting hot and burning off oil deposits. The signs to look for are leaks of water or oil which will be obvious if serious. Check also the exhaust pipe and manifold connections, as these do not always 'find' their exact gas tight position until the warmth and vibration have acted on them, and it is almost certain that they will need tightening further. This should be done of course, with the engine stopped.
5 When normal running temperature has been reached adjust the engine idling speed, as described in Chapter 3. Run the engine until the fan cuts in and then switch off. Check that no oil or coolant is leaking with the engine stationary.
6 Allow at least two hours for the engine to cool down and then retighten the cylinder head bolts after removing the rocker cover. Follow the bolt tightening sequence and, starting with the first, completely slacken the bolt and retighten it to the specified final tightening torque before loosening the second bolt. Repeat until all bolts have been retightened.
7 Recheck the valve clearances with reference to Section 37, then refit the rocker cover.
8 Road test the car to check that the timing is correct and that the engine is giving the necessary smoothness and power. Do not race the engine – if new bearings and/or pistons have been fitted it should be treated as a new engine and run in at a reduced speed.

43 Fault diagnosis – engine

Symptom	Reason/s
Engine will not turn over when starter switch is operated	Flat battery Bad battery conditions Bad connections at solenoid switch and/or starter motor Starter motor jammed Defective solenoid Starter motor defective
Engine turns over normally but fails to fire and run	No sparks at plugs No fuel reaching engine Too much fuel reaching engine (flooding)
Engine starts but runs unevenly and misfires	Ignition and/or fuel system faults Incorrect valve clearances Burnt out valves Blown cylinder head gasket, dropped liners Worn out piston rings Worn cylinder bores
Lack of power	Ignition and/or fuel system faults Incorrect valve clearance Burnt out valves Blown cylinder head gasket Worn out piston rings Worn cylinder bores
Excessive oil consumption	Oil leaks from crankshaft oil seal, timing cover gasket and oil seal, rocker cover gasket, crankcase or gearbox joint Worn piston rings or cylinder bores resulting in oil being burnt by engine (smoky exhaust is an indication) Worn valve guides and/or defective valve stem
Excessive mechanical noise from engine	Wrong valve to rocker clearance Worn crankshaft bearings Worn cylinders (piston slap) Slack or worn timing chain and sprockets Worn transfer gears and/or bearings

Chapter 2 Cooling and heating systems

Contents

Specifications

Type of system . . . . Pressurised and sealed with centrifugal circulation pump, thermostat and electric cooling fan

Coolant capacity . . . . 9.8 pints (5.6 litres)

Coolant . . . . Mixture of water and antifreeze, Peugeot 9730.43 or equivalent, in proportions dependent on protection requirements. Cars with aluminium matrix radiators must use antifreeze Peugeot 9730.70, minimum 40%, with water mixture

Expansion tank . . . . Plastic, attached to engine bulkhead and incorporating pressurising valve

Radiator . . . . Corrugated fin and tube type with hot tank left-hand side and cool tank right-hand side

Fan . . . . Electric, thermostatically controlled to run at 88°C (190°F) and above
Standard fan . . . . 60W, Part No 1250.58
Recommended fan for 104ZS when caravan towing . . . . 100W, Part No 1250.59

Water pump . . . . Belt driven, centrifugal type

Drivebelt tension . . . . 1% stretch, ie 200 mm free length tightened to 202 mm, see text

Thermostat
Type . . . . Wax
Operating temperature:
    Starts to open . . . . 82°C (180°F)
    Fully open . . . . 94°C (201°F)

Torque wrench settings

	lbf ft	kgf m
Water pump to cylinder block bolts	10	1.4
Alternator mounting:		
Bolts in slotted bracket	13	1.75
Alternator pivot bolt	33	4.5

1 General description

1 The engine cooling water is circulated by a thermo syphon water pump assisted system and the coolant is pressurised.
2 The system comprises a radiator, a water pump, a fan, a thermostat, also top and bottom hoses and heater hoses. There is one drain plug located on the right-hand side underneath the cylinder block and another at the bottom of the radiator on the left-hand side.
3 The system functions in the following manner. Cold water from the bottom of the radiator circulates up the lower radiator hose to the water pump where it is pushed round the water passages in the cylinder block, helping to keep the cylinder liners and pistons cool.
4 The water then travels up into the cylinder head and circulates round the combustion spaces and valve seats absorbing more heat, and then, when the engine is at its correct operating temperature, travels out of the cylinder head, past the open thermostat into the upper radiator hose and so into the radiator hot tank on the left-hand side.
5 The water travels across the radiator where it is rapidly cooled by

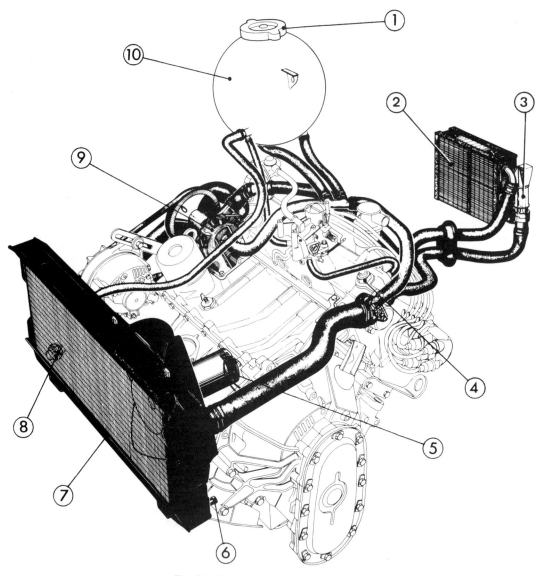

Fig. 2.1 The cooling system (Sec 1)

1 Filler cap	4 Coolant temperature	6 Radiator drain plug	control switch
2 Heater matrix	sender switch	7 Radiator	9 Water (coolant) pump
3 Heater control valve	5 Cooling fan motor	8 Cooling fan thermal	10 Expansion tank

the in-rush of cold air created by both the fan and the motion of the car. The water, now much cooler, reaches the cool tank side of the radiator and the cycle is repeated.

6   When the engine is cold the thermostat (which is a valve which opens and closes according to the temperature of the water) maintains the circulation of the same water in the engine.

7   Only when the correct minimum operating temperature has been reached does the thermostat begin to open, allowing water to return to the radiator.

8   The carburettor body contains waterways and is connected to the cooling system by small diameter pipes. This ensures that carburettor warm up is rapid and optimum combustion conditions soon reached.

9   The fan is powered by an electric motor which is only energised when the cooling water is hot. By this means the fan is only driven when it is really needed, with a consequent reduction in noise and power consumption.

2   Cooling system – draining

1   *It is dangerous to remove a cooling system filler cap when the*

system is hot owing to the risk of scalds from escaping steam or hot coolant. Remove the filler cap from the expansion tank by turning it anti-clockwise. If the engine is hot and it is not possible to wait for it to cool, cover the filler cap with a thick rag and then turn it very slightly until pressure in the system has had time to be released. With the pressure released the cap can then be removed.

2   Turn the heater control knob to the red spot (heat on) position.

3   If antifreeze mixture is used in the cooling system, position suitable containers, under the two drain plugs, in which to collect the liquid for re-use. Remove the plugs from the left bottom side of the radiator (photo) and from the right underside of the cylinder block.

4   When the coolant has stopped draining, probe the plug holes with a piece of wire to make sure that they have not become blocked with particles of rust or sediment.

3   Cooling system – flushing

1   In time the cooling system will gradually lose efficiency as the radiator becomes choked with rust, scale deposits from the water and other sediment. This is why old cars suffer so much from overheating

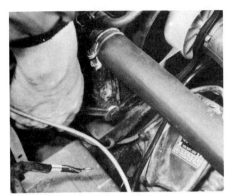

2.3 Removing the radiator drain plug (battery removed for clarity)

5.4 The thermal switch in the radiator controls the cooling fan

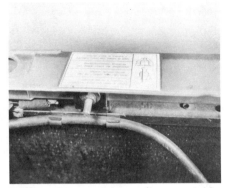

5.5 The radiator retaining nut (fan removed for clarity)

compared with newer cars. To restore cooling system efficiency it is necessary to flush the system clean. First drain the system, as explained in the previous Section, and remove the thermostat, as explained in Section 8; reconnect the hose in which the thermostat is housed. Disconnect the radiator top hose connection and, with the drain plugs removed, direct a flow of water through the radiator using a garden hosepipe. Protect the engine assembly by covering it with a sheet of plastic. When rust-free water emerges from the drain holes, direct the hosepipe into the radiator top hose and also into the expansion tank filler neck. Continue flushing until you are satisfied that the system is clean. On completion, refit the thermostat and reconnect the radiator top hose.

2   In badly contaminated systems, or where overheating has been a problem, the system should be reverse flushed. This involves forcing water the wrong way round the system to dislodge deposits which are not moved by conventional flushing. This can be done by disconnecting the radiator bottom hose, after having flushed the system normally, and with suitable adaptors connecting the garden hosepipe first to the bottom connector on the radiator and then to the bottom hose. If any doubt remains about the inner cleanliness of the radiator, it should be removed so that it can be flushed and agitated at the same time. See Section 5 for radiator removal and refitting. After reverse flushing, carry out a normal flow direction flush before refitting the thermostat and reconnecting the system hoses.

4   Cooling system – filling

1   Before attempting to fill the cooling system, refit and tighten the cylinder block and radiator drain plugs. Check that all hose connections are tight. The method of filling depends on whether or not your car has two manual bleed screws in the system, one in the radiator de-aerator hose and another in the carburettor preheater inlet hose. These bleed screws are fitted to models made in 1978 and after.

Models without bleed screws

2   Check that the heater control knob is set to heat on (red spot).
3   Remove the expansion tank filler cap and fill the system slowly to reduce the chances of air locks forming. If your radiator has a filler plug in the top, this should be removed until the radiator is full, when the plug should be refitted. Fill the system until the expansion tank is about half full or the level is up to the indicator visible through the filler neck. Repeated squeezing of the large coolant hoses will induce surging in the coolant in the system which will help to dislodge air bubbles. Refit the cap tightly and proceed to paragraph 5.

Models with bleed screws

4   Undo the attachment bolts securing the expansion tank to the structure and, with all hoses still connected, suspend the tank as high as possible from the raised bonnet with wire or string. Open the two bleed screws and fill the system through the expansion tank filler neck. When air-free coolant flows from the bleed screws, tighten them and continue filling the system until the tank is half full. Refit the filler cap tightly and refit the expansion tank into its mounting.

All models

5   After filling the system, run the engine until the cooling fan motor

engages. Where bleed screws are fitted, open them until air-free coolant flows and retighten them. Stop the engine and allow to cool. Top up the coolant level in the expansion tank, as necessary.
6   Finally inspect the system for leaks, especially if any part of the cooling system has been disturbed for repair or overhaul.

5   Radiator – removal, inspection and refitting

1   The radiator can be removed complete with the electrically driven cooling fan if there is no need to disturb the fan. If the fan must be removed, refer to Section 10.
2   Drain the cooling system as described in Section 2 and disconnect the battery earth terminal.
3   Detach the radiator top and bottom hoses and detach the small diameter vent hose between the top of the radiator and the expansion tank.
4   Disconnect the electric wiring from the thermal switch in the radiator at the lower right-hand side (photo). Disconnect the fan motor leads at the junction block in the vicinity of the front of the battery.
5   Unscrew and remove the single retaining nut at the top centre of the radiator (photo), and carefully lift the radiator clear after moving the top back slightly.
6   With the radiator assembly removed it is easier to examine for leaks which will show up as corroded or stained areas. Repairing a radiator by resoldering is a skilled job and should not be attempted by anyone without experience – it is very easy to make a bad situation much worse. Either get the radiator repaired by a specialist or try to salvage one from a breaker's yard.
7   Clean the inside of the radiator out by flushing, see Section 3, and also clean the matrix, removing all the dead flies and bugs which reduce the radiator's efficiency. Take this opportunity to inspect the hoses and clips, making sure that all are fit for further use.
8   Refitting the radiator is the reverse of the removal procedure. Ensure that the bottom location pegs fit correctly on installation. Refer to Section 4 for refilling the system.
9   A number of 104GL and ZL cars were produced in 1977 with radiators incorporating an aluminium matrix and plastic material water tanks. These cars have an identifying label attached to the radiator and to the upper part of the chassis front frame. *Extra care must be exercised with these radiators to avoid damage* and, when removing hoses, a twisting action should be employed as metal tools would damage the hose connections. If you intend to leave the radiator empty for more than 48 hours it should be flushed out with plain water and, if possible, dried with compressed air. *Avoid flushing these radiators with any caustic or alkaline product* as corrosion would quickly result. See Section 9 concerning the use of antifreeze in this type of radiator.

6   Water pump – removal, inspection and refitting

1   Refer to Section 2 and drain the system. It is not necessary to empty the system providing the level is lower than the pump on completion.
2   Slacken the alternator mountings and remove the drivebelt.

6.7 Renewing the water pump/cylinder block O-ring seal

6.9 Refitting the water pump

3   Slacken the hose clips and disconnect the coolant hoses from the pump.
4   Undo the three bolts securing the pump to the cylinder block and remove the pump.
5   With the pump on the bench clean the exterior thoroughly. Clean the interior passages as far as possible.
6   Check the pump shaft for smooth rotation in its bearings and for freedom from sideways play. A small amount of endfloat on the shaft is normal.
7   Examine as far as possible for internal corrosion and also for signs of fluid leakage. Remove and discard the O-ring sealing the joint between the pump and cylinder block, and fit a new seal (photo).
8   Evidence of excessive wear, corrosion or damage such as cracks in the pump body will require renewal of the pump as no dismantling or repair is possible.
9   Refitting the pump is the reverse of the removal procedure. Tighten the three securing bolts to the specified torque (photo).

7   Drivebelt – tension

1   The correct tensioning of the drivebelt will ensure that it has a long and useful life. Beware, however, of over-tightening as this can cause excessive wear in the water pump and alternator bearings.
2   The tension of the drivebelt is adjusted by altering the position of

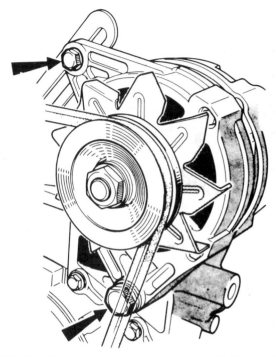

Fig. 2.2 The alternator mounting bolts (arrowed). The top bolt locates in the slotted bracket (Sec 7)

the alternator which is determined by the slotted support handily placed above it.
3   Peugeot recommend an easy way of checking the tension which has the great merit that something is actually measured. On the drivebelt between the alternator and the water pump make two marks with chalk or wax crayon 200 mm apart with the belt unstretched.
4   Slacken the nut and bolt securing the alternator to the slotted support, but do not loosen it completely,* as some friction in swinging the alternator is helpful in tensioning the belt. Also slightly loosen the lower pivots of the alternator and the slotted bracket (Fig. 2.2).
5   With a piece of wood as a lever between the engine and the mounting bracket end of the alternator, move the alternator up to tighten the drivebelt so that the marks on the belt stretch to 202 mm apart. Tighten the alternator securing bolts. *It is important not to lever on the alternator body* as internal damage could result.
6   The securing bolts should be tightened to the torque loads quoted in the Specifications at the front of this Chapter. Note that the bolts and nuts should have the following washers:

   (a) *Alternator pivot bolt and nut – flat washer under the bolt head and internal star lockwasher under the nut*
   (b) *Alternator bolt and nut in slotted bracket – spring lockwasher under the bolt head, flat washer and internal star lockwasher under the nut*
   (c) *Slotted bracket pivot bolt – double star lockwasher under the head*

8   Thermostat – removal, testing and refitting

1   The thermostat is located at the engine end of the coolant hose running from the cylinder head to the top of the radiator.
2   Partially drain the cooling system as described in Section 2.
3   Slacken the hose clips at the engine end of the hose and detach the hose from the casting (photo).
4   Extract the thermostat from the hose, taking care not to damage it (photo).
5   The thermostat can easily be tested for correct functioning if this should be in doubt. Boil a pan of water and suspend the thermostat on a piece of cord. Lower the thermostat into the hot water and it should be seen to open on immersion. Remove the thermostat and allow it to cool and it should be seen to close. This is only a simple function test but it will identify a failed thermostat. When renewing this component

8.3 Removing the top hose from the cylinder head to gain access to the thermostat

8.4 Removing the thermostat from the top hose

8.5 The cooling system thermostat, marked 82°C, the opening temperature

10.2 Two of the four fan assembly attachment screws (arrowed)

10.3 The fan motor end cap removed to reveal the brushes

11.1a The early type of expansion tank with filler cap removed

make sure that the replacement is the correct item for your model as thermostats are made for a wide range of different models and conditions (photo). You can drive without a thermostat in an emergency: no harm will result but the engine will not warm up properly.

6   Refitting the thermostat is the reverse procedure to removal.

9 Antifreeze mixture

1   It is a sensible precaution to keep the cooling system filled with antifreeze mixture instead of plain water. Apart from the obvious protection against damage caused by low temperatures, suitable antifreeze liquids are available containing an inhibitor against corrosion which, of course, works all year round.

2   Some models of the 104 GL and ZL versions were originally equipped with radiators having an aluminium matrix. These can be identified by labels on the upper front frame and on the radiator. *It is essential that these cars are only filled with antifreeze mixture of the specified grade* and never with plain water or other type antifreeze solutions.

3   Antifreeze should be mixed in accordance with the manufacturer's instructions on the container and the proportion of liquid to water should be chosen to meet the local weather conditions. In the absence of any other instructions use 1 litre (1.76 pints) antifreeze in the system for protection down to -7°C (19°F), 2 litres (3.52 pints) in temperatures down to -18°C (-0.4°F), or 3 litres (5.28 pints) in temperatures down to -35°C (-31°F). Cars with aluminium matrix radiators must have at least 40% antifreeze content, ie 2.25 litres (3.96 pints); using the special antifreeze liquid, all the year round.

4   Before filling the system with antifreeze mixture check that all the hoses are in sound condition and that all hose clips are tight. Antifreeze has a searching action and will leak more readily than plain water.

5   Renew the coolant mixture every 2 years, as the inhibitor in the solution will by then be of little value. When it is necessary to top up the cooling system, use a mixture of the same strength as that in the system.

10 Radiator electric fan – removal and refitting

1   Disconnect the battery earth terminal and disconnect the fan motor leads at the junction block near the front of the battery.

2   Unscrew and remove the four attachment screws retaining the fan assembly to the radiator and remove the assembly from the car (photo).

3   Further dismantling of the fan unit depends on the problem. The motor brushes can be inspected by prising off the two spring clips retaining the end cap to the motor body. Note, as this is a permanent magnet motor, *do not dismantle the motor where there are any ferrous metal filings* as they could cause serious damage if they contaminate the motor internally. If the brushes are worn, new ones will be required (photo). In this case it may be necessary to have the motor overhauled by a specialist as it is not likely that spares will be available.

4   Reassembly, if the unit was dismantled, and refitting to the car are the reverse of the dismantling procedures. Run the engine up to normal operating temperatures and check the fan for correct functioning.

11 Expansion tank – general

1   Early cars are fitted with a roughly triangular shaped black plastic expansion tank located at the left rear of the engine compartment. Later cars have a white spherical plastic tank located in the same place. The purpose of the tank is to accommodate surplus coolant from the system as it expands on heating and return it to the system on cooling. Any air in the system can also separate out in the expansion tank and be vented to atmosphere if pressure builds up beyond the relief valve setting in the filler cap. Normally no trouble should be experienced with the tank but it is a simple job to remove it for cleaning or to gain access to something else (photos).

2   Before removing the expansion tank, drain off sufficient coolant to permit tank removal without spillage, see Section 2 for drainage procedure. Identify each of the hoses connected to the tank so that

11.1b Later cars are fitted with a spherical expansion tank

14.4 The heater location in the car, showing the coolant supply and return pipes

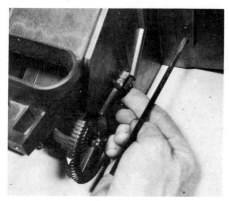

14.5a To open the heater casing release the spring clips on the sides and ...

14.5b ... undo the retaining screws (heater upside down). Then ...

14.5c ... lift off the upper half-case and ...

14.5d ... lift the matrix out of the lower half

14.5e The control valves simply lift out

14.5f When assembling the heater make sure that the spring and ball detents are fitted

14.5g Carefully locate the control rods in the control knobs when fitting the front panel

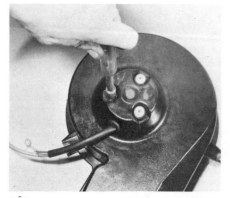

14.9a Undo the three retaining nuts ...

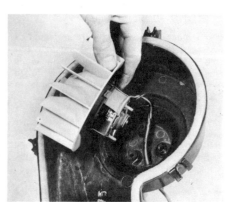

14.9b ... to release the heater fan motor from its casing

they can be reconnected to their proper locations on reassembly and then disconnect the hoses. Undo and remove the tank attachment bolts, noting the position of washers and spacers, where fitted, and remove the tank.

3   Refit in the reverse order. Before refitting, wash out any sediment and scum with hot water and check the condition of hoses and clips.

12 Cooling fan thermal switch – removal and refitting

1   The cooling fan is controlled by a thermal switch (and also, on early models, a relay). The switch is located on the right-hand side rear face of the radiator (photo 5.4).

2   To remove the switch, first drain the coolant from the system as described in Section 2, and disconnect the battery earth lead.

3   Disconnect the electrical leads from the switch and unscrew the switch from the radiator.

4   Refitting is the reverse of the removal procedure. Refill the system as described in Section 43 and run the engine up to its normal operating temperature to check the fan for correct functioning, and to check for leaks.

13 Coolant temperature sender unit – removal and refitting

1   The coolant temperature sender unit is located in the cylinder head between the coolant outlet connection (at the distrbituor end of the head) and the carburettor mounting (See Chapter 1, photo 41.26 (a)).

2   Before removing the sender unit, drain sufficient coolant from the system to avoid spillage when the unit is removed, as described in Section 2, and disconnect the battery earth cable.

3   Disconnect the electrical wires from the sender unit terminals; unscrew and remove the unit from the cylinder block.

4   Refitting is the reverse of the removal procedure; refill the system as described in Section 4. Run the engine up to normal operating temperature and check for leaks.

14 Heating system – general

1   The heater is located centrally under the facia and it supplies warm air for interior heating or windscreen demisting. Hot coolant is piped from the engine through a heater matrix and back to the engine when a manually operated valve mounted on the left side of the matrix is opened. The valve is controlled by the left-hand knob on the heater control panel – blue spot, cold, and red spot, hot. With the car in motion, air is forced through the system when the right-hand knob on the control panel is turned clockwise. When the car is stopped, or when additional hot air is required, an electrically driven fan, located under the facia on the right-hand side, can be switched on to high or low speed.

2   Normally the heater components give very little trouble and require negligible maintenance. An occasional check of the hoses and connections for condition and leaks is all that is usually required. Should it be necessary to remove any part of the system, proceed as follows.

Heater matrix

3   Partially drain the cooling system (see Section 2) to permit removal of the heater without spillage. Alternatively, fit clamps to the two heater hoses, taking care not to damage the hoses. Disconnect the two hoses at the left-hand side of the heater. Be prepared to catch a small quantity of coolant as the connections are broken.

4   Undo and remove the heater assembly attachment fasteners; there are two nuts at the front on studs fixed to the structure and a nut and bolt to the left and right ends of the heater control panel. Lower the assembly and remove from the car; hold the left side high to retain the coolant in the matrix (photo).

5   The assembly holding the matrix is all plastic and it can be removed easily by undoing the retaining screws and clips. Work methodically and lay out the parts as they are removed so that reassembly is simplified. With the matrix removed, examine it for leaks and clean the air passages free of dust and fluff (photos).

Heater valve

6   To gain access to the heater valve it is probably easier and quicker to remove the whole assembly as described for the heater matrix. The valve is attached to the left side of the matrix. A leaking valve will need to be renewed as repairs are not practicable.

Heater fan and motor

7   The heater fan assembly is awkwardly located under the facia and just forward of the right-hand air vent.

8   To remove the fan assembly, first disconnect the battery earth cable and then the electrical lead and earth wire from the fan assembly. Undo and remove the assembly retaining nuts and withdraw the unit. It will be necessary to move other wires out of the way and manoeuvre the assembly out.

9   Remove the shroud by undoing the three retaining nuts, but be careful not to lose the specially shaped anti-vibration rubber washers. For comments on servicing the fan motor see paragraph 3 of Section 10 dealing with the radiator fan. The heater fan motor, although smaller, is also a permanent magnet motor (photos).

10   Reassembly is the reverse of removal but make sure that the anti-vibration washers are correctly reassembled. On completion test the fan for correct functioning.

15 Fault diagnosis – cooling system

Symptom	Reason/s
Loss of coolant	Loose clips on hoses Hoses perished or leaking Radiator leaking Filler/pressure cap spring weak or seal ineffective Blown cylinder head gasket Cracked cylinder block or head
Overheating	Insufficient coolant in system Pump ineffective due to slack drivebelt Radiator blocked either internally or externally Kinked or collapsed hose causing coolant flow restriction Thermostat not working properly Engine out of tune Cylinder head gasket blown Engine not yet run-in Exhaust system partially blocked Engine oil level too low
Engine running too cool	Faulty, incorrect or missing thermostat

Chapter 3 Fuel and exhaust systems

Contents

Specifications

Fuel pump
Type . . . .   Mechanical, driven from camshaft

Fuel tank
Capacity . . . .   8.8 galls (40 litres)

Fuel filters . . . .   Gauze mesh, located in fuel pump and carburettor inlet

Air cleaner . . . .   Renewable element

Carburettor types
104, 104GL and ZL (954 cc):
    From start to Feb 1974 . . . .   Solex 32 HNSA (manual choke)
    From Feb 1974 . . . .   Solex 32 HSA (manual choke)
104SL (1124 cc) . . . .   Solex 32 PBISA (manual choke)
104S and ZS . . . .   Solex 32 TMMIA (automatic choke)

Carburettor specifications

Type 32 HNSA:	PEU 83	
Main jet (Gg)	122.5 to 127.5	
Idling jet (g)	49.5 to 55.5	
Constant richness idling jet (gCo)	32 to 38	
Needle valve (P)	1.2 mm dia	
Float (F)	14g	
Accelerator pump injector (i)	45	
Correction jet (a)	180 to 190	
Venturi (K)	26 mm dia	
Econostat orifice (Ce)	40 to 60	
Accelerator pump setting gauge	5 to 6	
Type 32 HSA:	**PEU 93 to 93/4**	**PEU 109 to A109/1**
Venturi (K)	25 mm dia	25 mm dia
Main jet (Gg)	117.5 to 122.5	112.5 to 117.5
Correction jet (a)	165 to 175	150 to 170
Idling jet (g)	43 to 53	38 to 48
Accelerator pump injector (i)	35 to 55	30 to 40
Needle ball valve (P)	1.2 mm dia	1.2 mm dia
Float (F)	7.5 g	7.5 g
Constant CO jet (gCo)	25 to 35	25 to 35
Econostat (E)	40 to 60	30 to 50
Accelerator pump setting gauge	3.5 to 4.5	6.5 to 7.5
Type 32 PBISA:	**PEU 101**	
Venturi (K)	25 mm dia	
Main jet (Gg)	125 to 130	
Correction jet (a)	140 to 170	
Idling jet (g)	37 to 47	
Pump injector (i)	30 to 50	
Ball needle valve (P)	1.5 mm dia	
Float (F)	5.7 g	
Constant CO jet (gCo)	25 to 35	

Econostat (E)	30 to 70	
Accelerator pump setting gauge	4.5 to 5.5	

Type 32 TMMIA:	**PEU 100 to 100/1**	**PEU 150 and 150/1**
Venturis (K)	24 mm dia	24 mm dia
Main jets (Gg)	120 to 125	120 to 125
Correction jets (a)	170 to 190	170 to 190
Idling jets (g)	38 to 48	38 to 48
Pump injectors (i)	30 to 40	30 to 40
Ball needle valve (P)	1.7 mm dia	1.7 mm dia
Float (F)	5.2 g	5.2 g
Constant CO orifice (gCO)	25 to 35	25 to 35
Econostat orifice (Ce)	90 to 110	90 to 110

Torque wrench settings

	lbf ft	**kgf m**
Needle valve assembly (32 TMMIA carb)	11.8	1.6

1 General description

The Peugeot 104 fuel system is conventional in layout and operation. The fuel tank is located at the rear of the car under the luggage
compartment. Fuel is drawn from the tank by an engine-driven
diaphragm pump which is mounted at the top of the timing chain
cover. The pump is actuated by a pushrod from an eccentric cam
mounted on the camshaft. The pump incorporates a mesh filter.

The Solex carburettor, with either single or twin barrels depending
on model, is attached to the cylinder head which has an integral induction manifold. The carburettor body is warmed by connections to the
engine cooling system.

Intake air is drawn through an air filter with a renewable element.
A manual valve is provided to select air warmed by the exhaust pipe in
cold weather or unheated air in warm weather (photo). Some models
incorporate an automatic preheating device.

The conventional exhaust system, incorporating a front and a rear
silencer, conducts exhaust gases from the exhaust manifold to
atmosphere. Heat shields are located over each silencer under the car
floor.

2 Air filter element – removal and refitting

1 The air filter element must be renewed at the mileage intervals
prescribed in the Routine Maintenance Section at the beginning of the
book. In severe environmental conditions such as hot dusty conditions the element should be changed more frequently.
2 If the filter element is not changed regularly it may become
clogged and consequently restrict the air passage to the carburettor air
intake. This will upset the air-to-fuel mixture ratio, normally governed
by the carburettor settings, causing the engine to lose tune.
3 The air filter is located in the front right-hand corner of the engine
compartment and the element is easily changed. Undo the hose clip
securing the air intake hose on the filter case endplate and then undo
and remove the endplate retaining nut.
4 Lift the endplate off and remove the old air filter element.
5 Before inserting the new filter element, wipe the inside of the case
and endplate clean using non-fluffy cloth.
6 Insert the new element and check that it is seated correctly. Refit
the endplate and its retaining nut and then reconnect the air intake
hose to the endplate (photo).

3 Fuel pump – removal, servicing and refitting

1 Disconnect the inlet and outlet pipes from the pump.
2 Unscrew the pump retaining bolts and carefully lift it clear of the
timing cover flange and remove the old gasket (photo).
3 Unscrew the top retaining screws and remove the top cover
(photo).
4 Extract the filter and coil spring (photo).
5 To remove and inspect the diaphragm assembly undo the five
screws and separate the upper and lower body sections (photo).
6 The diaphragm can now be removed for inspection (photo). Renew
it if it is torn or damaged in any way.
7 Use an air line and blow through the filter. Remove any sludge
build up from the main chambers.
8 Reassemble in the reverse order ensuring that the screws are
evenly tightened and the diaphragm is located correctly between the
body section flanges. Refit the top cover using a new gasket.
9 Refit the pump using a new gasket and check for leaks on the first
engine run.

1.1 The intake air selector valve at the Winter *(Hiver)* position. Some
models have a thermostatically controlled valve instead

2.6 Inserting a new air filter element

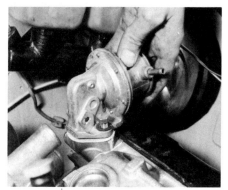

3.2 Removing the fuel pump

3.3 Remove the pump top cover

3.4 Take out the pump filter and spring

3.5 Separate the upper and lower sections

3.6 Removing the diaphragm assembly

4.1 The type number (32 HSA) and the modification standard (PEU 109) are stamped on the carburettor

5.8a Fit a new gasket before ...

5.8b ... fitting the carburettor

6.6 Adjusting the volume (Va) screw on the 32 HSA carburettor

4 Solex carburettors – general

1   Four types of Solex carburettors are fitted to Peugeot 104 models for the UK market, although a number of others are fitted to other models in the marque. The four we are concerned with are the 32 HNSA, 32 HSA, 32 PBISA and the 32 TMMIA. Modifications to these instruments are indicated by a Peugeot marking such as PEU 83, PEU 100 and so on. The type number and Peugeot marking are stamped on each carburettor (photo). As interchangeability is affected, your Peugeot dealer should be consulted if you are contemplating changing your carburettor.

2   The 32 HNSA carburettor is fitted to the earliest Peugeot 194 models and is a sidedraught carburettor with a constant richness idling device and manually operated choke. It is designed for 954 cc engines.

3   The 32 HSA carburettor replaced the 32 HNSA, to which it is broadly similar, in early 1974. Like its predecessor it is a single barrel

sidedraught carburettor with constant richness idling and a manually operated choke. An Econostat system is incorporated which enriches the mixture at high rpm and high airflow without affecting it at low rpm and low airflow. A mechanical accelerator pump injects additional fuel into the choke tube whenever the throttle is opened. The carburettor is designed for 954 cc engines.

4   The 32 PBISA carburettor is a single barrel downdraught carburettor with a manually operated choke and uniform CO idling device. It also has an Econostat and a mechanical accelerator pump. This carburettor is designed for 1124 cc engines.

5   The 32 TMMIA carburettor is a compound downdraught instrument having its two throttles linked by toothed quadrants. It also incorporates an Econostat and a mechanical accelerator pump and, in addition, it has an automatic cold start device operated by a wax expansion capsule. There are two separate idling circuits, one being an adjustable mixture idling circuit and the other a uniform CO circuit. This carburettor is designed for 1124 cc engines.

5 Carburettor – removal and refitting

1 Carburettor removal requires either partial draining of the cooling system or clamping the inlet and outlet coolant hoses as near as possible to their connections to the carburettor, so that coolant is not spilled when they are disconnected.
2 Detach the air cleaner tube by unscrewing the retaining clip.
3 Unscrew the fuel supply pipe retaining clip and pull the pipe from its connection at the carburettor. Plug the pipe to prevent spillage of fuel and the ingress of dirt.
4 Pull free the vacuum advance pipe which leads to the distributor.
5 Unscrew the choke cable retainer and pull the cable free.
6 Disconnect the throttle linkage from the balljoint.
7 Unscrew the retaining nuts and carefully lift the carburettor from

Fig. 3.1 The mixture screw (W) and the volume screw (Va) on the 32 HNSA carburettor (Sec 6)

Fig. 3.2 The mixture screw (W) and the volume screw (Va) on the 32 HSA carburettor (Sec 6)

the manifold. Cover the manifold inlet with some clean rag to prevent the ingress of dirt etc.
8 Refitting the carburettor is a direct reversal of the removal procedure. A new gasket must be used. When the carburettor is installed reconnect the choke cable and throttle linkage. Ensure that the choke cable is correctly adjusted giving a small amount of free play when the choke is off but allowing it to be fully applied (photos).
9 Top up the coolant as applicable and bleed the system as described in Chapter 2.
10 Adjust the carburettor to give the correct idle speed as described later.

6 Carburettor – adjustments

1 Generally speaking unless the carburettor is obviously out of tune or is malfunctioning it is not advisable to tamper with it. On any account *do not* touch the throttle stop screw or the idle fuel screw as they have been preset at the factory and are accurately adjusted to give optimum results.
2 The only adjustment normally required is to the idle adjustment screw.
3 Correct adjustment of the carburettor cannot be achieved unless the engine is in generally good condition. The valve clearances must be correct and the ignition system must also be in good condition and adjusted correctly.
4 Run the engine up to its normal operating temperature before any adjustments are made. The air filter must be connected during adjustments.
5 If a tachometer is available connect this up so that the correct engine idle speed can be achieved. This is recommended even if your car is equipped with a tachometer as standard equipment.
6 Assuming the carburettor is in reasonable condition, the idle speed adjustment is set by turning the volume screw Va as required. When unscrewed the idle speed is increased, whilst tightening will reduce the idle speed (photo).
7 Turn the screw slowly and progressively and when the correct idle speed is obtained, open the throttle a couple of times and check that when it closes again the idle speed is correct. If not, check that the throttle and choke cable connections are operating correctly and do not stick open.
8 If a new or overhauled carburettor has been fitted, the procedure is slightly different as the fuel mixture W may also need adjustment. First turn the volume control screw Va to give a high idling speed as indicated below, then turn the fuel mixture screw W to increase the engine speed as much as possible. Reset the volume control screw Va to the high idling speed indicated. Repeat this procedure until the speed obtained is the same on both screws as indicated. Then adjust the fuel mixture screw W to reduce the engine speed to normal idling speed as indicated (photo).

6.8 Adjusting the mixture (W) screw on the 32 HSA carburettor

Fig. 3.3 The mixture screw (W) and the volume screw (Va) on the 32 PBISA carburettor (Sec 6)

Fig. 3.4 The volume screw (Va) on the 32 TMMIA carburettor (Sec 6)

Carburettor	Initial setting Va	Normal idling
32 HNSA and 32 HSA	940 rpm	900 rpm
32 PB15A	950 rpm	900 rpm
32 TMM1A	980 rpm	900 rpm

Note: *Some carburettors are fitted with 'tamperproof' plugs which must be removed before making an adjustment*

7 Carburettor – dismantling, overhaul and reassembly

1   The carburettor should not normally need to be dismantled except for cleaning and checking the float level.

2   If the carburettor is to be dismantled, remember that it is a relatively delicate instrument and therefore requires careful handling. Use the correct tools for the job and do not interchange jets or clean them out with wire or any other such item which could score and damage them permanently.

3   Before dismantling any part of the carburettor, first clean it on the outside and prepare a clean work area where the parts can be laid out in order of dismantling for inspection.

4   *DO NOT* remove or disturb in any way the throttle stop screw (covered with plastic cap) or the idle fuel screw.

5   When taking anything mechanical apart – and this applies particularly to carburettors – it is always sound policy to make sure that the pieces are put back exactly where they came from, even though they may appear to be interchangeable. This can be done by marking or labelling, by putting various pieces into boxes or tins so that they don't get mixed up, or by carefully laying the pieces out on clean paper.

6   Identify the relevant illustrations with the particular carburettor on which you are working and there should be little difficulty in dismantling. Start by removing brackets and levers and then remove obvious assemblies. It is a good idea to limit the extent ot dismantling to the particular purpose in mind. If you only intend to clean out the float chamber, don't disturb those parts which do not have to be removed for this job. Always make a point of cleaning the small filter which is located in the fuel inlet connection.

7   The respective chambers, passages and jet seatings can be brush cleaned using clean petrol and should then be blown dry with compressed air. Clean and blow through the jets in a similar manner. Do not under any circumstances use emery paper, wire wool or hard scrapers for cleaning!

8   Inspect for blockages and check the float is not punctured. Ensure that the needle valve operates freely. Renew any defective or suspect items but check that replacement parts are available before disposing

Fig. 3.5 The mixture screw (W) on the 32 TMMIA carburettor (Sec 6)

of the old parts – they may be usable as a temporary repair.

9   If the throttle butterfly spindle or choke flap spindles are worn in the body then serious consideration should be given to renewing the complete carburettor. This wear is an indication that the carburettor is due for replacement, and it would be false economy to refit the original carburettor. Air leaks around worn spindles make it impossible to adjust the carburettor correctly and poor performance and economy will result.

10   Reassembly is a reversal of the dismantling sequence, whenever possible use new gaskets and washers where fitted.

11   Check and adjust as necessary the following items during assembly.

Float level check

12   The makers have designed gauges for checking the correct float level setting and these are illustrated in Fig. 3.14. They are all used in a similar fashion. With the top of the carburettor separated from the remainder, invert the top and support it horizontally. Position the gauge, which can easily be made of a piece of scrap sheet metal, as shown in the relevant illustration, noting whether or not the gasket should be in position. The float should abut the gauge; if it does not, adjustment can be made on the float arm hinge (32 HNSA, 32 HSA and 32 PB1SA carburettors) or by adjusting the gasket thickness under the float needle assembly nut (32 TMMIA carburettor). Tighten the needle valve assembly to the specified torque.

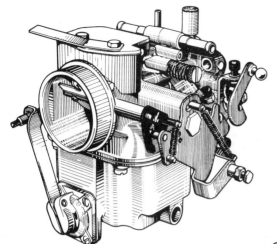

Fig. 3.6 Exploded view of the 32 HNSA carburettor (Sec 7)

Key to all exploded views

a	Correction jet	Gg	Main jet
Cc	Econostat fuel calibrated orifice	i	Accelerator pump injector
E	Econostat	K	Venturi
F	Float	P	Needle ball valve
g	Idling jet	Va	Volume control screw
gCo	Constant CO jet	W	Mixture screw

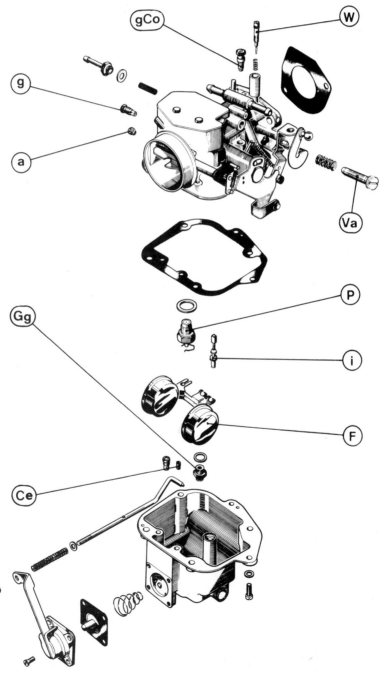

54

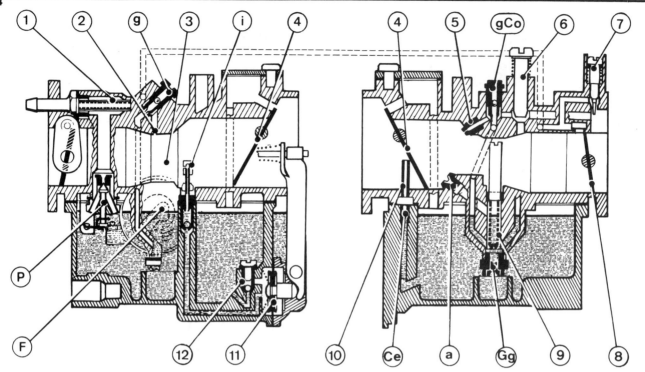

Fig. 3.7 Sectioned diagram of the 32 HNSA carburettor (Sec 7)

1 Fuel inlet filter
2 Calibrated orifice
3 Venturi
4 Choke
5 Calibrated orifice
6 Volume control screw (Va)
7 Mixture screw (W)
8 Throttle
9 Jet assembly
10 Econostat
11 Accelerator pump
12 Accelerator pump valve

Note: *See Fig. 3.6 for remainder of key. Do not dismantle the venturi*

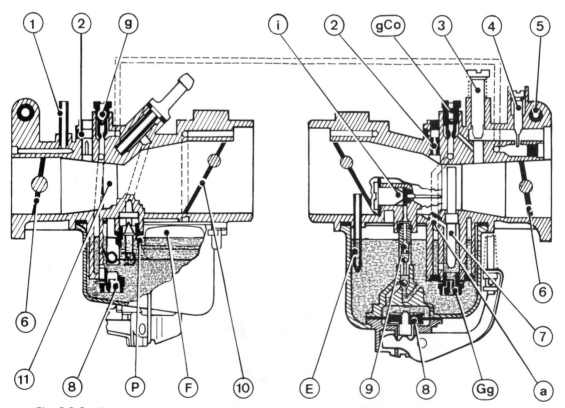

Fig. 3.8 Sectioned diagram of the 32 HSA carburettor (Sec 7). See Fig. 3.6 for remainder of key

1 Vacuum advance tube
2 Calibrated air orifice (idling and CO)
3 Volume control screw (Va)
4 Mixture screw (W)
5 Cooling system connection
6 Throttle
7 Jet assembly
8 Accelerator pump
9 Accelerator pump valve
10 Choke
11 Venturi

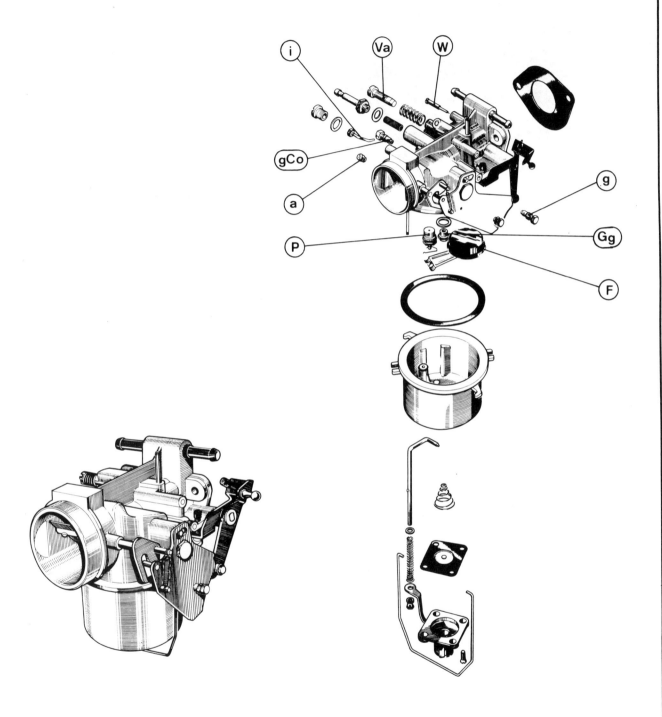

Fig. 3.9 Exploded view of the 32 HSA carburettor (Sec 7). See Fig.
3.6 for key

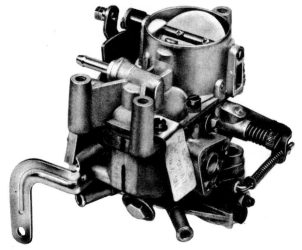

Fig. 3.10 Exploded view of the 32 PBISA carburettor (Sec 7). See Fig. 3.6 for key

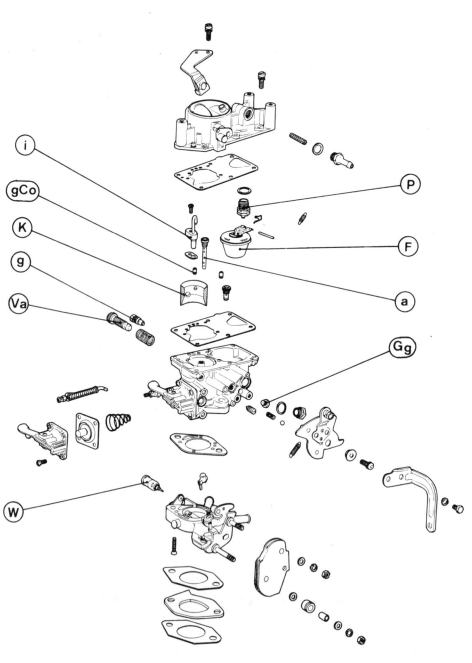

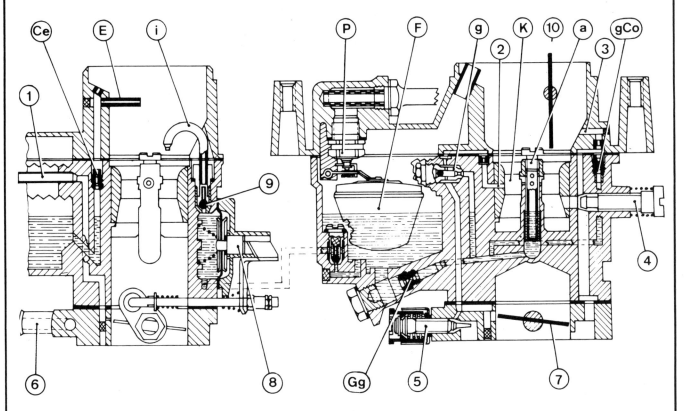

Fig. 3.11 Sectional diagram of the 32 PBISA carburettor (Sec 7)

1 Vacuum advance tube
2 Calibrated air orifice
   (normal idling circuit)
3 Calibrated air orifice
   (constant CO circuit)
4 Volume control screw (Va)
5 Mixture screw (W)
6 Cooling system connection
7 Throttle
8 Accelerator pump
9 Accelerator pump valve
10 Choke

Note: *See Fig. 3.6 for remainder of key*

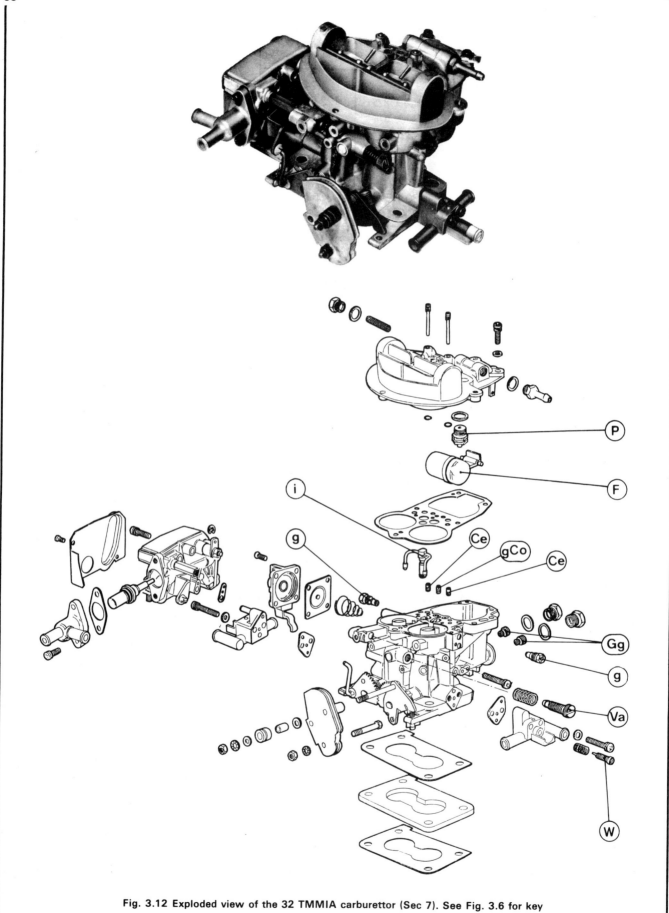

Fig. 3.12 Exploded view of the 32 TMMIA carburettor (Sec 7). See Fig. 3.6 for key

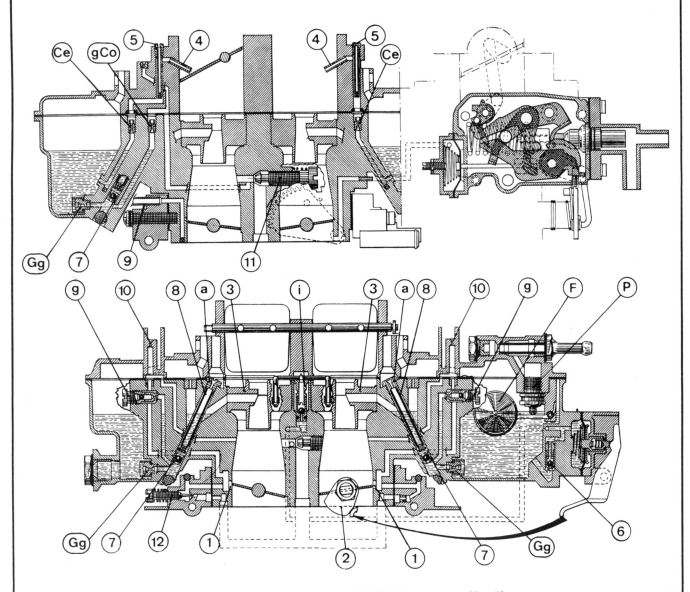

Fig. 3.13 Sectional diagram of the 32 TMMIA carburettor (Sec 7)

1 By-pass
2 Pump cam
3 Venturi diffuser
4 Econostat

5 Econostat air
calibrated orifice
6 Pump valve
7 Ball seat

8 Emulsion tube
9 Vacuum tube
10 Idling air bleed
orifice

11 Volume control
screw (Va)
12 Mixture screw (W)

Note: *See Fig. 3.6 for remainder of key. Do not dismantle the venturis (Items 3) or the correction jets (a)*

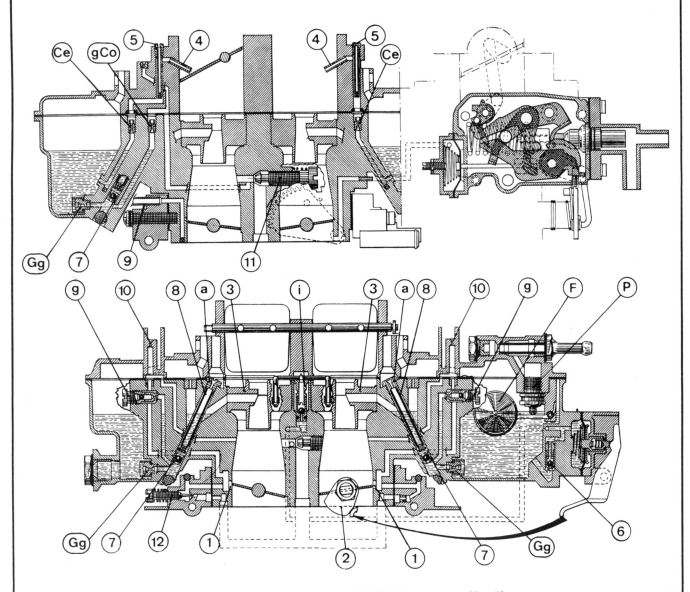

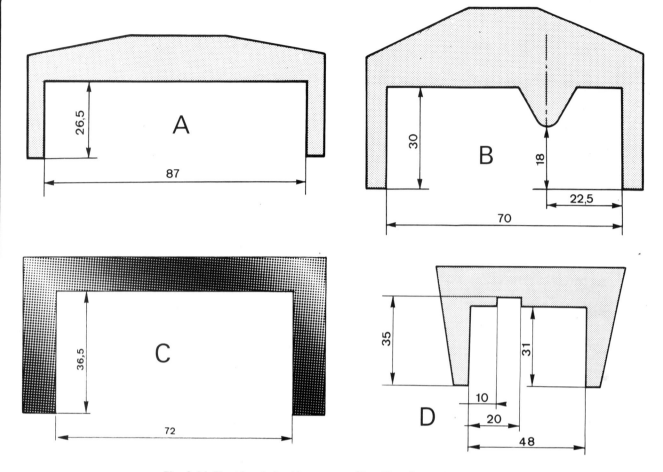

Fig. 3.14 Float level checking gauges (Sec 7) – dimensions in mm

A   32 HNSA carburettor
B   32 HSA carburettor
C   32 PBISA carburettor
D   32 TMMIA carburettor

Fig. 3.15 Checking the float level on the 32 HNSA carburettor. Note that the gasket is removed (Sec 7)

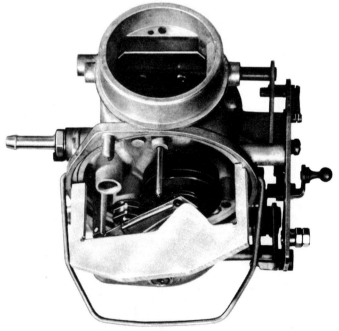

Fig. 3.16 Checking the float level on the 32 HSA carburettor. Note that the gasket is removed (Sec 7)

Fig. 3.17 Checking the float level on the 32 PBISA carburettor. Note that the gasket is in position between the gauge and upper body (Sec 7)

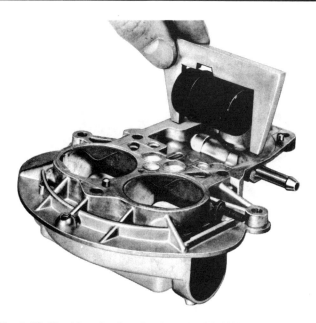

Fig. 3.18 Checking the float level on the 32 TMMIA carburettor. Note that the gasket is removed (Sec 7)

Fig. 3.19 The float and needle valve assemblies removed to change the gasket on the 32 TMMIA carburettor (Sec 7)

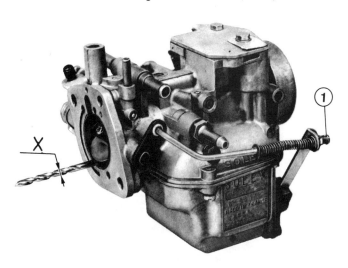

Fig. 3.20 Adjusting the accelerator pump stroke, 32 HNSA carburettor (Sec 7)

X   Drill shank used as gauge rod - see text
1   Adjusting nut

Accelerator pump stroke

13 To carry out this check a gauge rod of a set diameter will be required. The size differs for each carburettor (except the 32 TMMIA, for which no pump stroke adjustment is required). The sizes are as follows, and relevant drill sizes are quoted which can be used as gauges:

Carburettor	Gauge rod dia (mm)	Equivalent drill sizes
32 HNSA	5 to 6	$\frac{7}{32}$ in or No 3
32 HSA:		
PEU 93	3.5 to 4.5	$\frac{5}{32}$ in or No 22
PEU 108	6.5 to 7.5	$\frac{9}{32}$ in or letter J
PEU 109	6.5 to 7.5	$\frac{9}{32}$ in or Letter J
32 PBISA	5 to 6	$\frac{7}{32}$ in or No 3

If a drill is used, the shank must be undamaged and free of burrs

14 The gauge rod, or drill shank, is inserted between the carburettor bore and the butterfly valve. In this position the accelerator pump is adjusted by unscrewing the nut on the operating rod a few turns and, holding the butterfly valve lightly in contact with the gauge rod or drill, retightening the nut until it just makes contact with the pump lever, see Figs. 3.20, 3.21 or 3.22.

Other adjustments

15 No other adjustments are possible on these carburettors without the use of special checking jigs or instruments. These will be held by your Peugeot agent and it is recommended that, if you require these adjustments to be made as a result of disturbing the original settings or because of poor performance, you should take the carburettor to your agent for his attention. The adjustments are as follows:

(a) Throttle normal idling position (NIP) (except 32 HNSA)
(b) Positive opening (PO) (except 32 HNSA)
(c) Mixture, using an exhaust gas analyser (engine running)
(d) Choke opening after starting (COAS) (32 TMMIA only, engine running)

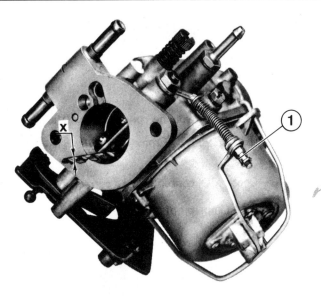

Fig. 3.21 Adjusting the accelerator pump stroke, 32 HSA
carburettor (Sec 7)

x Drill shank used as gauge rod - see text
1 Adjusting nut

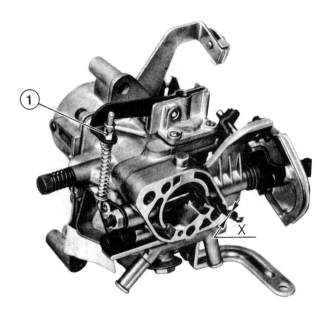

Fig. 3.22 Adjusting the accelerator pump stroke, 32 PBISA
carburettor (Sec 7)

x Drill shank used as gauge rod - see text
1 Adjusting nut

8 Choke cable – removal and refitting

1   Disconnect the inner cable from the carburettor by loosening the
retaining nut on the pivot bolt. Withdraw the cable by pulling the
choke knob.
2   Fit a new inner cable in the reverse sequence. Lubricate the cable
before fitting and ensure that it is correctly adjusted. With the knob
pushed in, the choke should be fully closed and there should be a slight
clearance behind the knob, thus ensuring that the choke has full movement. Pull the knob and check that the choke is fully open.
3   To change the outer cable, undo the nut behind the dash panel and
pull the assembly out, easing the outer cable through the grommet in
the bulkhead (photo). Fit the new cable in the reverse way and adjust
the control as already described.

Fig. 3.23 The choke cable connection at the carburettor (32 HSA)
(Sec 8)

8.3 The choke control being removed from the dash panel (instrument
panel removed for clarity only)

9 Throttle cable – removal and refitting

1   Disconnect the cable from the carburettor by undoing the retaining nut on the pivot bolt.
2   Disconnect the cable fitting from the foot pedal. The holes in the
sleeve are larger than the pedal rod and, when loose, the fitting simply
slides off. Remove the cable from the fitting and pull the cable out of
the outer cover (photo).
3   Before fitting a new cable, lubricate it with general purpose
grease. Ensure that it is correctly adjusted. The throttle should be
closed when the foot pedal is not quite on its stop (that is,
undepressed) resulting in a tension in the cable. Check that the throttle
on the carburettor is fully open before the foot pedal contacts the floor.
4   The throttle cable outer cover can be changed when the inner
cable is changed simply by removing it from its terminal mountings
and fitting the new one in the reverse way.

10 Exhaust system – general

1   The exhaust system is conventional in its working and extremely
simple to repair. It is wise to use original type exhaust clamps and
proprietary made systems (photos).
2   When any one section of the exhaust system needs renewal it

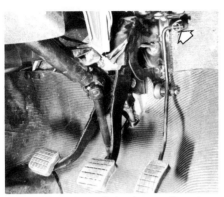
9.2 The cable sleeve fitting (arrowed) on the throttle foot pedal

10.1a The exhaust pipe support stay, original installation

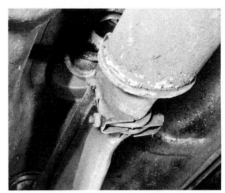
10.1b The joint between the front exhaust pipe and front silencer

10.1c The exhaust pipe safety strap, original installation

10.1d The rear silencer front hanger and joint

10.1e The rear silencer hanger, original installation

often follows that the whole lot is best replaced.

3   It is most important when fitting exhaust systems that the bends and contours are carefully followed and that each connecting joint overlaps the correct distance. Any stresses or strain imparted, in order to force the system to fit the hanger rubbers, will result in early fractures and failures.

4   When fitting a new part of a complete system it is well worth removing *ALL* the system from the car and cleaning up all the joints so that they fit together easily. The time spent struggling with obstinate joints whilst flat on your back under the car is eliminated and the likelihood of distorting or even breaking a section is greatly reduced. Do not waste a lot of time trying to undo rusted and corroded clamps

and bolts. Cut them off. New ones will be required anyway if they are that bad.

5   Use an exhaust joint sealant when assembling pipe sections to ensure that the respective joints are free from leaks.

6   When fitting the new system, only semi-tighten the retainers initially until the complete system is fitted, then when you have checked it for satisfactory location, tighten the securing bolts/nuts. If the hangers are stretched, perished or broken they must be renewed otherwise the system will vibrate, leading to leaks, premature wear or even fractures.

7   Figs. 3.24 and 3.25 illustrate the original and later systems installed on the Peugeot 104. It should be noted that most parts are

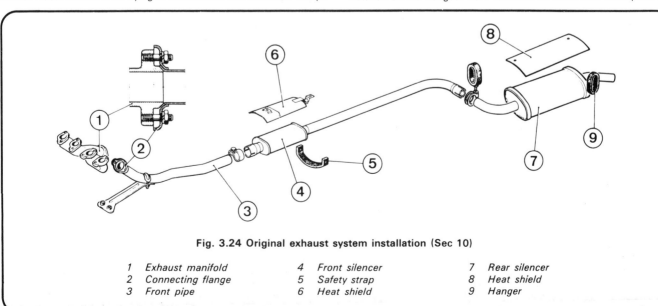
Fig. 3.24 Original exhaust system installation (Sec 10)

1 Exhaust manifold
2 Connecting flange
3 Front pipe
4 Front silencer
5 Safety strap
6 Heat shield
7 Rear silencer
8 Heat shield
9 Hanger

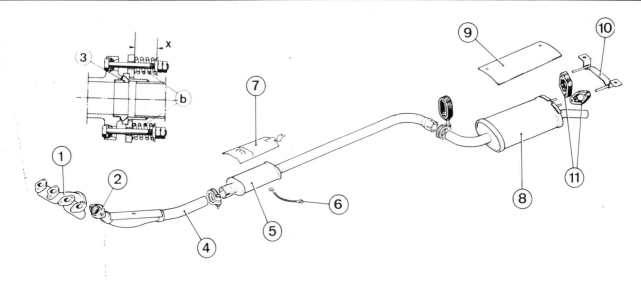

Fig. 3.25 Modified exhaust system fitted to some later models (Sec 10)

1 Exhaust manifold	4 Front pipe	7 Heat shield	10 Rear silencer support
2 Coupling	5 Front silencer	8 Rear silencer	11 Hangers
3 Collar	6 Safety cable	9 Heat shield	

Note: *The springs (b) of the cone type coupling must be compressed to give a dimension X of 22 mm (0.867 in)*

11.2 The fuel gauge sender unit is accessible when the floor bung is removed

11.6 A fuel tank retaining bolt

not interchangeable between these two systems.

11 Fuel tank – removal and refitting

1   The fuel tank is located at the rear of the car directly below the boot floor. Its removal is simple if a little messy.
2   Disconnect the battery and detach the fuel gauge sender unit (photo).
3   Place a suitable container below the drain plug in the bottom of the tank and drain the fuel into it. Store the fuel in a sealed container in a safe place.
4   Jack up the rear of the car and support with axle stands or blocks.
5   Remove the filler cap and remove the screws holding the filler neck in position. These are visible with the cap removed.
6   Undo and remove the bolts in the fuel tank flange which secure the tank to the brackets on the car (photo). Remove the tank by sliding it to one side to clear the brackets on the other side and lowering it

from the car, disconnecting the fuel feed pipe.
7   Refitting is the reverse of the removal procedure.

12 Fuel tank – cleaning and repair

1   With time it is likely that sediment will collect in the bottom of the fuel tank. Condensation, resulting in rust, and other impurities, will accumulate and will usually be found in the fuel tank of any car more than three or four years old.
2   When the tank is removed it should be vigorously flushed out with hot water and detergent and, if facilities are available, it should be steam cleaned.
3   Even though it is empty, residual petrol fumes in a tank make it extremely dangerous. *Never weld, solder or bring a naked light close to any fuel tank* unless it has been drained and cleaned as described in the previous paragraph for at least two hours.

13 Fault diagnosis – Fuel system

Unsatisfactory engine performance and excessive fuel consumption are not necessarily the fault of the fuel system or carburettor. In fact they more commonly occur as a result of ignition and timing faults. Before acting on the following it is necessary to check the ignition system first. Even though a fault may lie in the fuel system it will be difficult to trace unless the ignition is correct. The faults below, therefore, assume that this has been attended to first (where appropriate)

Symptom	Reason/s
Smell of petrol when engine is stopped	Leaking fuel lines or unions Leaking fuel tank
Smell of petrol when engine is idling	Leaking fuel line unions between pump and carburettor Overflow of fuel from float chamber due to wrong level setting, ineffective needle valve or punctured float
Excessive fuel consumption for reasons not covered by leaks or float chamber faults	Worn jets Over-rich jet setting Sticking mechanism
Difficult starting, uneven running, lack of power, cutting out	One or more jets blocked or restricted Float chamber fuel level too low or needle valve sticking Fuel pump not delivering sufficient fuel

Chapter 4 Ignition system

Contents

Specifications

Spark plugs
Type . . . . AC 42 LTS or Champion BN9Y (taper seat)
Electrode gap . . . . 0.024 in (0.6 mm)

Coil
All models up to April 1978 . . . . Ducellier 2789
Bosch 0221 1230 12
Femsa BI 12.55
Sev-Marchal 3H
All models April to December 1978 . . . . Ducellier 3805
Since December 1978 . . . . Ducellier 520019 (temperature sensitive resistor)
Input voltage (all types) 12V

Distributor
Rotation . . . . Anti-clockwise
Firing order 1-3-4-2
Contact points gap . . . . 0.016 in (0.4 mm)
Dwell angle . . . . 54° to 60°

Ignition timing

	Static advance (° BTDC)	Advance curve (see text)
XV3 engine (954 cc):		
Serial No up to 5330000	5°	M72
5330001 to 5465000	5°	M88
5465001 to 5618569	0°	M93
5618569 onwards	5°	M111
XW3 engine (1124 cc):		
9.2:1 compression ratio	5°	M96
8.2:1 compression ratio:		
Up to April 1978	0°	M93
April 1978 onwards	5°	M111
XW3S engine (1124 cc):		
Serial No up to 5554000	11°	M83
5554001 onwards	11°	M106

Torque wrench setting

	lbf ft	kgf m
Spark plugs	11 to 14	1.5 to 1.9

1 General description

In order that the engine may run correctly it is necessary for an electrical spark to ignite the fuel/air mixture in the combustion chamber at exactly the right moment in relation to engine speed and load.

Basically the ignition system functions as follows. Low tension voltage from the battery is fed to the ignition coil, where it is converted into high tension voltage. The high tension voltage is powerful enough to jump the spark plug gap in the cylinder many times a second under high compression pressure, providing that the ignition system is in

good working order and that all adjustments are correct.

The ignition system comprises two individual circuits known as the low tension (LT) circuit and high tension (HT) circuit.

The low tension circuit (sometimes known as the primary circuit) comprises the battery, lead to ignition switch, lead to the low tension or primary coil windings and the lead from the low tension coil windings to the contact breaker points and condenser in the distributor.

The high tension circuit (sometimes known as the secondary circuit) comprises the high tension or secondary coil winding, the heavily insulated ignition lead from the centre of the coil to the centre of the distributor cap, the rotor arm, the spark plug leads and the spark plugs.

The complete ignition system operation is as follows. Low tension voltage from the battery is changed within the ignition coil to high tension voltage by the opening and closing of the contact breaker points in the low tension circuit. High tension voltage is then fed, via a contact in the centre of the distributor cap, to the rotor arm of the distributor. The rotor arm revolves inside the distributor cap, and each time it comes in line with one of the four metal segments in the cap, these being connected to the spark plug leads the opening and closing of the contact breaker points causes the high tension voltage to build up, jump the gap from the rotor arm to the appropriate metal segment and so via the spark plug lead, to the spark plug where it finally jumps the gap between the two spark plug electrodes, one being earthed.

The ignition timing is advanced and retarded automatically to ensure the spark occurs at just the right instant for the particular load at the prevailing engine speed.

The ignition advance is controlled both mechanically and by a vacuum operated system. The mechanical governor mechanism comprises two weights which move out under centrifugal force from the central distributor shaft as the engine speed rises. As they move outwards they rotate the cam relative to the distributor shaft, and so advance the spark. The weights are held in position by two light springs, and it is the tension of these springs which is largely responsible for correct spark advancement.

The vacuum control comprises a diaphragm, one side of which is connected, via a small bore tube, to the carburettor, and the other side to the contact breaker arm. Depression in the induction manifold and carburettor, which varies with engine speed and throttle opening, causes the diaphragm to move so moving the contact breaker plate and advancing or retarding the spark.

The timing marks on this engine differ from established practice in that they refer to No 2 and No 3 cylinders, not to No 1. This is to minimise the effect of any flexing of the crankshaft.

2 Contact breaker points – adjustment

1 To adjust the contact breaker points so that the correct gap is obtained first release the clip(s) securing the distributor cap and lift away the cap. Clean the inside and outside of the cap with a dry cloth. It is unlikely that the four segments will be badly burned or scored but if they are the cap must be renewed. If only a small deposit is on the segments it may be scraped away using a small screwdriver.
2 Push in the spring-loaded carbon brush located in the top of the cap several times to ensure that it moves freely. Ideally the brush should protrude by at least 0.25 inch (6.35 mm).
3 Adjusting the contact breaker points is extremely awkward due to the difficulty in gaining access as they are mounted in the distributor at the left-hand end of the cylinder head. Cars produced after early 1978 have a distributor with external adjustment for the contact breaker

points, although special test equipment is necessary to adjust the points to give the correct dwell angle (the period in which the points remain closed). On cars without an externally adjustable contact breaker a mirror might prove useful in making the adjustment but, if a strobe timing light for refitting is available or can be borrowed, it would probably be worth taking the distributor off, after making reassembly alignment marks on the mounting flange and cylinder head, and making the points adjustment in comfort on the bench. To make the adjustment, leave the outer bearing carrier in position and proceed as follows.
4 Gently prise the contact breaker points open, to examine the condition of their faces. If they are rough, pitted or dirty it will be necessary to remove them for resurfacing, or for replacement points to be fitted (photo).
5 Presuming the points are satisfactory, or that they have been cleaned or replaced, measure the gap between the points by turning the engine over until the contact breaker arm is on the peak of one of the four cam lobes. A 0.016 inch (0.40 mm) feeler gauge should now just fit between the points.
6 If the gap varies from this amount adjust as follows.

Distributor without external adjustment

7 Slacken the locking screw and adjust the contact gap by moving the fixed contact in the appropriate direction. When the required gap has been obtained, tighten the securing screw and check the gap again (photo).

Distributor with external adjustment

8 Using a 7 mm open-ended or box spanner on the adjusting nut (Ducellier), or a 3 mm Allen key inserted through the hole in the plastic plug to engage with the adjuster (Paris-Rhône), adjust to achieve the required gap. Recheck after adjusting.

All models

9 If the adjustment has been made with the distributor in situ, refit the rotor arm and distributor cap, and clip the spring retainer(s) into position. Where the distributor was removed to make the adjustment, refer to Section 5 for the refitting procedure.

3 Contact breaker points – removal and refitting

1 Changing the contact breaker points will require removal of the distributor because of inaccessibility. Refer to Section 5 for the procedure for removing and refitting the distributor.
2 With the distributor removed, unscrew the bearing carrier retaining screws, remove the circlip and then remove the carrier (photo). The rest of the procedure depends on what type of distributor you have on your car.

2.4 The contact breaker points viewed through the bearing carrier

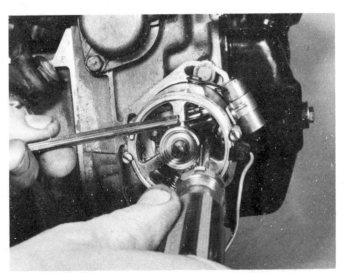

2.7 Adjusting the contact breaker points

3.2 Removing the bearing carrier

3.3 The retaining clip being removed

3.4 Removing the toothed cam spring clip

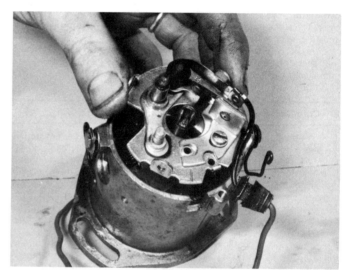
3.5 The contact breaker assembly being removed

Distributor without external adjustment

3   Remove the retaining circlip on the driveshaft (photo).
4   Mark the toothed cam to identify its setting with the vacuum capsule plunger so that, on reassembly, it can be refitted in its original position. Then remove the spring clip and disconnect the toothed cam (photo).
5   Ease the LT cable grommet out of the casing and remove the contact breaker assembly (photo). Refitting is the reverse of the removal procedure, but ensure that the toothed cam is refitted in its original position.

Externally adjustable distributor – Ducellier (Fig. 4.1)

6   Unscrew and remove the adjustment nut (3) and the two screws (4). Take out the adjustment rod (5) and its spring. Slide the grommet (6) out of the distributor body and remove the blanking plug (7). Remove the retaining lug (8). Undo and remove the fixed contact retaining screw (9) and remove the fixed contact. Remove the spring clip (10), taking care not to lose it, and remove the moving contact. Fitting the new contact set is the reverse of the removal procedure.

Externally adjustable distributor – Paris-Rhône (Fig. 4.2)

7   Undo and remove the contact breaker retaining screw (3), disconnect the spring clip (4) and remove the contact breaker assembly. Fitting the new contact set is the reverse of the removal procedure, but take care to align the adjuster (5) with its holder (6).

All models

8   After removing the contact breaker points, refit the bearing carrier and tighten the two retaining screws. Refit the circlip and then adjust the contact breaker gap, as explained in the previous Section, before refitting the distributor.

4   Condenser – removal, testing and refitting

1   The purpose of the condenser (sometimes known as a capacitor) is to ensure that when the contact breaker points open there is no sparking across them which would waste voltage and cause wear.
2   The condenser is fitted in parallel with the contact breaker points. If it develops a short circuit, it will cause ignition failure, as the points will be prevented from interrupting the low tension circuit. If it develops an open circuit it will also cause malfunction, if not total failure.
3   If the engine becomes very difficult to start, or begins to misfire after several miles running, and the breaker points show signs of excessive burning then the condition of the condenser must be suspect. A further test can be made by separating the points manually (using an insulated screwdriver) with the ignition switched on. If this is accompanied by a strong blue flash it is indicative that the condenser has failed in the open circuit mode.
4   Without special test equipment, the only sure way to diagnose

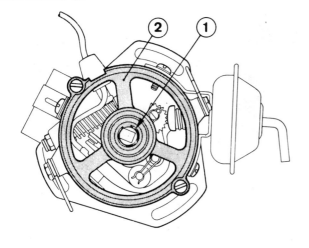

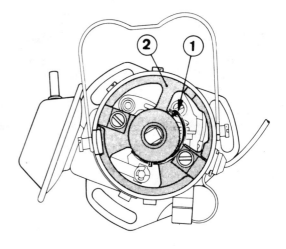

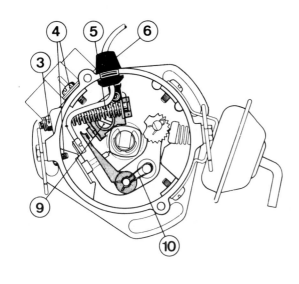

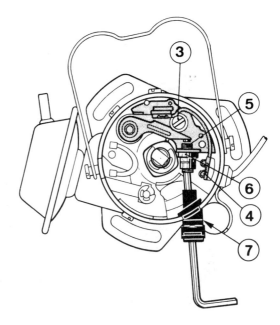

Fig. 4.2 The Paris-Rhone externally adjustable distributor (Sec 3)

1 Anti-vibration clip	5 Adjuster contact
2 Bearing carrier	6 Adjuster support
3 Retaining screw	7 Plug
4 Spring clip	

condenser trouble is to replace a suspected unit with a new one, noting if there is any improvement.

5 To remove the condenser from the distributor, first detach the condenser lead from the LT terminal post on the side of the distributor body.

6 Undo and remove the securing screw, or screws depending on model, noting the locations of the washers, and remove the condenser (photo).

7 Refitting of the condenser is simply the reverse of the removal procedure.

5 Distributor – removal and refitting

1 Apart from replacing the contact points, the distributor will need removal if there are any indications that the rotor shaft bearings are worn, (giving contact gap adjustment difficulties) or if it is to be dismantled for general cleaning and checking.

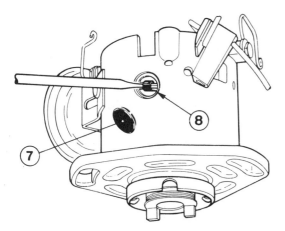

Fig. 4.1 The Ducellier externally adjustable distributor (Sec 3)

1 Driveshaft circlip	6 Cable grommet
2 Bearing carrier	7 Plug
3 Adjusting nut	8 Retaining lug
4 Screws	9 Retaining screw
5 Spring and adjusting rod	

4.6 Removing the condenser securing screw

5.7 The offset distributor drive slots in the camshaft

6.1 A distributor dismantled

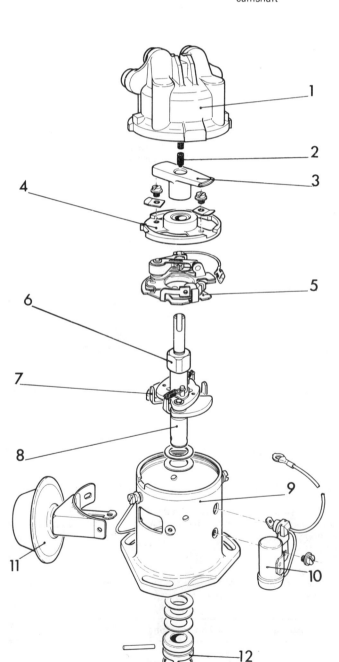

2   Before removing the distributor it will help prevent further confusion if the engine is positioned with the flywheel timing mark at TDC (see Section 7). In this way if the engine is accidentally rotated whilst the distributor is removed, it can be repositioned.
3   Detach the plug leads from the spark plugs and the coil HT lead from the distributor cap or coil. Remove the cap by unclipping the spring clip or clips, depending on model.
4   Undo the LT lead at the coil – this should be a screw-on connector, and pull off the vacuum advance pipe from the distributor.
5   Before removing the distributor scribe an alignment mark between the distributor flange and the cylinder head. This will assist correct reassembly.
6   Unscrew the retaining screws and withdraw the distributor. As it is removed note the offset drive lugs on the base of the rotor shaft which enable it to be correctly positioned on reassembly.
7   Refitting is a direct reversal of the removal procedure. Check that the rubber O-ring between the flange and cylinder head surface is in good condition and renew if necessary. Align the offset spindle lugs with the slots in the end of the camshaft and fit the distributor, turning the rotor shaft a little either way to enable the lugs and slot to engage (photo). Do not forget to refit the HT lead location bracket under the retaining bolt head. Align the marks scribed on the flange and cylinder head before tightening the retaining bolts. If a new distributor unit is being fitted, set the timing as described in Section 7.

6   Distributor – overhaul

1   It has been found from practical experience that overhauling a distributor is not worthwhile even if all parts are available. The usual items needing attention are such parts as the distributor cap, rotor arm, contact breaker points and condenser (very rare). After these have been considered there is not a great deal left to wear except the shaft assembly, bush and automatic advance system. If one of these parts is worn then it is reasonable to assume the remainder are, so, all in all, it is best to obtain a guaranteed service exchange unit which could work out cheaper than purchasing a complete set of individual parts (photo).
2   If it is intended to fit a new distributor it is important that the correct one for your car is used. Peugeot identify distributors by an Advance Curve number. The curve is a graphical plot of the amount of advance, both centrifugal and vacuum, against distributor (rpm) or intake depression as appropriate. A typical curve is shown in Fig. 4.4. If you are in doubt which one applies to your car, consult your Peugeot agent.

Fig. 4.3 Exploded view of distributor (Sec 6)

1 Distributor cap	mechanism
2 Carbon brush	8 Distributor driveshaft
3 Rotor arm	9 Distributor case
4 Bearing carrier	10 Condenser (capacitor)
5 Contact breaker assembly	11 Vacuum advance capsule
6 Cam	12 Drive dog
7 Centrifugal advance	

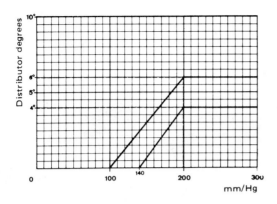

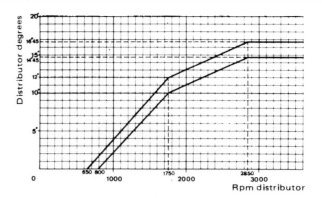

Fig. 4.4 An example of distributor vacuum (left) and centrifugal (right) advance curves, in this case M111 (Sec 6)

7 Ignition timing

1   It is necessary to time the ignition when it has been upset due to overhauling or dismantling which may have altered the relationship between the position of the pistons and the moment at which the distributor delivers the spark. Also, if maladjustments have affected the engine performance it is very desirable, although not always essential, to reset the timing starting from scratch. In the following procedures it is assumed that the intention is to obtain standard performance from the standard engine which is in reasonable condition. It is also assumed that the recommended fuel octane rating is used.

2   To set the initial advance (static timing) first check that the contact breaker points are correctly adjusted (Section 2).

3   Remove the plastic cover from the flywheel timing aperture, located just forward of the clutch cable return spring and adjuster, and rotate the engine so that the TDC mark on the periphery of the flywheel is aligned with the O-mark on the timing plate. Pistons No 2 and 3 are at TDC now. If it is wished simply to check the initial advance setting, it is immaterial whether No 2 or No 3 is on the firing stroke. If for some reason it is necessary to know which cylinder is firing, remove the spark plugs and place a temporary bung over the plug hole in question. Pressure will be felt in the cylinder as the piston approaches TDC on the firing stroke.

4   An alternative indication of which cylinder is firing is given by the position of the rotor arm, which will be pointing to either No 2 or No 3 cylinder contact in the distributor cap when the timing marks are aligned.

5   The initial, or static, ignition advance setting is given in the Specifications at the beginning of the Chapter. Turn the crankshaft so that the TDC mark on the flywheel is aligned with the specified static ignition timing mark on the timing plate with No 2 or 3 cylinder on the compression stroke. Loosen the distributor retaining bolts and turn the distributor gently anti-clockwise then clockwise until the points are just opening. Tighten the retaining bolts (photos).

6   The accuracy of this operation can be improved by using a test light to indicate when the points open. Connect a 12 volt bulb in parallel with the contact breaker points (one lead to earth and the other to the distributor low tension terminal). Switch on the ignition and turn the distributor body anti-clockwise then clockwise until the bulb just lights up, indicating that the points have opened. Tighten the distributor retaining bolts. Check the setting by turning the crankshaft back a few degrees and carefully turn it in the normal direction of rotation until the light just lights. Check that the flywheel mark is exactly opposite the timing plate static ignition advance mark.

7   Set in this manner the timing should be approximately correct, but further minor adjustments may be necessary following a road test. If a strobe light is available a more accurate setting can be made with the engine running. Follow the makers' directions for connecting the strobe light leads to No 2 or No 3 plug lead. Disconnect the vacuum advance pipe and fit a temporary plug on the suction side. Mark the TDC line on the flywheel with a little white paint to make it easier to see. Start the engine and run at a speed not exceeding 800 rpm (slow running). Shine the strobe light on the timing plate and adjust the distributor position so that the TDC mark aligns exactly with the static timing setting for your engine. When removing the strobe light, don't forget to reconnect the vacuum advance pipe after removing the temporary plug.

7.5a The TDC mark on the flywheel aligned with the 5° static advance slot in the timing plate

7.5b The timing plate on an engine with no ignition static advance

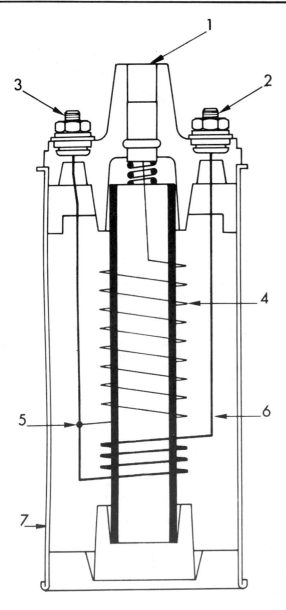

Fig. 4.5 The ignition coil (Sec 8)

1	HT outlet to distributor		connection
2	Contact breaker LT connection	4	Secondary windings
		5	Common connection
3	Battery positive LT	6	Primary windings
		7	Case

8 Ignition coil – general

1 The maintenance of the coil is minimal and is limited to periodically wiping its surfaces clean and dry and ensuring that the lead connectors are secure. High voltages generated by the coil can easily leak to earth over its surface and prevent the spark plugs from receiving the electrical pulses. Water repellent sprays are now available to prevent dampness causing this type of malfunction (photo).

2 Wipe clean and spray the HT leads and distributor cap also.

3 Testing of the coil is covered in the faults Section at the end of this Chapter.

4 Some cars are fitted with a temperature sensitive resistor, mounted on the coil, to overcome starting difficulties when cold or in damp conditions. The effect is to boost the HT current when starting. This type of coil can be fitted retrospectively to any model, and when old type spares are used up, will be the only type available from dealers.

8.1 The coil is mounted just behind the battery tray

9 Spark plugs and HT leads

1 The spark plugs should be cleaned and their gaps reset after 5000 miles (7500 km). At 10 000 miles (15 000 km) the plugs should be renewed.

2 *It is most important that the plugs in these engines are not over-tightened.* The plugs have tapered seats and are fitted without a sealing washer. A special plug spanner is provided which has a short handle in order to limit the torque which can be applied in use. If this spanner is not available it is recommended that a torque spanner with extension and socket is used when fitting plugs. In addition care must be taken not to cross the threads on installation – remember that the cylinder head is made of soft aluminium alloy which can easily be damaged. Don't be tempted to use a conventional plug spanner as, in this case, an overtightened plug might be impossible to remove.

3 Cleaning plugs is best left to your local garage where proper cleaning equipment will be available. It is suggested that two sets of plugs are used. With one set installed you can get the other set cleaned at leisure and you will have a spare, clean set always available for emergency use. Don't forget to discard them when their life is up as it is false economy to use old plugs.

4 The spark plug gap is of considerable importance, as, if it is too large or too small, the size of the spark and its efficiency will be seriously impaired. The spark plug gap should be set to the figure given in the Specifications at the beginning of this Chapter.

5 To set it, measure the gap with a feeler gauge, and then bend open, or close, the outer plug electrodes until the correct gap is achieved. The centre electrode should never be bent as this may crack the insulation and cause plug failure if nothing worse. Before fitting each plug, fit the plug extension, making sure that it is clean, dry and securely tightened to the plug (Fig. 4.6).

6 The HT leads and their connections at both ends should always be clean and dry and, as far as possible, neatly arranged away from each other and nearby metallic parts which would cause premature shorting in weak insulation. The metal connections at the ends should be a firm and secure fit and free from any signs of corrosive deposits. If any lead shows signs of cracking or chafing of the insulation it should be renewed. Remember that radio interference suppression is required when renewing any leads.

10 Fault diagnosis – ignition system

1 There are two main symptoms indicating faults. Either the engine will not start or fire, or the engine is difficult to start and misfires. If it is a regular misfire, ie the engine is only running on two or three cylinders the fault is almost sure to be in the secondary, or high tension circuit. If the misfiring is intermittent, the fault could be in either the high or low tension circuit. If the car stops suddenly or will not start at all, it is

Measuring plug gap. A feeler gauge of the correct size (see ignition system specifications) should have a slight 'drag' when slid between the electrodes. Adjust gap if necessary

Adjusting plug gap. The plug gap is adjusted by bending the earth electrode inwards, or outwards, as necessary until the correct clearance is obtained. Note the use of the correct tool

Normal. Grey-brown deposits, lightly coated core nose. Gap increasing by around 0.001 in (0.025 mm) per 1000 miles (1600 km). Plugs ideally suited to engine, and engine in good condition

Carbon fouling. Dry, black, sooty deposits. Will cause weak spark and eventually misfire. Fault: over-rich fuel mixture. Check: carburettor mixture settings, float level and jet sizes; choke operation and cleanliness of air filter. Plugs can be re-used after cleaning

Oil fouling. Wet, oily deposits. Will cause weak spark and eventually misfire. Fault: worn bores/piston rings or valve guides; sometimes occurs (temporarily) during running-in period. Plugs can be re-used after thorough cleaning

Overheating. Electrodes have glazed appearance, core nose very white – few deposits. Fault: plug overheating. Check: plug value, ignition timing, fuel octane rating (too low) and fuel mixture (too weak). Discard plugs and cure fault immediately

Electrode damage. Electrodes burned away; core nose has burned, glazed appearance. Fault: pre-ignition. Check: as for 'Overheating' but may be more severe. Discard plugs and remedy fault before piston or valve damage occurs

Split core nose (may appear initially as a crack). Damage is self-evident, but cracks will only show after cleaning. Fault: pre-ignition or wrong gap-setting technique. Check: ignition timing, cooling system, fuel octane rating (too low) and fuel mixture (too weak). Discard plugs, rectify fault immediately

Fig. 4.6 The spark plug and extension (Sec 9)
a Tapered seat

likely that the fault is in the low tension circuit. Loss of power and overheating, apart from faulty carburation settings, are normally due to faults in the distributor or incorrect ignition timing.

2   The suggestions given in the following two sections are for guidance purposes and should not be considered to cover every aspect of the ignition system.

Engine fails to start

3   If the engine fails to start and the car was running normally when it was last used, first check that there is fuel in the petrol tank. If the engine turns over normally on the starter motor and the battery is evidently well charged, then the fault may be in either the high or low tension circuit. First check the HT circuit. **Note:** If the battery is known to be fully charged, the ignition light comes on, and the starter motor fails to turn the engine, **check the tightness of the leads on the battery terminals** and the secureness of the earth lead at its **connection to the body.** It is quite common for the leads to have worked loose, even if they look and feel secure. If one of the battery terminal posts gets very hot when trying to work the starter motor this is a sure indication of a faulty connection to that terminal.

4   One of the commonest reasons for bad starting is wet or damp spark plug leads and distributor. Remove the distributor cap. If condensation is visible internally dry the cap with a rag and also wipe over the leads. Refit the cap.

5   If the engine still fails to start, check that current is reaching the plugs, by disconnecting each plug lead in turn at the spark plug end, and holding the end of the cable with insulating material about $\frac{3}{16}$ inch (5 mm) away from the cylinder block. Spin the engine on the starter motor.

6   Sparking between the end of the cable and the block should be fairly strong with a strong regular blue spark. If current is reaching the plugs, then remove them and clean and regap them to the specified clearance. The engine should now start.

7   If there is no spark at the plug leads take off the HT lead from the centre of the distributor cap and hold it to the block as before. Spin the

engine on the starter once more. A rapid succession of blue sparks between the end of the lead and the block indicates that the coil is in order and that the distributor cap is cracked, the rotor arm faulty, or the carbon brush in the top of the distributor cap is not making good contact with the rotor arm. Possibly, the points are in bad condition. Clean and reset them as described in this Chapter, Section 2.

8   If there are no sparks from the end of the lead from the coil check the connections at the coil end of the lead. If it is in order start checking the low tension circuit.

9   Use a 12V voltmeter or a 12V bulb and two lengths of wire. With the ignition switched on and the points open, test between the low tension supply lead on the switch side of the ignition coil and earth. No reading indicates a break in the supply from the ignition switch. Check the connections at the switch to see if any are loose. Refit them and the engine should run. A reading shows a faulty coil or condenser, or broken lead between the coil and the distributor, or a fault in another system.

10   Detach the condenser from the side of the distributor and with the points open test between the moving point and earth. If there now is a reading then the fault is in the condenser. Fit a new one and the fault is cleared.

11   With no reading from the moving point to earth, take a reading between earth and the distributor side of the ignition coil. A reading here shows a broken lead which will need to be replaced between the coil and distributor. No reading suggests that the coil has failed and must be renewed, after which the engine will run once more. Remember to refit the condenser lead to the points assembly. For these tests it is sufficient to separate the points with a piece of dry paper while testing with the points open.

Engine misfires

12   If the engine misfires regularly run it at a fast idling speed. Pull off each of the plug caps in turn and listen to the note of the engine. Hold the plug cap in a dry cloth or with a rubber glove as additional protection against a shock from the HT supply.

13   No difference in engine running will be noticed when the lead from the defective circuit is removed. Removing the lead from one of the good cylinders will accentuate the misfire.

14   Remove the plug lead from the end of the defective plug and hold it about $\frac{3}{16}$ inch (5 mm) away from the block. Re-start the engine. If the sparking is fairly strong and regular the fault must lie in the spark plug or in the engine itself.

15   The plug may be loose, the insulation may be cracked, or the points may have burnt away giving too wide a gap for the spark to jump. Worse still, one of the points may have broken off. Either renew the plug, or clean it, reset the gap, and then test it.

16   If there is no spark at the end of the plug lead, or if it is weak and intermittent, check the ignition lead from the distributor to the plug. If the insulation is cracked or perished, renew the lead. Check the connections at the distributor cap.

17   If there is still no spark, examine the distributor cap carefully for tracking. This can be recognised by a very thin black line running between two or more electrodes, or between an electrode and some other part of the distributor. These lines are paths which now conduct electricity across the cap thus letting it run to earth. The only answer is a new distributor cap.

18   Apart from the ignition being incorrect, other causes of misfiring have already been dealt with above in dealing with the failure of the engine to start. To recap – these are that

(a) *The coil may be faulty giving an intermittent misfire*
(b) *There may be a damaged lead or loose connection in the low tension circuit*
(c) *The condenser may be defective*
(d) *There may be a mechanical fault in the distributor (broken driving spindle or contact breaker spring)*

19   If the ignition timing is too far retarded, it should be noted that the engine will tend to overheat, and there will be a quite noticeable drop in power. If the engine is overheating and the power is down, and the ignition timing is correct, then the carburettor should be checked, as it is likely that this is where the fault lies.

Chapter 5 Clutch

Contents

Specifications

Type .... Diaphragm spring, single dry plate, cable operation

Operating lever clearance .... $1\frac{1}{4}$ turns of adjusting screw – $\frac{1}{4}$ turn on fitting new cable assembly

Torque wrench settings

	lbf ft	kgf m
Flywheel bolts with thread locking compound	50	6.8
Clutch cover Allen headed screws	7.25	1.0
Clutch housing bolts	9.0	1.2
Starter to housing bolts	13.0	1.75

---

1 General description

The clutch is a cable-operated single dry-plate diaphragm type.

The clutch pedal pivots in a bracket mounted under the facia and operates a cable to the clutch release arm. The release arm operates a thrust bearing (clutch release bearing) which bears on the diaphragm spring of the pressure plate. The diaphragm then releases or engages the clutch driven plate which floats on a splined shaft. This shaft (the engine output shaft) is part of the transfer gear assembly which is mounted on the clutch housing. The drive passes via an intermediate pinion to the gearbox input shaft.

The clutch release mechanism consists of a fork and bearing which are in permanent contact with the release fingers on the pressure plate assembly. The fork pushes the release bearing forwards to bear against the release fingers, so moving the centre of the diaphragm spring inwards. The spring is sandwiched between two rings which act as fulcrum points. As the centre of the spring is pushed in, the outside of the spring is pushed out, so moving the pressure plate backwards and disengaging it from the clutch disc.

When the clutch pedal is released, the diaphragm spring forces the pressure plate into contact with the friction linings on the clutch disc and at the same time pushes the clutch disc a fraction of an inch forwards on its splines so engaging the clutch disc with the flywheel. The clutch disc is now firmly sandwiched between the pressure plate and the flywheel, so the drive is taken up.

As wear takes place on the clutch disc the clearance between the release bearing and the diaphragm decreases. This wear can be compensated for by adjusting the screws and locknut on the clutch operating lever.

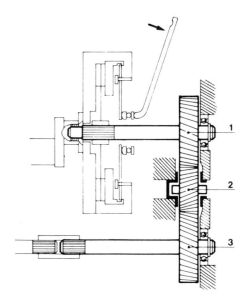

Fig. 5.1 Illustration showing the relative positions of the clutch and the transfer gear assembly (Sec 1)

1   Engine output shaft   2   Intermediate gear
3   Gearbox input shaft

---

2 Clutch – adjustment

1   Clutch adjustment will be necessary to compensate for the wear of the clutch lining. This will result in less free play at the rod between the clutch operating lever and the release bearing arm.

2   To make the adjustment, unhook the return spring from the clutch operating lever, loosen the locking nut on the adjusting screw and then turn the adjusting screw until there is just no clearance between the operating lever and the pushrod. Now turn the screw back $1\frac{1}{4}$ turns to provide the working clearance. If the adjustment is being made after fitting a new cable and outer casing, the screw should be turned back only $\frac{1}{4}$ turn.

3   Retighten the locknut, rehook the return spring onto the clutch operating lever and check the clutch operation.

3   Clutch cable – removal and refitting

1   The clutch cable connects the clutch pedal to the operating lever/rod assembly. It is a simple item to replace. To remove proceed as follows.

2   Unscrew the clutch lever adjustment screw locknut and slacken the adjustment.

3   Inside the car, unhook the cable from the clutch pedal. Release the other end of the cable from the clutch operating lever.

4   Undo the two split-pin style clips holding the outer sheath to the exhaust pipe bracket and work the cable and grommet out of the bulkhead. Remove the cable assembly.

5   Refitting is a direct reversal of the removal procedure. When fitted readjust the operating lever clearance as given in Section 2.

4   Clutch – removal

1   Should it become necessary to renew the friction plate or examine the clutch assembly, the clutch housing and the transfer gear casing will have to be removed. This cannot be done with the engine installed owing to limited access and the lengths of the shafts mounted in the transfer gear case. Although it might just be possible to remove the clutch housing and transfer gear case with the engine partially removed and swung over to the right-hand side of the engine bay, this is untried. It would be much simpler in the long run to remove the engine from the car completely and attend to the clutch on the bench or on a cleared floor space.

2   Refer to Chapter 1 and follow the instructions given to remove the engine, but omit any work other than that relating to a simple removal and refitting of the engine.

3   With the engine removed, detach the clutch lever spring and remove the actuating rod. Unscrew and remove the housing retaining bolts, noting their respective locations. Remove the engine lifting bracket, noting its position. Remove the left-hand engine mounting where applicable, and the starter.

4   Carefully tap on the casing lugs and prise the assembly free. Withdraw the clutch housing and the transfer gear casing by supporting its weight and pulling it straight out and in line with the shafts so that no strain is put on either the input or output shafts. Remove the old gasket.

5   Mark the position of the clutch unit in relation to the flywheel to facilitate reassembly. Progressively loosen the six Allen headed screws retaining the clutch unit to the flywheel so as to relieve the diaphragm spring pressure without distorting it.

6   When the screws are removed the cover and the driven plate can be removed (photo).

5   Clutch – inspection and renovation

1   The clutch driven plate should be inspected for wear and for contamination by oil. Wear is gauged by the depth of the rivet heads below the surface of the friction material. If this is less than 0.025 in (0.6 mm) the linings are worn enough to justify renewal.

2   Examine the friction faces of the flywheel and clutch pressure plate. These should be bright and smooth. If the linings have worn too much it is possible that the metal surfaces may have been scored by the rivet heads. Dust and grit can have the same effect. If the scoring is very severe it could mean that even with a new clutch driven plate, slip and juddering and other malfunctions will recur. Deep scoring on the flywheel face is serious because the flywheel will have to be removed and machined by a specialist, or renewed. This can be costly. The same applies to the pressure plate in the cover although this is a less costly affair. If the friction linings seem unworn yet are blackened and shiny then the cause is almost certainly due to oil. Such a condition also requires renewal of the plate. The source of oil must be traced also. It could be due to a leaking seal on the transmission input shaft (photos) or from a leaking crankshaft oil seal (see Chapter 1 for details of renewal).

3   If the reason for removal of the clutch has been because of slip and the slip has been allowed to go on for any length of time it is possible that the heat generated will have adversely affected the diaphragm spring in the cover with the result that the pressure is now uneven and/or insufficient to prevent slip, even with a new friction

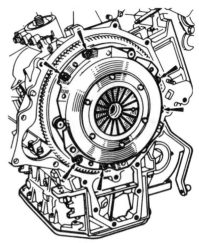

Fig. 5.2 The clutch cover retaining bolts (arrowed) (Sec 4)

plate. It is recommended that under such circumstances a new assembly is fitted.

4   Although it is possible to dismantle the clutch cover assembly and, in theory, renew the various parts the economics do not justify it. Clutch cover assemblies are available on an exchange basis. It will probably be necessary to order an assembly in advance as most agencies other than the large distributors carry stocks only sufficient to meet their own requirements. However, it is possible to get assemblies from reputable manufacturers other than Peugeot, Borg and Beck for example, but be specific as to your requirements.

6   Clutch – refitting

1   Support the driven plate centrally between the flywheel and the cover. The offset side of the driven plate (the side where the boss has the larger diameter) faces outwards (photo).

2   Align the marks made on the flywheel and cover prior to removal and retain the cover in position on the flywheel with the bolts (hand tight only).

3   It is now necessary to align the centre of the driven plate with that of the flywheel. To do this use a special alignment tool or alternatively use a suitable diameter bar inserted through the driven plate into the flywheel spigot bearing, but take care not to damage the output shaft seal. It is possible to align the driven plate by eye, but difficulty will probably be experienced when refitting the output shaft. If the transfer gears have been separated from the clutch housing the driven plate can be aligned using the engine output shaft located in its normal running position (photo).

4   With the driven plate centralized the cover bolts should be tightened diagonally and evenly to the specified torque. Ideally new spring washers should be used each time a replacement clutch is fitted. When the bolts are tight remove the centralizing tool (photo).

5   Before refitting the clutch housing, check the condition of the release bearing and operating mechanism, renewing any parts as necessary (photo) (see Section 9).

7   Clutch housing – refitting

1   Before refitting the housing, check that the mating surfaces are clean and dry. Smear the bearing surface of the withdrawal pad on the diaphragm spring with medium grease.

2   Place a new gasket over the location dowels and then carefully offer the clutch housing/transfer pinion unit to the engine and insert the output and input shafts (photos).

3   To assist the respective shaft splines to engage, rotate the flywheel and gearbox input shaft alternately until they slide home into position with the housing flush,

4   Insert the retaining bolts, remembering to replace any fittings retained by them. Tighten the bolts progressively to the specified torque. Refit the plastic protector, actuating rod and return spring (photos). Refit the starter and, where applicable, the left-hand engine mounting.

4.6 The clutch cover

5.2a Using a piece of tube, nut, bolt and washers to insert a new engine output shaft sleeve/seal

5.2b The sleeve/seal fitted

6.1 Note the correct way round for fitting the driven plate

6.3 Using the engine output shaft to align the driven plate

6.4 Tighten the cover bolts diagonally and progressively. Note the use of the special adaptor for the torque wrench

6.5 Fitting a new release bearing

7.2a Install a new gasket over the location dowels and ...

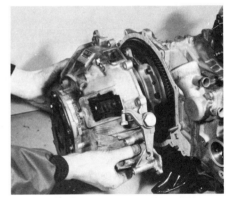
7.2b ... offer up the clutch housing

7.4a Tighten the retaining bolts ...

7.4b ... fit the plastic protector and ...

7.4c ... the clutch operating cable bracket

7.4d Fit the actuating rod and ...

7.4e ... the return spring

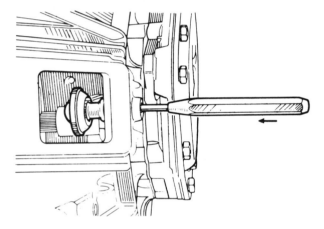

Fig. 5.3 Drifting out the clutch lever balljoint (Sec 9)

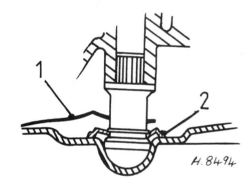

Fig. 5.4 Location of the fork spring blade (Sec 9)

1   Spring blade   2   Rubber cover

8   Engine/transmission unit – relocation and final assembly

1   With the clutch housing fully installed the engine/transmission unit can be relocated on its mountings and the various fittings reconnected. This procedure is a direct reversal of the removal sequence and further information is given in Chapter 1.
2   Readjust the clutch as described in Section 2.
3   Top up the engine/transmission oil and engine coolant. Bleed the cooling system after topping up (see Chapter 2). After starting the engine check for leaks from the joints and connections.

9   Clutch actuating rod/fork and release bearing – removal, inspection and refitting

1   The clutch actuating rod can be removed by slackening the operating adjustment and unhooking the return spring.
2   To remove or overhaul the withdrawal bearing and fork the clutch

housing must be removed. This is described in Section 4.
3   With the housing removed the withdrawal fork and bearing can be withdrawn from the output shaft for inspection.
4   Do not clean the bearing with fluid as it will harm the bearing. Wipe it clean and check for excessive wear or play. Always renew if in doubt.
5   Inspect the fork retaining balljoint and if obviously distorted or worn renew it. Drift the balljoint from the housing using a suitable diameter drift (Fig. 5.3). Fit the new one together with a new rubber cup by driving it carefully into position using a soft faced hammer. Support the housing during this operation to prevent it being damaged.
6   To refit the fork, fit the spring blade so that it is located under the rubber cover as shown in Fig. 5.4.
7   Position the release bearing over the engine output and engage the retainers behind the fork fingers. The release bearing can be slid along the sleeve whilst holding the fork.
8   Check the fork and bearing for correct operation and then refit the housing – see Section 7. Readjust the clutch operating clearance on completion – see Section 2.

10 Fault diagnosis – clutch

Symptom	Reason/s
Judder when taking up drive	Loose engine/gearbox mountings or over-flexible mountings Badly worn friction surfaces or friction plate contamination with oil carbon deposit Worn splines in the friction plate hub or on the engine output shaft
Clutch spin (or failure to disengage) so that gears cannot be meshed	Clutch actuating cable clearance too great Clutch friction disc sticking because of rust on splines (usually apparent after standing idle for some length of time) Damaged or misaligned pressure plate assembly Incorrect release bearing fitted
Clutch slip (increase in engine speed does not result in increase in car speed – especially on hills)	Clutch actuating cable clearance from fork too small resulting in partially disengaged clutch at all times Clutch friction surfaces worn out (beyond further adjustment of operating cable) or clutch surfaces oil-soaked

Chapter 6 Transmission

Contents

Specifications

Gearbox

Type	BH3 (408) or BH2
Number of gears	4 forward, 1 reverse
Synchromesh	All forward gears
Ratios:	
1st	3.883:1
2nd	2.296:1
3rd	1.502:1
4th	1.042:1
Reverse	3.568:1
Engine-to-gearbox transfer gears:	
Engine output shaft	27 teeth
Gearbox input shaft	34 teeth
Reduction ratio	1.259:1
Lubrication	Common with engine (see Chapter 1)

Final drive

Type	Integral with gearbox. Helical gear crownwheel and pinion
Differential end thrust	Copper faced thrust washers
Differential bearing	Shell type
Ratio	Varies with model, year and country, consult your Peugeot agent (Initial ratio 4.067:1)

Torque wrench settings

	lbf ft	kgf m
Bellcrank lever pivot bolt (1)	10	1.4
Detent retaining plugs (3)	9	1.25
Case bolts:		
Initial load:		
7 mm	11.25	1.6
8 mm	7.5	1.0
10 mm	14.5	2.0
Final load		
7 mm	11.25	1.6
8 mm	14.5	2.0
10 mm	33.75	4.7
Primary shaft nut:		
Initial load (to set tapered bearings)	14.5	2.0
Final load	6.5	0.9
Pinion shaft nut	16.0	2.25

1 General description

The Peugeot 104 is fitted with a four-speed manual gearbox mounted transversely directly beneath and in line with the engine. The transmission housing is cast in aluminium alloy and besides the gears, also contains the differential and final drive units. Drive to the gearbox from the engine is via transfer gears which are mounted separately on the outside of the clutch housing.

The gearbox has a conventional two shaft constant-mesh layout. There are four pairs of gears, one for each forward speed. The gears on the primary shaft are fixed to the shaft, while those on the secondary or pinion shaft float, each being locked to the shaft when engaged by the synchromesh unit. The reverse idler gear is on a third shaft. The gear selector forks engage in the synchromesh unit; these slide axially along the shaft to engage the appropriate gear. The forks are mounted on selector shafts which are located in the base of the gearbox.

The helical gear on the end of the pinion shaft drives directly onto

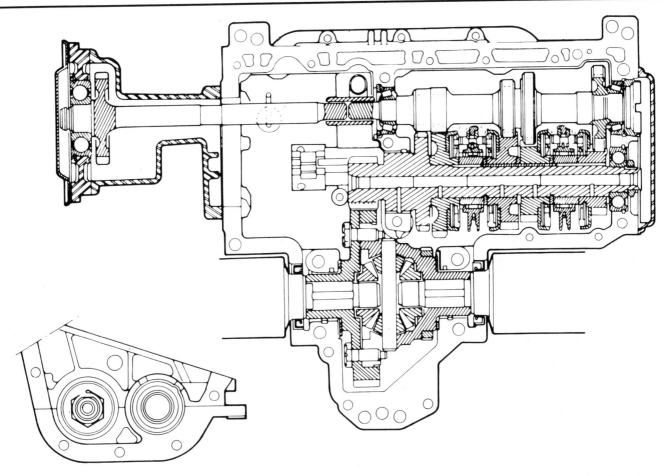

Fig. 6.1 Sectional view of the transmission system including the gearbox input shaft. Inset, end view on input face (Sec 1)

the crownwheel mounted on the differential unit. The latter differs from normal practice in that it runs in shell bearings and the end thrust is taken up by thrust washers in a similar manner to the engine crankshaft.

Although the transmission system employed is relatively simple there are nevertheless a few words of warning which must be stressed before any potential dismantlers start work, to let them know what they are letting themselves in for.

First of all decide whether the fault you wish to repair is worth all the time and effort involved. Secondly, if the transmission unit is in a very bad state then the cost of the necessary component parts may well exceed the cost of an exchange factory unit. Thirdly, be absolutely sure that you understand how the transmission unit works.

Special care must be taken during all dismantling and assembly operations to ensure that the housing is not overstressed or distorted in any way.

When dismantled, check the cost and availability of the parts to be renewed and compare this against the cost of a replacement unit, which may not be much more expensive and therefore a better proposition.

On reassembly, take careful note of the tightening procedure and torque settings. This is most important to prevent overtightening, distortion and oil leakage.

2 Transmission unit – removal

1   It is necessary to remove the engine and transmission assemblies as a combined unit. Refer to Chapter 1 where this work is described in Section 4.
2   With the unit removed from the car, considerable dismantling is necessary before the transmission can be separated from the engine. Follow the relevant procedures in Chapter 1 as follows:

Section 5 – Engine dismantling
Section 8 – Removal of clutch housing and transfer gears
Section 9 – Removal of timing cover
Section 10 – Separation of engine and gearbox

3 Transmission unit – dismantling

1   Before proceeding according to the directions given below, first read Section 1 (General description). It is assumed that the unit is out of the vehicle and on the bench. (It is not advisable to dismantle it on the floor. It will do the kitchen table no harm as it is not heavy). Do not throw away gaskets when dismantling for they will act as a guide for the fitment of the new ones supplied in the gasket set which should have already been purchased. Always renew all gaskets, locking washers and roll pins. Clean the outside casing thoroughly, all the nooks and crannies, and allow to dry. Start work with clean hands and a plentiful supply of clean rag.
2   To separate the upper and lower gearbox half-housings first unscrew and remove the bolts (see Fig. 6.2) from the upper housing.
3   Now invert the gearbox, undo the three bolts retaining the guard plate and remove the plate. Remove the bottom cover plate retaining bolts and remove the bottom plate. Unscrew the retaining pin and locknut and withdraw the speedometer drive pinion.
4   Unscrew the four retaining bolts and remove the oil pump suction filter. Pull the gauze strainer out carefully noting the O-ring.
5   Unscrew and remove the bottom housing bolts as shown in Fig. 6.3 and carefully separate the two half-housings.
6   The gear train assemblies and the differential unit are now accessible for inspection and removal if further dismantling is required. Simply lift out the appropriate assembly. If the bearing shells are removed mark them with their location in case they are to be reused. Unless new bearings have been fitted recently and are in good condition it is sensible to renew them.

82

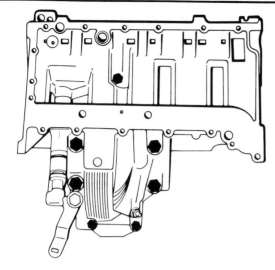

Fig. 6.2 The upper half-housing bolt positions (Sec 3)

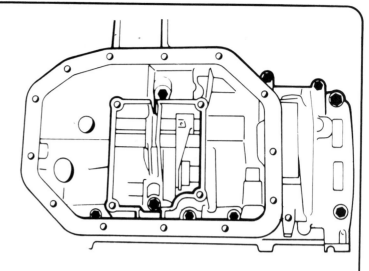

Fig. 6.3 The lower half-housing bolt positions (Sec 3)

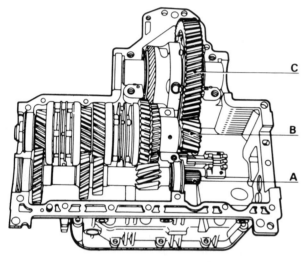

Fig. 6.4 Arrangement of shafts and differential (Sec 3)

A Primary shaft
B Secondary (pinion) shaft
C Differential unit

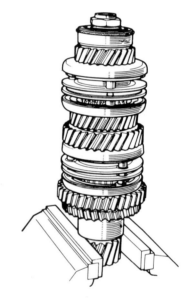

Fig. 6.5 Support the pinion shaft in a soft-jawed vice (Sec 3)

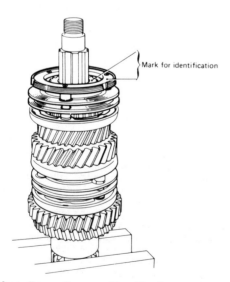

Mark for identification

Fig. 6.6 Before dismantling put identification marks on mating parts for reassembly in correct positions (Sec 3)

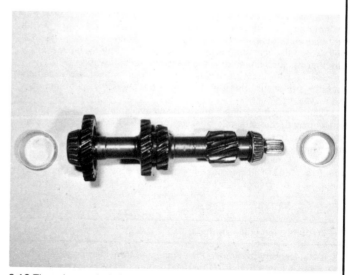

3.18 The primary shaft. Keep each outer track with its own taper bearing

Secondary (pinion) shaft – dismantling

7 If the secondary (or pinion) shaft is to be dismantled, first support it vertically in a soft-jawed vice as shown (Fig. 6.5).

8 The end nut must now be unscrewed. This will have been (or should have been) staked on its inner protruding flange to lock it in position. Tap out the intended portion of flange and then unscrew the nut to remove.

9 The bearing must now be withdrawn. This is a press fit onto the shaft and will require the use of a suitable bearing puller to remove it. Take care not to damage the adjacent 4th speed gear. Note that the bearing is fitted with the snap-ring groove outwards.

10 With the bearing removed, withdraw the distance washer and the 4th speed gear.

11 Before removing the 3rd/4th speed synchromesh unit it should be suitably marked for identification so that it is nor confused with the 1st/2nd gear synchromesh unit which is identical.

12 Withdraw the 3rd/4th synchromesh unit, complete with hub.

13 Remove the assembly from the vice and invert to remove the key from within the wide spline groove.

14 Rotate the distance washer to align with shaft splines and then withdraw it.

15 Withdraw the 3rd speed gear, distance washer and the 2nd speed gear.

16 Rotate and remove the washer from the shaft groove and then withdraw the 1st/2nd gear synchromesh unit and hub after marking them for position.

17 Remove the 1st speed gear.

Primary shaft – dismantling

18 The primary shaft runs in taper roller bearings. The outer tracks of the bearings are easily removed once the gear unit is lifted clear but keep the cups separate (photo).

19 If the inner track and races are to be removed, (this is only necessary if they are to be removed) a suitable bearing puller will be needed. Take care not to damage the roller cage during removal just in case a replacement bearing is not readily available.

Selector mechanism – dismantling

20 The selector mechanism can only be dismantled after the primary and secondary shaft assemblies have been removed from the gearbox.

21 The selector mechanism is shown in Fig. 6.7. Commence dismantling by unscrewing the three selector detent ball and spring retaining plugs (Fig. 6.8). Extract the springs and balls and keep them with their respective plugs.

22 Use a suitable drift and drive out the roll pins from the reverse gear selector fork, the 1st/2nd gear selector fork and the 3rd/4th speed selector fork.

23 Extract the reverse selector shaft and its interlock disc (Fig. 6.9).

24 Remove the 3rd/4th gear selector fork, then the 1st/2nd and 3rd/4th gear selector shafts. Withdraw the 1st/2nd gear selector fork.

Reverse sliding gear – removal

25 The gear can be removed after withdrawing the shaft (located in the gearbox casting by a roll pin). Drive the roll pin out with a punch, extract the shaft, gear, and stop collar. Note which way round the gear faces.

Gear shift control lever

26 Drive out the roll pin holding the control finger to the shaft using a suitable punch and then withdraw the selector shaft control finger. Remove the external control arm. Withdraw the half-bushes and remove the shift control lever and shaft together with the spacer, spring and thrust bush.

---

4 Differential unit – general

1 Apart from lifting it from the gearbox half-housing, cleaning it out and giving it a general external inspection, the differential unit should not be dismantled or interfered with (Fig. 6.10).

2 If on inspection it is found to be defective or is suspect, have your Peugeot dealer examine it or fit a new unit.

3 The crownwheel is mounted on the differential unit, which also incorporates the drivegear for the speedometer cable. The unit runs in shell bearings and is located by thrust washers.

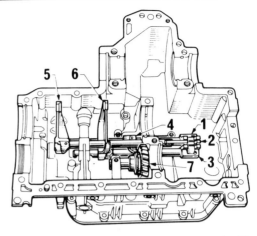

Fig. 6.7 Arrangement of selector shafts and forks (Sec 3)

1	Reverse selector shaft	5	3rd/4th selector fork
2	3rd/4th selector shaft	6	1st/2nd selector fork
3	1st/2nd selector shaft	7	Reverse idler gear
4	Reverse gear selector fork		

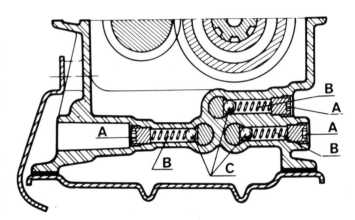

Fig. 6.8 The selector rod detent plugs (A), springs (B), and balls (C), showing their relative positions in the gearbox (Sec 3)

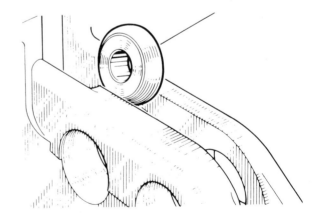

Fig. 6.9 The reverse shaft interlock disc (Sec 3)

---

5 Transmission components – inspection

1 Having removed and dismantled the transmission, the various components should be thoroughly washed with a suitable solvent, or with petrol and paraffin, and then wiped dry. Take great care not to damage the mating faces of the half-housings.

2 Check the transmission half-housings for cracks or damage particularly near the bearings or selector rod bushes. The housings are

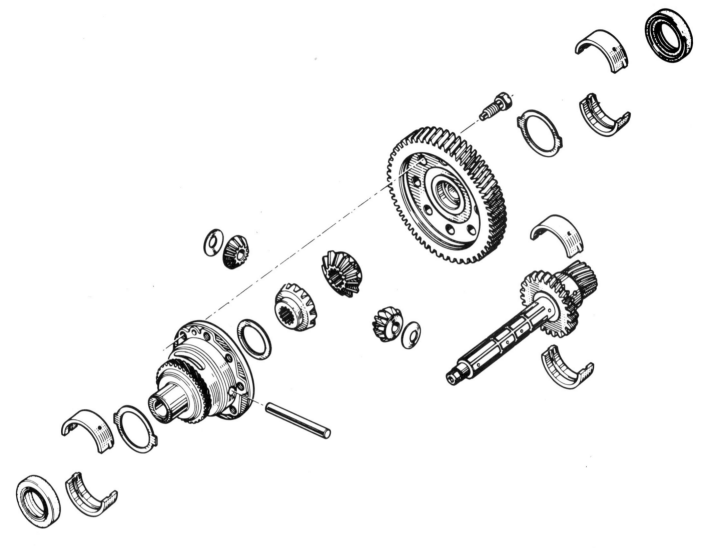

Fig. 6.10 Exploded view of the differential unit (Sec 4)

a matched pair and cannot be renewed individually. The mating faces
must not be more than 0.004 in (0.10 mm) out of true.
3   Components requiring particular attention will have been noted as
a result of the performance of the transmission prior to dismantling.
4   Check the gears for chips of uneven wear. The pinion shaft gears
should be a good sliding fit on the shaft.
5   Check the pinion shaft for wear on the splines or bearing surfaces.
6   Carefully inspect the synchromesh units (photo). If weak synchromesh has been experienced, renew the synchromesh units and
carefully inspect the synchronising face on the pinion shaft gears.
7   Examine the gearbox bearings. The primary shaft taper roller bearings are normally reliable and hard wearing. Check them for wear,
scoring and freedom of rotation which should be perfectly smooth.
Check the pinion shaft ball bearings for excessive play between the
inner and outer races. Hold the bearing by its inner race and spin the
outer race — the movement should be smooth with no signs of harsh-
ness or binding. Check the shell bearings at the pinion end of the
mainshaft and either side of the differential, taking care not to get
them mixed up. They must be in good condition showing no signs of
scoring or excessive wear. In view of their low cost and ease of fitting
it is suggested that they be renewed as a matter of course. The
differential thrust washers should also be renewed at this stage —
again the replacement cost is relatively low.
8   Check that the nylon speedometer drive gearwheel is in good condition and running easily in its bush.
9   Check the selector forks for wear. Measure them with a pair of

5.6 When inspecting each synchromesh unit keep the hub in correct
relationship with its synchro unit

calipers and compare their ends with the thickest point; if in doubt renew them. They should be only fractionally worn.
10 Check the gear shift mechanism. The tongue which also slots into the top of the selectors wears quite rapidly, often resulting in non-selected gears and sloppy action.
11 Blow through the oilways to ensure that they are clear before reassembly.

6 Transmission unit – reassembly

1 All components must be spotlessly clean prior to assembly, as must the upper and lower half-housings. Lubricate the respective sub-assemblies as they are installed, particularly the bearings and moving parts.
2 As with the dismantling process, the various subassemblies are dealt with in turn.

Pinion shaft assembly

3 First check that the shaft and its bearing surfaces are perfectly clean. Commence by fitting the 1st speed gear (photos).
4 Slide the synchromesh unit down the shaft to fit against the 1st speed gear (photo). If the original synchromesh unit is being used it must be fitted facing the same direction as before. The spacer pins of the synchromesh unit are marked on one side with 2 lines (Fig. 6.11), and when the hub is installed these lines must face the 1st speed gear.
5 Slide the distance washer down the shaft and align with the groove around the splines (photo). Adjust the washer position to allow the key to be installed in the wide groove between the shaft splines (Fig. 6.12). Check that the key can be fitted.
6 Slide the 2nd speed gear into position as shown (photo). Fit the next distance washer (photo) and again position to allow the key to pass through between the shaft splines.
7 Slide the 3rd gear into position (photo), and as before fit a distance washer (photo).
8 Now slide the key down the wide groove of the shaft with its

6.3a With the pinion shaft mounted in a soft-jawed vice ...

6.3b ... and using plenty of clean oil ...

6.3c ... fit the first speed gear

6.4 Slide the 1st/2nd sychromesh unit down the shaft

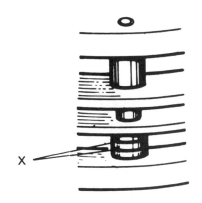
Fig. 6.11 The synchro hub spacer markings (X) (Sec 6)

6.5 Fit the distance washer and then turn it to align the wide key slot

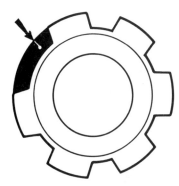
Fig. 6.12 End view of the pinion shaft showing the wide groove (arrowed) (Sec 6)

6.6a Slide the second speed gear into position

6.6b Again fit a distance washer and turn into alignment with the wide groove

6.7a Then fit the third speed gear ...

6.7b ... followed by its distance washer

6.8 Then fit the key in the wide groove

6.9 Fit the 3rd/4th synchromesh unit ...

6.10a ... followed by the fourth speed pinion ...

6.10b ... and its distance washer

6.11 When fitting the ball bearing make sure that the snap-ring is uppermost

6.12a Tighten the retaining nut to the specified torque and ...

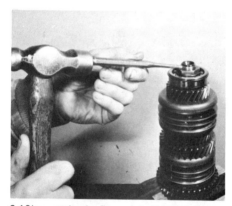
6.12b ... stake the flange into the shaft flat

6.13 Fit the bearing shells into the lower half case

6.14 Refit the reverse idler gear, shaft and stop collar, then ...

6.15 ... tap the roll pin home

tapered end inwards (photo). Check that when the key is fully installed it does not protrude beyond the last distance washer, fitted against 3rd gear. If the key does not fit fully home the chances are that a distance washer has moved and is obstructing the key.

9 Slide the 3rd/4th synchromesh unit into position on the shaft. If using the old unit it must be fitted facing the same direction as before, with the two lines on the spacer pins facing the 3rd speed gear (photo).

10 Fit the 4th speed pinion and its distance washer (photos).

11 The ball bearing is now pressed into position on the shaft. The snap-ring grooves must be offset outwards as shown (photo). Support the shaft and press or drift the bearing carefully into position using a suitable diameter tube against the bearing inner race flange. If the snap-ring was removed this should now be fitted.

12 Refit the nut and tighten to the specified torque. The nut is locked in position by staking the flange against the flat section of the shaft, using a punch (photos).

Reverse idler gear assembly and selector shafts

13 Before fitting the reverse gear fit the lower half bearing shells to the bottom half-case. The bearings must be perfectly clean as must be their respective recesses. If the old shells are being refitted they must be located in their original positions (photo).

14 Insert the reverse idler gear shaft into the housing and, as it is inserted, fit the sliding gear and stop collar as shown (photo).

15 Turn the shaft and position it to align the roll pin holes through the shaft and housing. Tap a new roll pin into position to locate the shaft (photo). Check that the gear slides and rotates freely.

16 Slide the 3rd/4th selector shaft into position with its selector slot upwards. As it is pushed through the housing, locate the 1st/2nd selector fork on the shaft (photo). Fit the 3rd/4th selector fork on the end of the shaft, and with the holes carefully aligned, drift the new roll pin into position, checking that the selector slot is still facing upwards (photo).

17 Slide the 1st/2nd selector shaft into position. As it is pushed through, locate the reverse selector fork in the groove on the reverse idler gear and pass the 1st/2nd shaft through the aperture in the reverse fork. Fit the 1st/2nd selector fork onto the end of its shaft and tap the new roll pin into the aligned holes to secure (photos).

18 Turn the lower half-case over and align the recesses in the rods to allow the interlock disc to be fitted (photo). Fit the reverse selector shaft and turn the case back the right way up. Align the reverse

Fig. 6.13 Positioning the 3rd/4th selector shaft (Sec 6)

1 3rd/4th selector fork and roll pin
2 1st/2nd selector fork
3 3rd/4th selector shaft

6.16a Locate the 1st/2nd selector fork on the 3rd/4th selector shaft

6.16b Securing the 3rd/4th selector fork to its shaft with a roll pin

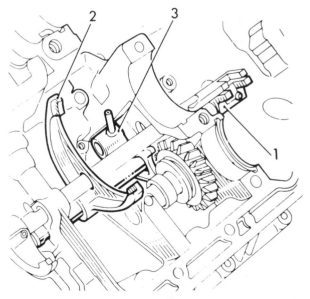

Fig. 6.14 The relationship of the 1st/2nd selector shaft (1), the 1st/2nd selector fork (2) and the reverse selector fork (3) (Sec 6)

6.17a Slide the 1st/2nd selector shaft into position and then ...

6.17b ... tap in a new roll pin to secure the selector fork

6.18a Insert the interlock disc and then ...

6.18b ... fit the reverse selector shaft

6.18c Pinning the reverse selector fork to its shaft

6.19a A detent ball, spring and retaining plug

6.19b After the ball insert the spring, followed by ...

6.19c ... the retaining plug and then ...

6.19d ... tighten to the specified torque

6.20 Fitting the bearing shells to the upper half-case

6.21a Fitting the speedometer drive pinion and ...

6.21b ... its retaining pin

6.22a Inserting the selector shaft

6.22b The four half bushes, spring and spacer bush ...

6.22c ... fitted on the selector shaft

selector and reverse selector fork holes and drift a new roll pin in to secure (photos).

19 Refit the three detent balls, springs and retaining plugs in their respective locations. Clean each plug and coat the thread with a sealant before fitting and then tighten to the specified torque (photos).

Selector mechanism assembly

20 Before assembling the selector mechanism in the upper half-case, fit the upper half bearing shells to the case. As with the lower half shells, they must be perfectly clean, their recesses must be clean and shells for re-use must go back into their original positions (photo).

21 Next fit the speedometer drive pinion. Fit a new O-ring seal and secure the assembly with its retaining pin and locknut. Make sure that the pin enters the hole in the pinion housing. Do not tighten the locknut until the cable is reconnected (photos).

22 Fit a new O-ring seal to the selector shaft and lubricate it with clean engine oil. Fit the longer of the two bushes to the shaft and insert the shaft into the case (photo). Before the shaft enters the inner bearing, fit the four half bushes and spring and the shorter of the two bushes, and then push the shaft into the inner bearing (photos).

23 Now the selector finger can be fitted to the end of the shaft. Align it as shown in Fig. 6.15 with the roll pin holes coinciding. Drift new roll pins into position (photo). The larger (7 mm diameter) pin is fitted and then the smaller (4 mm diameter) pin is drifted into its bore to secure. Operate the shaft to check it.

24 The bellcrank lever can now be fitted to the case. Grease the pivot bolt and, with the washers arranged as shown in Fig. 6.16, tighten the pivot bolt to the specified torque (photos).

General transmission assembly

25 The sub-assemblies can now be refitted into the bottom half-case. Lubricate all bearings and shells with clean engine oil.

26 Insert the differential thrust washers. Each washer has a coppered face and this must be positioned to face the differential. It will also be apparent that the lugs of the washer are of different sizes and are asymmetrically positioned so that they sit on the mating face of the half-housing when the washer is correctly installed (photo). Lubricate the washers and fit them into position on the differential, then lower

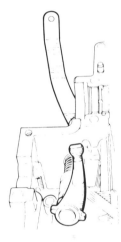

Fig. 6.15 The correct alignment of the selector finger and lever before inserting the roll pins (Sec 6)

the differential unit into position in the lower half-housing (photo). Check that it rotates freely and that the washers are fully seated.

27 The pinion shaft assembly is now lowered into position as shown (photos). The shell bearings must be well lubricated and the selector forks must engage with their respective grooves as the gear assembly is lowered into position. Check that the snap-ring in the end bearing is seated in the location groove of the housing.

28 Lubricate the taper roller bearings of the primary shaft and fit the outer races. Position the thrust washer and carefully lower the shaft into the lower half-housing (photo).

29 Before refitting the top half-housing, check that the gears rotate freely and that the case joint flanges are perfectly clean. Generously lubricate the gear assemblies with clean engine oil (photo).

6.23 Pinning the selector finger to the selector shaft with concentric roll pins

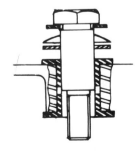

Fig. 6.16 Arrangement of washers on the bellcrank lever pivot bolt (Sec 6)

6.24a The bellcrank lever and its pivot bolt, bushes and washers ...

6.24b ... being tightened after assembly into the case

6.26a Assembling a differential thrust washer with copper face towards the differential unit. Note the offset and different sized tabs

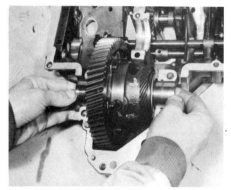

6.26b Refitting the differential in the lower half-case

6.27a Lubricate the bearings and ...

6.27b ... refit the pinion shaft assembly ...

6.28 ... followed by the primary shaft. Note the thrust washer (arrowed)

6.29 Check the assembly before fitting the upper half-case

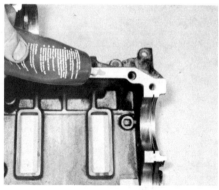

6.30 Clean the mating faces and apply sealant, then ...

6.31 ... lower the upper half-case into position

30 Smear an even amount of sealant (Rhodorsil CAF33 or equivalent) over the joint faces (photo).

31 Check that you have not left any tools or loose articles inside the housing and carefully lower the upper half-housing into position (photo). Check that the selector finger is correctly located in the shafts.

32 Insert and hand tighten the top housing fixing bolts, then refer to Fig. 6.17 and tighten the bolts to the appropriate initial torque, according to their size (see Specifications).

33 Invert the gearbox and insert the bottom retaining bolts as shown in Fig. 8.18. Hand tighten them first, then tighten them to the appropriate initial torque (see Specifications).

34 Screw the special nut into position at the end of the gearcase in the primary shaft aperture. This will adjust the endfloat of the primary shaft and give the correct preload to the taper roller bearings. When the nut is in position recheck the torque settings of the number 3 and 5 housing bolts and if satisfactory select a gear. Self-locking grips clamped onto the selector rod will assist here.

35 Rotate the gear train by turning the pinion shaft nut (clockwise) and at the same time tighten the primary shaft nut. As assistant will be required here to support the gearbox. Peugeot dealers use a special peg socket to tighten the bearing adjustment nut and unless this can be borrowed or hired you will have to fabricate one that is suitable for use with your torque wrench. First tighten the nut to the initial torque then slacken it off and re-tighten to the fixed torque (see Specifications) (photos).

36 Now reselect neutral and check the torque necessary to rotate the pinion shaft. A figure of 3.75 to 6.0 lbf ft (0.5 to 0.8 kgf m) should be necessary to start turning it. Bend over the nut flange to lock in position (photo).

37 When the above is achieved, retighten the upper housing retaining bolts to the appropriate final torques (see Specifications).

38 Invert the gearbox again and retighten the bottom housing retaining bolts to their final torque settings.

39 To complete the gearbox assembly, refit the oil pump suction filter unit and tighten the four bolts to the specified torque (photos).

40 Refit the bottom plate, using a new gasket. Fit the flat washers

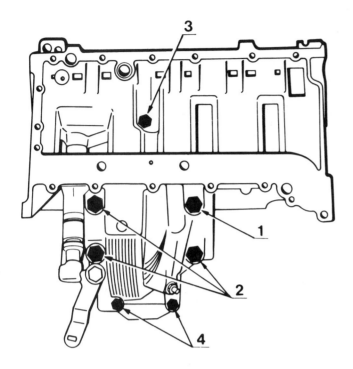

Fig. 6.17 The bolts in the top half-housing must be tightened to different torques – see specifications (Sec 6)

| 1 | 10 mm x 90 mm | 3 | 8 mm x 55 mm |
| 2 | 10 mm x 65 mm | 4 | 7 mm x 30 mm |

Fig. 6.18 The bolts in the bottom half-housing must also be tightened to different torques (Sec 6)

| 5 | 8 mm x 75 mm | 7 | 7 mm x 75 mm |
| 6 | 8 mm x 55 mm | 8 | 7 mm x 30 mm |

under the bolts and tighten to the specified torque (photos).
41 Refit the sump guard plate (photo).
42 Carefully tap the oil seals into position in the differential housing if not already fitted (photo).
43 The gearbox is now ready for refitting to the engine.

6.35a With an assistant turning the gear train, tighten the primary shaft nut

6.35b A home-made adaptor for tightening the primary shaft nut

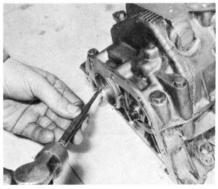

6.36 Bending the nut flange to lock the nut

6.39a Fit the oil suction filter and ...

6.39b ... tighten the retaining bolts to the specified torque

6.40a Refit the bottom plate and ...

6.40b ... the drain plug with a new washer

6.41 After fitting the sump guard plate ...

6.42 ... complete the assembly by fitting new oil seals in the differential housing

10.1 The gearchange lever with floor covering removed

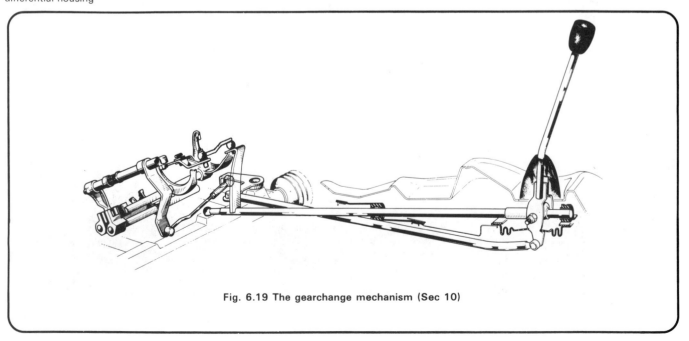

Fig. 6.19 The gearchange mechanism (Sec 10)

7 Transmission to engine – reassembly

Refer to Chapter 1, where full instructions are given for refitting the gearbox to the engine.

8 Engine/transmission – refitting

Refer to Chapter 1, where full refitting instructions are given.

9 Differential oil seal – renewal

1 The differential oil seals can be removed and refitted with the engine/transmission unit in position in the car, but the driveshafts will obviously have to be removed. This operation is covered in Chapter 7.
2 With the driveshafts withdrawn the old oil seals can be extracted from the differential housing using a suitable screwdriver.
3 Clean out the seating before fitting a new seal. Lubricate the seal to assist assembly and drift carefully into position, with the lip facing inwards.
4 Always take care not to damage the oil seals when removing or refitting the driveshafts.

10 Floor gearchange mechanism – adjustment

1 Access to the gearchange lever is gained by lifting the floor covering and moulding (photo). Overhaul consists of checking the pivots and bushes for wear or damage and renewing the assembly if it has a major defect. However, unless there has been gross neglect or the car has covered a very high mileage, it is unlikely that renewal will be necessary.
2 If the original mechanism adjustment has been lost, or resetting is necessary following renewal of parts, this is accomplished on the two transverse links located near the steering rack.
3 To adjust the upper transverse link, loosen the clamp nut on the sliding joint at its left end and ensure that the gearbox selector rods are in the neutral position. Have an assistant move the gearchange lever from left to right over neutral position and note the movement of the transverse rod in the clamp bolt. At the midway point of this movement tighten the clamp nut, thus ensuring that gear lever movement is centralised with that of the selector rods. Check the movement after tightening the clamp nut.
4 The lower transverse link is initially adjusted to a length of 160 mm (6.3 in) between balljoint centres. Further adjustment may be necessary on this link to obtain full movement of the gearbox selector rods when the gearchange lever is moved in the fore and aft direction. Tighten the adjuster locknut on completion.
5 After making any adjustment to the gearchange mechanism, check that all gears can be selected cleanly with the engine running.

11 Fault diagnosis – transmission

1 Transmission faults can be divided into two main groups, the first being a definite failure preventing the transmission from operating. The second may be partial failure or unusual noises caused by a worn or damaged component.
2 In the first instance the problem is almost certain to be an internal gearbox fault in which case it will be necessary to remove and dismantle the transmission for inspection and rectification.
3 The only possible external fault could be in the gear lever control linkage. The selector rod between the lever and transmission may have been distorted or damaged. Adjustment may also be lost due to the transverse rod clamp nut coming loose (see previous Section). This is most unlikely but is worth a check.
4 In the second instance of partial failure such as difficulty in engaging a gear, noises and/or vibrations, it should first be confirmed that the problem is actually with the transmission. Strange noises caused by a component malfunction may carry through to the car and mislead the unsuspecting operator into an incorrect diagnosis. Check the basics first, items such as the selector rod adjustment and the clutch operating clearance. Difficulty in changing gear may be caused by a worn or incorrectly adjusted clutch.
5 Noises can be traced to a certain extent by doing the test sequence as follows.
6 Find the speed and type of driving that makes the noise. If the noise occurs with engine running, car stationary, clutch disengaged, gear engaged: the noise is not in the transmission. If it disappears after the clutch is engaged in neutral, halted, it is the clutch.
7 If the noise can be heard faintly in neutral, clutch engaged, it is in the gearbox or transfer gears. It will presumably get worse on the move, especially in some particular gear.
8 Final drive noises are only heard on the move. They will only vary with speed and load, whatever gear is engaged.
9 Noise on corners implies excessive tightness or excessive play of the bevel side gears or idler pinions in the differential, but first suspect the front wheel bearings.
10 In general, whining is gear teeth at the incorrect distance apart. Roaring or rushing or moaning is bearings. Thumping or grating noises suggest a chip out of a gear tooth.
11 If subdued whining comes on gradually, there is a good chance the transmission will last a long time to come.
12 Whining or moaning appearing suddenly, or becoming loud should be examined quickly.
13 If thumping or grating noises appear, stop at once. If bits of metal are loose inside, the whole transmission, including the casing, could quickly be wrecked.
14 Synchromesh wear is obvious. You just beat the gears and crashing occurs.
15 If uncertain about a problem, get a second qualified opinion before dismantling – you may save yourself some time, effort and possibly money.

Chapter 7 Driveshafts, hubs, wheels and tyres

Contents

Specifications

Driveshafts . . . .
Glaenzer reinforced shafts with constant velocity universal joints on inner and outer ends; inner end splines permit axial movement

Wheel bearings
Front . . . . Twin track ball bearings
Rear . . . . Two tapered roller bearings

Wheels
Type . . . . Pressed steel disc, 3-stud fixing
Size . . . . 4B13 or 4½B13
Maximum rim run-out . . . . 0.040 in (1 mm)

Tyres
Type . . . . Radial ply, tubeless

Sizes and pressures:

	Front bars (lbf/in²)	Rear bars (lbf/in²)
104GL – 135SR13	1.9 (27)	2.1 (31)
104S – 145SR13	1.8 (26)	2.1 (31)
104SL – 145SR13	1.8 (26)	2.0 (29)
104ZS – 145SR13	1.8 (26)	2.1 (31)
104ZL – 135SR13	1.9 (27)	2.2 (32)

For motorway use, or when fully laden, increase above pressures by 0.1 bar (1.5 lbf/in²)

Torque wrench settings

	lbf ft	kgf m
Driveshaft/hub nut	180	25
Wheelnuts	43	6
Anti-roll bar bracket bolts:		
8 mm dia (early cars)	9	1.25
10 mm dia (later cars)	32	4.5
Track control arm link pin nut	25	3.5
Anti-roll bar/track control arm nut	40	5.5
Locknut (if fitted)	7	1.0

1 General description

The drive to the front wheels of the Peugeot 104 is transmitted directly from the final drive unit to the front hubs by the driveshafts. Constant velocity universal joints are fitted at each end and accommodate the steering and suspension angular movements. The inner joints also plunge to allow the changes of length that accompany suspension and steering movement.

Little maintenance is possible, even changing the rubber bellows is a specialised operation best entrusted to your Peugeot dealer.

The driveshafts are splined to the front hubs. These run on double row ball-races located in the hub carrier at the base of the MacPherson struts.

The rear hubs run on conventional taper-roller bearings on individual stub axles.

2 Driveshafts – removal and refitting

1 Undo and remove the two bolts holding each of the anti-roll bar retaining brackets. Remove the brackets and retrieve the packing plate from each mounting.

2 Remove the anti-roll bar attachment nut on the side to be disconnected if only one driveshaft is being removed, or remove both attachment nuts if applicable. On early models the nut is secured with a thin locknut but on later models the roll bar has a pin through it. Remove the locknut or pin, then remove the attachment nut followed by the steel and the rubber washers.

3 Undo and remove the nut securing the inner end of the track control arm (through which the end of the anti-roll bar fits) to the chassis cradle subframe.

4 With the handbrake applied, raise the front of the car and support

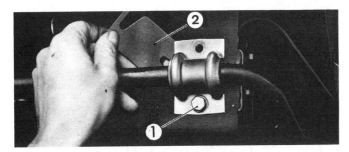

Fig. 7.1 The left-hand anti-roll bar mounting bracket (Sec 2)

1 Attachment bolt   2 Packing plate

Fig. 7.3 Freeing the end of the anti-roll bar from the track control arm (Sec 2)

A Early models with locknut
B Later models with locking pin
a Chamfered washer. Assemble with chamfer in direction shown

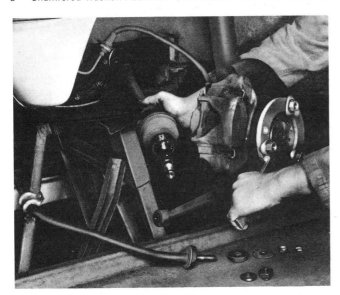

Fig. 7.5 Disconnecting the wheel hub from the driveshaft (Sec 2). Note the Peugeot tool for holding the wheel hub

Fig. 7.2 The track control arm (Sec 2)

1 Anti-roll bar attachment nut and locknut
2 Inner pivot pin attachment nut

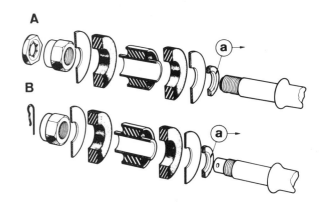

Fig. 7.4 The anti-roll bar end fitting assemblies (Sec 2)

it on chassis stands or blocks so that the front wheels hang free. Chock the rear wheels. Turn the steering wheel in the direction opposite to the driveshaft to be removed, remove the ignition key and engage the steering lock.

5 Remove the front roadwheel on the side concerned. Drain approx. 3.5 pints (2.0 litres) of engine oil into a clean container, then refit the drain plug.

6 Free the end of the anti-roll bar from the track control arm and retrieve the washers. Note their positions for reassembly.

7 Unscrew and remove the stub axle retaining nut. To prevent the hub from turning when loosening the nut, position a suitably padded bar between two wheel studs, taking care not to damage the threads.

8 Remove the pin securing the inner end of the track control arm to the subframe.

9 Disconnect the wheel hub from the driveshaft. Hold the shaft and manoeuvre the hub assembly free, taking care not to damage the seal bearing surfaces on the shaft. If the driveshaft is not to be removed, tie it up to the chassis to prevent it coming free from the engine.

10 To remove the driveshaft from the transmission, withdraw it carefully, keeping it horizontal until clear of the differential case. Be prepared for oil spillage as the shaft leaves the seal in the differential case.

11 When refitting the driveshaft, take special care when inserting it into the transmission to avoid damaging the oil seal (photo).

12 After the driveshaft has been engaged with the wheel hub, fit the track control arm inner pivot pin. Check that the arm is accurately located before inserting the pin. If necessary grip the arm with self-locking pliers to manoeuvre it into position. Fit the retaining nut, preferably a new one, but don't tighten it at this stage.

13 Fit the driveshaft-to-hub nut and washer and tighten the nut to the specified torque. Lock the nut by drifting the rim into the shaft recess.

14 Fit the roadwheel, tightening the retaining nuts to the specified torque, and refit the trim plate.

15 Unlock the steering and straighten the front wheels. Lower the vehicle to the ground, release the handbrake and rock the car forwards and backwards slightly to allow the assembly to assume its normal position.

16 It is now necessary to load the front end of the car so that the anti-roll bar mounting holes in the track control arms are horizontally in line with the bottom of the subframe. Peugeot have a special tool to pull the car downwards whilst it is raised on a car lift (Fig. 7.6). If you can get hold of a set of spring compressors this could be your solution: it may be possible to compress the front suspension springs sufficiently to achieve the right geometry. Failing that, if you have some well-developed friends perhaps they could be encouraged to add some weight, so to speak! With the track control arms lined up as required,

2.11 Avoid damaging the transmission case seals (right-hand shown) when refitting the driveshafts

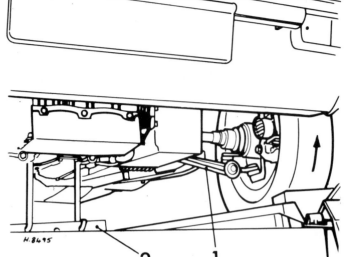

Fig. 7.6 Suspension position for connecting the anti-roll bar (Sec 2)

1   Horizontal alignment of the anti-roll bar mounting and bottom of the sub-frame
2   Peugeot tool for pulling vehicle downwards

push the front wheel back as far as it will go and wedge it in that position with a block under the front of the tyre. Engage the anti-roll bar with the suspension arm after fitting the appropriate washers. Note that the chamfered washer must have the chamfer against the face on the anti-roll bar. Fit the retaining nut but don't tighten it fully at this stage.

17 Fit the anti-roll bar retaining brackets to the subframe, making sure that the packing plate is located between each bracket and frame, and tighten the attachment bolts to the appropriate torque, depending on the size of the bolts.

18 Now tighten the following to their specified torques:

(a)   Track control arm link pin nut
(b)   Anti-roll bar attachment nut on track control arm
(c)   If appropriate, the locknut for the anti-roll bar attachment nut. Alternatively fit the locking pin to the anti-roll bar

19 Unclamp the spring compressors, or release the suspension load, as appropriate. Before the next engine run, check the oil level and top up as required.

3   Driveshaft joints – maintenance

1   As has been stated earlier, there is very little maintenance which can be carried out on the driveshaft joints. The joints can be dismantled by the do-it-yourself mechanic but he will find that he is unable to reassemble them.

2   Special tools are required to effect an efficient repair. Even replacing the rubber bellows and relubricating the joint is beyond the scope of ordinary tools. Under all circumstances it is more efficient to remove the driveshaft and then take it to a Peugeot garage (only) to have them effect any repair or maintenance. With the specific special tools available to them, all repairs to the joint can be carried out quickly and safely.

3   With the spider joints it is possible to have the bellows, yoke and spider itself replaced together or separately. However, experience shows that unless the bellows are punctured and lubricant allowed to escape so that the joint becomes dry, the outer universal joint wears at a far greater rate than the inner, consequently the shaft is nearly always replaced before the total life of the inner joint is reached.

4   Front wheel hub bearings – removal and refitting

1   The front hub bearings are twin track ball-races and removal for cleaning, inspection or replacement necessitates removing the wheel hub and brake disc.

2   The hub and disc unit will have to be separated from the strut assembly using a Peugeot special tool as it is not possible to use the usual sort of three or two legged puller. As the same tool is used for

extracting and inserting the bearings, as well as reassembling the hub and disc unit to the strut, it will be obvious that, either this tool must be borrowed or hired, or the job will have to be done by a Peugeot agent who will have the tool. As it is a simple matter to remove the MacPherson strut, and in any case removing the strut will make the job far easier, it is recommended that the strut is removed as explained in Chapter 10 and the assembly taken to the nearest Peugeot agent for servicing. The two oil seals will need renewing regardless of the condition of the bearings.

3   Reassembly is the reverse of the removal procedure. When tightening nuts and bolts, do so with the weight of the car on the suspension and tighten to the specified torque.

5   Rear wheel hub bearings – removal and refitting

1   Each rear wheel runs on a pair of tapered bearings, which must be renewed as a pair if the need arises.

2   Refer to Chapter 8 and remove the brake drum/hub assembly.

3   Remove the old seal from the stub axle by levering it out with a screwdriver (photo). Clean the axle and fit a new seal, making sure that the lip faces outwards towards the brake drum/hub.

4   There must be no traces of oil or grease on the brake drums or linings. If there is, clean the brake drums using a cloth soaked in a suitable grease solvent. *Do not blow any dust out with compressed air as it is a health hazard.* Linings affected by oil or grease, or worn linings, must be renewed; refer to Chapter 8 for details of the procedure.

5   Remove the outer and inner bearings from the hub, if they have not already been removed, and identify them so that they can be refitted to their original positions if they are still fit for use. When removing the inner bearing it will be necessary to use a suitable drift to release the oil seal thrust cup. Tap the inner track on diagonally opposite points to remove the cup squarely. Clean the bearings and their tracks. Examine them for signs of wear, overheating indicated by discolouration, damage and pitting. New bearings should be fitted if there is any evidence of deterioration or any doubt about their condition.

6   Remove the bearing tracks by drifting out using suitable drifts and supports for the drum/hub. Clean the bearing track housings in the drum/hub and fit new bearing tracks. Make sure that each track is fully bedded down in its recess (photo).

7   After fitting the two tracks, pack the new inner race with multi-purpose grease and fit it into its track. With great care, fit a new thrust

Fig. 7.7 Removing a rear brake drum/hub (Sec 5)

1 *Retaining nut*
2 *Washer*
3 *Outer tapered bearing*

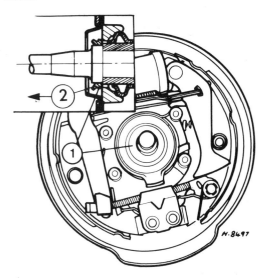

Fig. 7.8 The rear wheel stub axle seal (Sec 5)

1 *The seal located and in sectional view*
2 *Ensure that the seal lip faces outwards*

5.3 Removing the old seal from the stub axle

cup. *It is most important that the cup is perfectly square in the hub* and that the rubbing face, which contacts the seal on the axle stub, is in perfect condition. Any defect could lead to grease contaminating the brake shoes. The cup should be flush with the surface of the hub (photos) (Fig. 7.9).

8   On completion, re-check that the drum brake surface is perfectly clean and free of oil or grease.

9   Refit the brake drum/hub assembly as explained in Chapter 8.

6   Wheels – general

1   Because of the design of the suspension of the car the strength and the trueness of the roadwheels is critical, particularly at the front. Excessively fast wear on the wheel bearings and universal joints can often be attributed to buckled and deformed wheels. Check every 5000 miles, or when there is a sudden difference of feeling at the steering wheel, that the wheels are not buckled or dented. Check also that the front wheels are balanced.

2   If it is suspected that the wheels are out of balance have your local dealer rebalance them.

3   If a wheel is badly rusted or damaged in any way do not attempt to repair it – get a new replacement.

4   Do not overtighten the wheel nuts for this can deform the wheel. Always check that the inner side of the wheel is free from mud and grit for the accumulation of these can create imbalance.

5.6 Fitting a new outer bearing track

5.7a Fitting a new inner bearing and ...

5.7b ... a new thrust cup, which must be square to the axle on completion

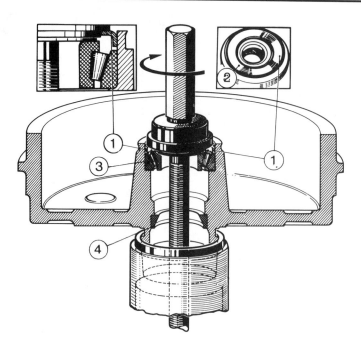

Fig. 7.9 Using a Peugeot tool to fit the rear wheel seal thrust cup
(Sec 5)

1 *The thrust cup*
2 *Make sure that this face is square with the wheel axis and*
   free of all damage
3 *Inner tapered bearing*
4 *Outer bearing track*

7 Tyres – general

In the same way that the condition and suitability of the wheels
fitted is critical so it is with the tyres. Because of the long suspension
travel and fully independent suspension it is always wise to fit radial
tyres on all wheels of these cars. Tyre wear is not great under any
circumstances but the front tyres wear faster than the rear. Do not fit
oversize tyres. The wheel rims are not readily able to take a larger
section tyre. See Specifications for suitability of tyres. Tyre pressures
are also important.

8 Fault diagnosis – driveshafts, hubs, wheels and tyres

Refer to Chapter 10.

Chapter 8 Braking system

Contents

Specifications

Type .... Front disc brakes, rear drum brakes. Cable operated handbrake to rear wheels only. All brakes self-adjusting for wear. Servo assistance on ZS models

Master cylinder
Type .... Single circuit (early models) or dual circuit (later models)
Piston diameter .... 19 mm (0.748 in)

Front disc brakes
Disc diameter .... 241 mm (9.49 in)
Disc thickness:
  New .... 10 mm (0.394 in)
  Minimum after resurfacing .... 8.5 mm (0.335 in)
  Minimum permissible .... 8 mm (0.315 in)
  Maximum variation in thickness between faces .... 0.02 mm (0.0008 in)
Maximum disc run-out measured 22 mm (0.866 in) from the rim ... 0.07 mm (0.0028 in)
Cylinder diameter .... 48 mm (1.89 in)
Minimum pad lining thickness:
  DBA (Bendix) .... 2.5 mm (0.098 in)
  Teves .... 2 mm (0.078 in)

Rear drum brakes
Drum internal diameter:
  New .... 180 mm (7.1 in)
  Maximum after resurfacing .... 181 mm (7.126 in)
  Maximum permissible .... 181.5 mm (7.146 in)
Maximum ovality on hub .... 0.10 mm (0.0039 in)
Maximum eccentricity (the difference between largest and smallest diameter) .... 0.10 mm (0.0039 in)
Maximum difference in diameters between the two rear drum brakes after resurfacing .... 0.15 mm (0.0059 in)
Lining width:
  Up to July 1977 .... 40 mm (1.575 in)
  After July 1977 .... 30 mm (1.181 in)
Cylinder diameter:
  DBA (Bendix) .... 23.8 mm (0.937 in)
  Girling .... 22 mm (0.866 in)

Note: *All pipe unions in the 104 hydraulic systems (all models) are metric thread (M10 x 100). Parts from other Peugeot models may be Whitworth threaded and **must not be fitted to 104 models***

Torque wrench settings

	lbf ft	kgf m
Wheel nuts:		
Steel wheels	43.4	6
Light alloy wheels	57.9	8
Rear axle nuts (see text):		
Initial	22	3
Final	3.5	0.5
Caliper bolts:		
Treves (recess headed bolts)	61.6	8.5
DBA Bendix (hexagon headed bolts)	50.7	7

1 General description

1   All models are fitted with a conventional braking system with discs on the front wheels and drums of the rear. Operation is hydraulic on all four wheels, with a cable-operated handbrake on the rear wheels.

2   The front discs are attached to the front hubs and wheel bearings. The caliper, which is mounted on the front edge of each disc, carries a pair of pads and a single operating cylinder. Wear indicators in the pads can be inspected without dismantling the assembly.

3   The rear drum brakes consist of a leading and trailing shoe arrangement operated by a single wheel cylinder. A self-adjusting mechanism is fitted to take up wear in the linings.

4   The hydraulic brakes are operated by a suspended foot pedal, located under the instrument panel, which operates a master cylinder. Some models have the brake circuit divided between the front and rear brakes with a dual circuit master cylinder and a dual reservoir. A brake servo unit is fitted to the ZS models.

5   A brake regulator is fitted in the rear brake circuit to prevent locking of the rear wheels. No servicing is possible on this unit: if it malfunctions it must be renewed.

6   A warning light, to indicate when the handbrake lever is applied, is fitted. On later models the warning light will also indicate when the fluid level in the hydraulic reservoir is low.

7   All work undertaken on the braking system must be to the highest standard. It is vitally important to maintain the integrity of the system and to use the right fasteners with correct locking devices where appropriate. Adjustments must be within specified limits where these apply and spare parts must be new or in faultless condition. *Absolute cleanliness when assembling hydraulic components is essential.* New seals and fresh hydraulic fluid must be used and any fluid drained or removed from the system must be discarded. Your life, and possibly the lives of others, could depend on these points: if you are in any doubt at all concerning what to do or how to do it, get professional advice or have the job done by an expert.

2 Routine maintenance

Every 250 miles (400 km) or weekly

1   Remove the hydraulic fluid reservoir cap, having cleaned thoroughly in its vicinity, and check the level of the fluid which should be just below the bottom of the filler neck. Some reservoirs are made of semi-transparent plastic and the fluid can be seen without removing the filler cap, but only rely on this check once you have satisfied yourself that an accurate indication in possible. Check also that the vent hole in the cap is clear. Any need for regular topping up must be viewed with suspicion and the whole hydraulic system carefully inspected for signs of leaks. A *small* fall in the level as the disc pads wear is normal.

Every 5000 miles (7500 km) or six-monthly

2   Inspect the front disc pads for wear. The grooves in the pads should still be visible, indicating that adequate pad material remains.

3   Check the operation of the brakes and inspect the hydraulic pipe unions and hoses for fluid leaks.

Every 10 000 miles (15 000 km) or annually

4   Remove the rear brake drums and carefully clean out the brake dust *taking care not to inhale it or disperse it.* Examine the shoe linings for wear and contamination. They must be renewed if hydraulic fluid or grease has got onto them and they should also be renewed if the material is worn down to the level of the rivet heads. If the rivets come into contact with the brake drums they will reduce braking efficiency by causing scoring which will also be expensive to rectify. Never interchange shoes to even out wear. Where oil or hydraulic fluid contamination has occurred, find the source and take appropriate action.

Every 20 000 miles (30 000 km) or two yearly

5   Check the operation of the handbrake and make sure that it is effective when applied.

Every 30 000 miles (45 000 km) or three yearly

6   Renew the brake fluid in the hydraulic system. Over a period of time the fluid degenerates as the inhibitors, which prevent corrosion and seal deterioration, decay. Also, the fluid is hygroscopic, it absorbs moisture. This affects both its boiling point and its congealing characteristics. It is false economy not to change the fluid on a regular basis, and could even be dangerous.

3 Bleeding the hydraulic system

1   The system should need bleeding only when some part of it has been dismantled which would allow air into the fluid circuit; or if the reservoir level has been allowed to drop so far that air has entered the master cylinder.

2   Ensure that a supply of clean non-aerated fluid of the correct specifications is to hand in order to replenish the reservoir(s) during the bleeding process. It is advisable, if not essential to have someone available to help, as one person has to pump the brake pedal while the other attends to each wheel. The reservoir level has also to be continuously watched and replenished. Fluid bled out should not be reused. A clean glass jar and a 9 – 12 inch length of $\frac{1}{8}$ inch internal diameter rubber tube which will fit tightly over the bleed nipples is also required.

3   Bleed the rear brakes first as these are furthest from the master cylinder. Where a dual circuit system is fitted bleed the rear brake system first, keeping both reservoir levels topped up, and then repeat the procedure on the front system.

4   Make sure the bleed nipple is clean and put a small quantity of fluid in the bottom of the jar. Fit the tube onto the nipple and place the other end in the jar under the surface of the liquid. Keep it under the surface throughout the bleeding operation.

5   Unscrew the bleed screw $\frac{1}{2}$ turn and get the assistant to depress and release the brake pedal in short sharp bursts when you direct him. Short sharp jabs are better than long slow ones because they will force any air bubbles along the line ahead of the fluid rather than pump the fluid past them. It is not essential to remove all the air the first time. If the whole system is being bled, attend to each wheel for three or four complete pedal strokes and then repeat the process. On the second time around operate the pedal sharply in the same way until no more bubbles are apparent. The bleed screw should be tightened and closed with the brake pedal fully depressed which ensures that no aerated fluid can get back into the system. Do not forget to keep the reservoir topped up throughout with fresh fluid.

6   When all four wheels have been satisfactorily bled, depress the foot pedal which should offer a firm resistance and give no trace of sponginess. The pedal must not go down under sustained pressure and if it does the master cylinder seals are likely to require replacement.

4 Brake adjustment

Front disc brakes

1   The front disc brakes are fully self-adjusting and therefore apart from the normal service checks they do not require any attention. The disc brake pads must be checked for wear periodically and if necessary, they must be renewed as described in Section 5.

Rear drum brakes

2   As with the front disc brakes the rear drum brakes are self-adjusting and do not require any attention apart from the occasional service check to inspect the linings. This involves removing the drums and is fully covered in Sections 7 and 8.

3   If the linings have been renewed or the handbrake cables have been detached or replaced, the rear brakes can be adjusted by simply applying pressure to the brake pedal several times. The handbrake cable adjustment should then be checked, as described below:

Handbrake adjustment

4   Raise the lever until the third notch in the ratchet is engaged.

5   Jack up the rear of the car and support it on stands, ramps or blocks. Chock the front wheels and engage a gear.

6   Adjust on the cable adjusters (located where the two rear wheel cables enter the flooring) until, by turning the wheels, the brakes can be felt just starting to bind (photo). Readjust if necessary, so that the arm at the back of the handbrake lever is at right angles to the centre line of the car, by loosening on one cable and tightening on the other (photo). Recheck the wheels for binding which should just be apparent

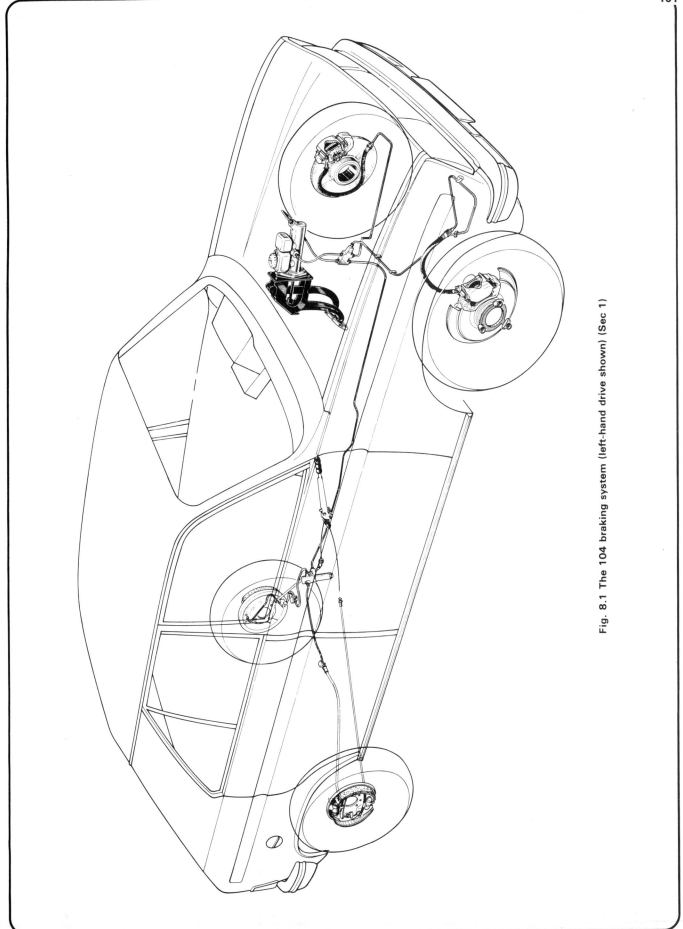

Fig. 8.1 The 104 braking system (left-hand drive shown) (Sec 1)

4.6a One of the handbrake cable adjusters (arrowed) and the brake regulator

4.6b The handbrake cable equaliser bar at the back of the handbrake lever

on both sides. Then tighten the cable adjuster locknuts.
7   Check the operation of the handbrake by ensuring that both wheels lock when the hand lever ratchet is on the 5th notch.
8   Lower the car to the ground.

5   Disc pads – inspection and renewal

1   Before dismantling any part of the brakes they should be thoroughly cleaned. Brush off as much road dirt as possible and finish off, using hot water and a mild detergent. *Do not* use paraffin, petrol or other solvents which could cause deterioration of the friction pads or piston seals.
2   Use ramps to raise the front of the car or jack it up and support on stands. Do not work on a car supported only on the wheel changing jack. Apply the handbrake to prevent movement of the car.
3   Inspection of the front brake disc pads requires no dismantling as they can be examined for wear by viewing from the front. This is made easier by turning the appropriate wheel outwards. Each pad has a groove to indicate the available depth of friction material. When the pads have worn down to the minimum permissible thickness specified, the grooves will no longer be visible and the pads must be renewed (photo). All four pads on the front brakes must be renewed when any one or more of them is worn.
4   To renew the pads first remove the front wheels and then, using a clean syringe, remove some of the fluid from the brake reservoir. When new pads are fitted the pistons must be repositioned back in the cylinders and, if fluid is not first removed from the system, it might overflow with possible damage to the car's paintwork – apart from the mess it will cause. Discard the fluid removed as it is not suitable for re-use in the system.

DBA Bendix brakes

5   With a pair of long-nosed pliers remove the figure-eight shaped clips from the keys (photo). Then slide the keys out of their slots (photo).
6   With the keys removed, the wheel cylinder can be removed from the caliper and, without disturbing the hose connection, swung to one side out of the way.
7   Remove the old pads from the caliper. Take careful note of the springs fitted to the top end of the pads, especially how they fit and the way round they are fitted.
8   Inspect the disc friction area. If it is badly scored, cracked, or excessively worn, the disc will have to be renewed, see Chapter 7 for details. Worn discs can be resurfaced by a specialist garage if the wear is within limits.
9   If the pads are not worn out but have a black, shiny surface, before refitting them roughen the surface with a piece of emery cloth, to remove this glaze but don't overdo it.

10   Visually check the condition of the caliper, the hydraulic hose and the cylinder assembly before fitting the pads. Examine the slides where the keys fit and remove any burrs with a hand stone, cleaning off any abrasive dust on completion. Clean the slide retaining springs and if they are corroded or damaged renew them.
11   Assemble the new springs to the pads in the same way as originally noted in paragraph 7. The crossing wire must be over the pad recess (photo).
12   Apply a fine film of Molykote 321R, or a suitable alternative dry, anti-friction agent, to the pad keys and set aside to dry (photo).
13   Hold the pair of pads face to face and, after checking that the springs are correctly fitted and at the top of the pads, assemble them to the caliper (photo).
14   Using a piece of wood, or a similar blunt tool, depress the piston fully into its bore in the cylinder and refit the cylinder on the caliper.
15   Slide the keys home, making sure that the wire springs locate *under* the slides on the cylinder. They must not be inserted between the keys and the slides.
16   Fit new figure-eight shaped clips to retain the keys in the slides.

Teves brakes

17   To remove the pads, extract the retaining clips from the pad pins and drift the pins out using a suitable pin punch of 3 mm (0.118 in) diameter (photo).
18   Extract the anti-rattle spring and then withdraw the inner disc pad first (photo).
19   Press the caliper unit towards the outside of the hub and remove the outer disc pad. Keep the two pads from each wheel separate.
20   Refer to paragraphs 8, 9 and 10 and follow the same procedures as far as they apply to the Teves brakes.
21   Refitting the pads is the reverse of the removal procedure, but before installing the pads spray them with Permatex PR 9730.61 anti-noise compound, or a suitable alternative. Don't let the spray contaminate the friction material though – use a piece of cardboard as a mask. Let the compound dry before fitting the pads.
22   Where the piston has a cutaway step incorporated, the step must be aligned as shown in Fig. 8.2. Note that the alignment differs for right or left-hand brake assemblies.
23   When assembled, check that the boss on the outside pad is properly located. Use new pad pin retaining clips if the old ones are rusty or distorted.

All front brakes

24   Repeat the procedure on the other front brake assembly and then refit the roadwheels, tightening the wheel nuts to the specified torque.
25   Top up the brake fluid reservoir using fresh fluid, and apply the footbrakes a few times to position the pistons. Top up the reservoir on completion if necessary and lower the car to the ground.
26   Remember that new pads need bedding in before they produce full efficiency, so exercise caution until they are fully effective.

5.3 The wear indicator grooves (arrowed) in the disc pads (DBA Bendix type)

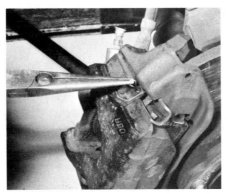

5.5a After removing the clips from the keys ...

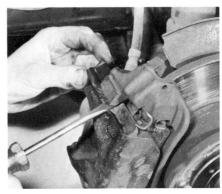

5.5b ... slide the keys out

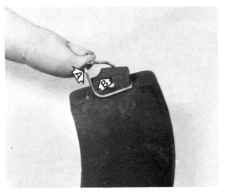

5.11 The crossing wire A must be over the recess B in the pad

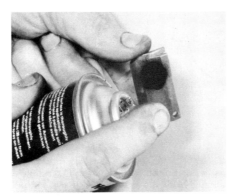

5.12 Spraying the keys with an anti-friction agent

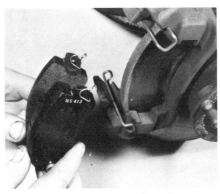

5.13 Assembling the pads to the caliper

5.17 Drift out the retaining pins

5.18 Remove the inner pad first

6 Disc brake calipers – removal, overhaul and refitting

1   To prevent excessive loss of hydraulic fluid when the front brake hoses are disconnected, remove the brake reservoir filler cap, and seal off the filler neck by placing a piece of thin polythene sheeting over the orifice and refitting the filler cap tightly. If the cap has a fluid low level indicator switch installed, use a piece of polythene large enough to accommodate the switch assembly when the cap is fitted.
2   Jack up the front of the car and support it on stands or ramps. Apply the handbrake.
3   Clean off all the road dirt from the brake unit and then disconnect the hydraulic hose from the wheel cylinder. Cover the end of the hose to stop dirt from getting in.
4   Refer to Section 5 and remove the disc brake pads.
5   Undo the two bolts securing the caliper assembly to the axle and remove the caliper (Fig. 8.3).

DBA Bendix brakes

6   With the assembly on the workbench remove the wheel cylinder and its bracket from the caliper. Depress the locking pin in the base to separate the cylinder from its bracket, taking care not to lose the locking pin and spring. A home made expander will be necessary to release the cylinder from its bracket (Fig. 8.4).
7   Prise the rubber dust cover off the cylinder and then extract the piston. This is best done by carefully blowing it out using an air line or tyre pump applied to the brake hose connection. Take care to prevent the piston flying out by wrapping the assembly in rags. If the piston is seized in the bore it could be difficult to remove without causing some damage, but try soaking the assembly in penetrating fluid and leaving it to work in. This may do the seal no good but it must be renewed in any case.
8   With the piston removed, extract and discard the seal from its groove in the cylinder bore. Clean all metal parts thoroughly in methylated spirit, but don't use any abrasive cleaning materials, and

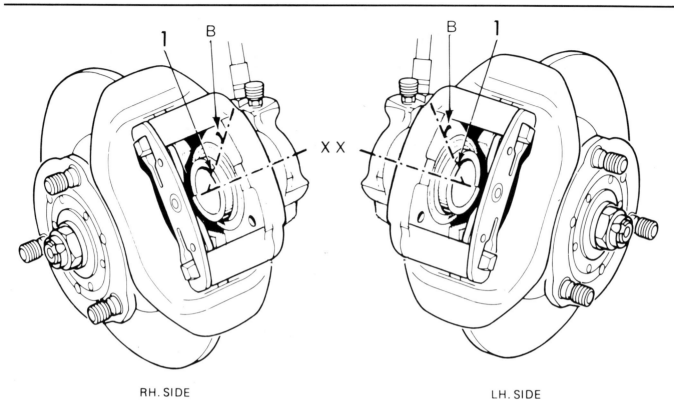

RH. SIDE   LH. SIDE

Fig. 8.2 The cutaway step on the Teves brakes is positioned with the step (1) in line with the hole (B) as shown. The opposing step should be aligned with the centre line of the caliper (X) (Sec 5)

Fig. 8.3 The two caliper retaining bolts (arrowed) – Teves brakes (Sec 6)

don't use a metal scraper which could scratch machined surfaces or anti-corrosive finish.
9   Closely examine the piston sliding surface for grooves, scores, ridges, corrosion pits and similar damage. If any damage is present a new piston must be fitted; on no account should you attempt to polish out any blemish. Examine all the component parts of the brake assembly for obvious damage, renewing parts where necessary.
10   Soak the new cylinder seal in fresh hydraulic fluid and lubricate the cylinder bore and the piston with the same fluid. Carefully fit the seal into the cylinder groove and then fit the piston, making sure that the

seal is not damaged. Wipe the assembly dry with clean rag and then fit the new rubber dust cover.

Teves brakes
11   After removing the brake caliper as described in paragraphs 1 to 5, with the assembly on a workbench, unclip the spring from the caliper bracket and then detach the bracket and caliper. The cylinder can be removed by tapping it free from its bracket with a soft-faced hammer if necessary.
12   Follow the procedures in paragraphs 7 to 10 to service the wheel cylinder.

DBA Bendix and Teves brakes
13   Reassembly and refitting of the brake calipers is the reverse of the removal sequence, but note the following points:

  (a) When fitting the caliper to the axle make sure that the threaded holes and the bolt threads are clean and coat the bolt threads with suitable thread locking compound. Tighten the bolts to the specified torque.
  (b) Fit the brake pads as described in Section 5 and note the instructions for positioning the pistons where they have have a cutaway step
  (c) Remove the bleed screw and prime the wheel cylinder with fresh brake fluid, tipping the cylinder in all directions to release trapped air before installation. Refit the bleed screw
  (d) Fit a new copper gasket to the hose union and make sure that there is no twist in the hose when connected. Check that the hose cannot come into contact with any part of the car when steering is applied and the car weight is on the wheels
  (e) Remove the piece of polythene from the brake reservoir filler cap and bleed the system as described in Section 3

7   Rear brake drums – removal and refitting

1   With the weight of the car on the wheels, remove the rear hub caps and slacken the wheel retaining nuts.
2   Jack up the rear of the vehicle and support it on axle stands or

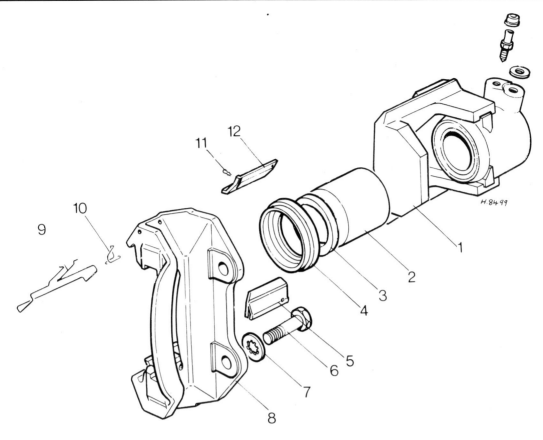

Fig. 8.4 Exploded view of the DBA Bendix front brake caliper assembly (Sec 6)

1 Sliding caliper	4 Rubber protector	7 Lockwasher	10 Pad spring
2 Piston	5 Lower key	8 Caliper support	11 Clip
3 Seal	6 Caliper retaining bolt	9 Spring	12 Upper key

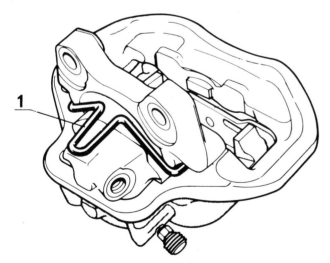

Fig. 8.5 The caliper retaining clip (1) – Teves brakes (Sec 6)

blocks. Do not work on a car supported only by the wheel changing jack. Chock the front wheels securely, engage a gear, and release the handbrake.

3   Undo the wheel nuts and remove the wheel. Prise off the dust cap from the centre of the drum. The axle nut is locked by deforming the rim into the axle slot. Use a punch to knock the deformation out and remove the axle nut, washer and outer bearing. Remove the brake drum.

4   If the drum resists removal the likely cause is that the brake shoes need retracting. Prise the plug from the backplate concerned (photo)

and insert a suitable screwdriver through the backplate hole. Apply pressure to the handbrake operating lever within the drum to disengage the nipple and push the lever rearwards, thus freeing the brake shoes. Refit the plug in the backplate hole.

5   With the hub off, carefully clean out the brake dust so as to disturb as little as possible. *It is important not to spread the dust in the atmosphere or inhale it* as it is a danger to health. An old paint brush and a damp cloth are useful for cleaning the assembly.

6   Examine the assembly for fluid leaks, grease contamination, condition of rubber cups on the cylinder and general condition of the moving parts. These should be no traces of fluid or grease. If there are, the appropriate seals will need renewal and, if the linings are contaminated, they will also need renewal. Inspect the linings for wear and if less than $\frac{1}{16}$ in or 2 mm material remains above the rivet heads – or is likely to remain before the next servicing – the linings should be renewed. Refer to Chapter 7 for details of renewing the bearings and seals in the brake drums.

7   Before refitting the drum, ensure that the bearings and the space between them are greased with a good quality general purpose grease. Refit the drum on the stub axle. Refit the outer bearing if it is not already fitted, followed by the safety washer and the retaining nut which should be a new one (photo).

8   Peugeot use a special tool to tighten the nut in a rather complicated procedure. A fairly accurate result can be obtained without the tool by following this suggested procedure.

9   Rotate the brake drum and tighten the retaining nut to the initial specified torque (see Specification). Slacken the nut off and, still rotating the drum, tighten the nut to the final specified torque. Stop rotating the drum and do not move the nut. Apply the footbrake two or three times (make sure that the brake drum on the other rear wheel is fitted before doing this!) and apply the handbrake. Now *slacken* the retaining nut through 30°; this is equivalent to half a flat on the nut. Keep the nut in this position and deform the sleeve on the nut into the slot in the

Fig. 8.6 The rear brake drum assembly (Sec 7)

1	Seal	4	Brake drum	7	Axle nut
2	Thrust cup	5	Outer roller bearing	8	Dust cap seal
3	Inner roller bearing	6	Safety washer	9	Dust cap

7.4 Remove this plug (arrowed) to gain access to the handbrake operating lever

7.7 Fitting the outer bearing in the brake drum

7.9a Tighten the retaining nut as explained in the text and then ...

7.9b ... lock the nut by peening into the shaft

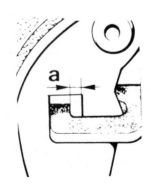

Fig. 8.7 Check the clearance (a) between the horizontal link and the shoe – DBA Bendix brakes (Sec 8)

8.4a The brake shoe assembly and ...

axle, using a hammer and pin punch to lock it (photo).
10 If it has not already been done, fit a new dust cap seal to the drum and fit the dust cap. Refit the wheels, leaving the final tightening of the wheel nuts until the car is on the ground. Lower the car to the ground and tighten the wheel nuts to the specified torque before fitting the hub caps.

8 Rear brake shoes – removal, inspection and refitting

1 Remove the brake drums as described in Section 7, and clean the assembly observing the precautions mentioned concerning brake dust.

DBA Bendix brakes

2 Remove the long spring under the wheel cylinder and then check the clearance between the horizontal link and the brake shoe which should be 1.0 to 1.2 mm (0.039 to 0.047 in) for assemblies marked M or T and 0.6 to 0.8 mm (0.024 to 0.032 in) for assemblies marked J or K. If the specified tolerance is exceeded the worn parts must be renewed.
3 Remove the brake shoe retaining springs. This can be done using a large bolt or an Allen key which will enter the spring. Push the bolt or key to extend the spring and unhook it from its anchorage. Repeat the procedure on the other shoe. These springs are prone to corrosion and must be renewed on reassembly.
4 Disconnect the handbrake cable from its lever on the rear shoe. Push the other lever with the self-adjuster ratchet on the bottom end rearwards to disengage the ratchet and disconnect the horizontal link from it. Allow the ratchet lever to return to its original position and remove the shoes assembly from the backplate (photos).
5 Make up a retaining clip from stout wire and locate it on the wheel cylinder to prevent the pistons moving (photo). Clean the assembly thoroughly after examining for leaks, and check the condition of the rubber protecting caps.
6 Brake shoes must be renewed in a set of four, that is both rear brakes complete. Two widths of brake shoes are supplied for 104 models depending on the date of manufacture – see Specifications.

When renewing shoes make sure that you get the correct ones for your car and, preferably, take a pattern with you to the spare parts store.
7 There are three different shoes in the set of four. The two trailing shoes are identical to each other with no stud at the bottom end. Hold the two leading shoes with the linings away from you and the stud in each web at the bottom, then the shoe with the stud on the right of the web belongs to the right-hand (offside) wheel and the one with the stud on the left of the web is the leading shoe for the left-hand (nearside) wheel.
8 Providing that it is in good condition, transfer the adjuster lever to the outer face of the new leading shoe using a new clip (photo). Then transfer the ratchet and spring, securing them with a new retaining ring (photo).
9 Similarly transfer the handbrake lever to the outer face of the new trailing shoe and lock it in place with a new clip.
10 Fit the horizontal link to the trailing shoe with the curved edges facing upwards, and attach the spring on the back. Note that the horizontal links are handed for left and right-hand assemblies.
11 Attach the bottom spring to the two shoes so that it lies on the outside faces. Offer the assembly to the backplate, making sure that the bottom spring locates behind the backplate bracket. Push the adjusting lever towards the stub axle and connect the horizontal link. Work the assembly into position on the backplate, removing the wheel cylinder clip in the process, until the upper ends of the shoes rest on the wheel cylinder. Then, using a pair of long-nosed pliers, refit the upper spring (photos). Push the adjusting lever fully forwards against the brake shoe.
12 Lever the handbrake lever forwards and connect the cable to the bottom end (photo).
13 Fit new shoe retaining springs using a long bolt or an Allen key to hook them into their anchorages (photo).
14 Fit a new seal to the stub axle, referring to Chapter 7, and then refit the brake drum referring to Section 7 in this Chapter. Operate the footbrake several times (after making sure that the drum is in position on the other wheel) to position the self-adjuster ratchet. As already mentioned for the front brake disc pads, new brake shoes need wearing in before they produce full braking efficiency and you should

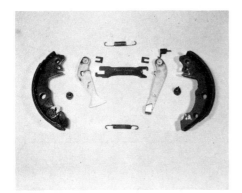

8.4b ... the component parts dismantled

8.5 Restrain the pistons with a temporary clip made of stout wire

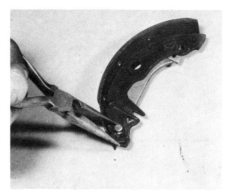

8.8a Securing the adjuster lever with a new clip

8.8b The ratchet and spring secured with a new retaining ring

8.11a Refitting the brake shoe assembly

8.11b Fitting the upper spring

8.12 The handbrake cable located in the handbrake lever

8.13 Using a large bolt to fit the shoe retaining springs

8.15a Girling drum brakes are very similar to Bendix ...

8.15b ... but the shoe retaining springs are different

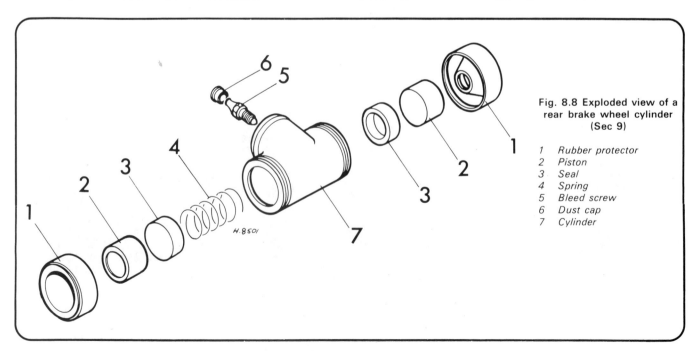

Fig. 8.8 Exploded view of a rear brake wheel cylinder (Sec 9)

1 Rubber protector
2 Piston
3 Seal
4 Spring
5 Bleed screw
6 Dust cap
7 Cylinder

H.8501

exercise care in driving until they are fully effective.

Girling brakes

15 The design of the Girling rear brakes is very similar to that of the DBA Bendix brakes (photo). The procedures described in the previous paragraphs are largely applicable. One of the main differences is that, instead of a fixed length horizontal link beneath the wheel cylinder, the Girling brake has an adjustable link and no dimensional clearance check is necessary. When assembling the brakes, use the adjuster on this link to set the diameter across the brake shoes to 179.5 mm (7.076 in) before refitting the drum. The white identified link must be fitted to the left-hand brake assembly and the yellow to the right. The shoe retaining springs are different to those already described (photo) and they need to be depressed and part rotated to release them, or engage them.

---

9 Rear wheel cylinders – removal, overhaul and refitting

1 Jack up the rear of the car and support it on axle stands. Chock the front wheels and engage a gear. Remove the brake drum as described in Section 7.

2 Remove the brake hydraulic reservoir filler cap and place a piece of polythene film over the filler neck, then replace the cap. Where a low level indicator switch is fitted use a piece of polythene, preferably thin, which is large enough to accommodate the switch housing under the cap. The plastic film will prevent a great loss of fluid when the rear brake hydraulic lines are undone.

3 Working on the inner side of the brake backplate, brush off all road dirt and clean around the hydraulic line connection, the bleed screw and the two bolts which secure the wheel cylinder to the backplate.

4 Carefully undo the hydraulic line connection to the wheel cylinder, and cover the pipe open end to stop dirt getting in.

5 Unscrew and remove the two wheel cylinder retaining bolts. Unclip the upper shoe return spring and, prising the brake shoes apart at the top, remove the wheel cylinder.

6 If the cylinder has been leaking and the brake linings are contaminated with fluid they must be renewed on *both* rear wheels. This procedure is described in Section 8.

7 Clean off the outside of the cylinder using methylated spirit and take it to a clean work area for dismantling.

8 Pull the rubber boots off each end of the cylinder and carefully extract the pistons, seal cups, and spring. Take careful note of the sequence of assembly of the individual parts and which way round they are fitted.

9 Inspect the cylinder bore carefully for any signs of grooving, scores, corrosion or similar damage. If any damage is present the cylinder must be renewed.

10 Providing that the cylinder is serviceable, clean it thoroughly with methylated spirits – don't use any abrasive material and don't use metal scrapers which could damage the cylinder bore. When clean, wipe the cylinder dry with clean, non-fluffy rag.

11 Sort out the new seals in the repair kit by matching them with the originals and immerse them in clean hydraulic fluid before assembly.

12 Lubricate the cylinder with clean hydraulic fluid and assemble the spring, pistons and cup seals. Take care not to damage the seals as you fit them into the cylinder. Fit the rubber boots and then wipe the assembly dry with clean rag.

13 Reassembly of the wheel cylinder to the brake backplate is the reverse of the dismantling procedure, but note the following:

    (a) *Take care not to cross-thread the brake pipe union when reconnecting it to the wheel cylinder*

    (b) *Refit the brake drum following the procedure described in Section 7*

    (c) *Bleed the brake hydraulic system and top up the reservoir, remembering to remove the piece of polythene, as described in Section 3*

    (d) *Operate the brake pedal on completion to centralise the brakes*

---

10 Hydraulic fluid pipes – inspection and renewal

1 Periodically, and certainly well in advance of the DoE (MoT)

Test, if due, all brake pipes, connections and unions should be carefully examined (Figs. 8.9 and 8.10).

2 Examine first all the unions for signs of leaks. Then look at the flexible hoses for signs of fraying and chafing (as well as for leaks). This is only a preliminary inspection of the flexible hoses as exterior condition does not necessarily indicate interior condition which will be considered later.

3 The steel pipes must be examined equally carefully. They must be thoroughly cleaned and examined for signs of dents or other percussive damage, rust and corrosion. Rust and corrosion should be scraped off and, if the depth of pitting in the pipes is significant, they will need replacement. This is most likely in those areas underneath the chassis and along the rear suspension arms where the pipes are exposed to the full force of road and weather conditions.

4 If any section of pipe is to be removed, first of all take off the fluid reservoir cap, place some polythene film over the filler neck aperture and secure with an elastic band. Sealing the system in this manner will minimise the amount of fluid dripping out of the system when the pipes are removed.

5 Rigid pipe removal is usually quite straightforward. The unions at each end are undone and the pipe drawn out of the connection. The clips which may hold it to the car body are bent back and it is then removed. Underneath the car exposed unions can be particularly stubborn, defying the efforts of an open ended spanner. As few people will have the special split ring spanner required, a self-grip wrench is the only answer. If the pipe is being renewed new unions will be provided. If not then one will have to put up with the possibility of burring over the flats on the union and use a self-grip wrench for replacement also.

6 Flexible hoses are always fitted to a rigid support bracket where they join a rigid pipe, the bracket being fixed to the chassis or rear suspension arm (photos). The rigid pipe unions must first be removed from the flexible union. Then the locknut securing the flexible pipe to the bracket must be unscrewed, releasing the end of the pipe from the bracket. As these connections are usually exposed they are more often than not rusted up and a penetrating fluid is virtually essential to aid removal. When undoing them, both halves must be supported as the bracket is not strong enough to support the torque required to undo the nut and can easily be snapped off.

7 Once the flexible hose is removed examine the internal bore. If clear of fluid it should be possible to see through it. Any specks of rubber which come out, or signs of restriction in the bore, mean that the inner lining is breaking up and the pipe must be renewed.

8 Rigid pipes which need replacement can usually be purchased at any local garage where they have the pipe, unions and special tools to make them up. They will need to know the pipe length required and the type of flare used at the ends of the pipe. These may be different at each end of the same pipe.

9 Installation of the pipes is a reversal of the removal procedure. The pipe profile must be pre-set before fitting. Any acute bends must be put in by the garage on a bending machine otherwise there is the possibility of kinking them and restricting the fluid flow.

10 With the pipes refitted, remove the polythene from the reservoir, top up and bleed the system as described in Section 3.

---

11 Master cylinder – removal, overhaul and refitting

1 If the wheel hydraulic cylinders are in order and there are no leaks elsewhere, yet the brake pedal still does not hold up under sustained pressure, then the master cylinder seals may be pressumed to be ineffective. To renew them the master cylinder must be removed. A repair kit is available from your Peugeot agent which will contain all the necessary parts to overhaul the unit.

2 Hydraulic fluid is harmful to paintwork. Try to avoid spillage and take steps to prevent any possible paint damage. Place a piece of plastic sheet and absorbent rags under the master cylinder prior to removal.

3 Wipe around the filler cap with clean rag and remove it. If a fluid level indicator switch is fitted disconnect the wire terminals first. With a clean plastic syringe remove as much fluid as possible and discard this fluid as it is unsuitable for re-use (photos).

4 Where dual circuit braking is fitted, disconnect the two supply pipes between the reservoir and the master cylinder. Open the spring clips and pull the pipes off the master cylinder connections.

5 Unscrew the hydraulic pipe unions from the master cylinder and

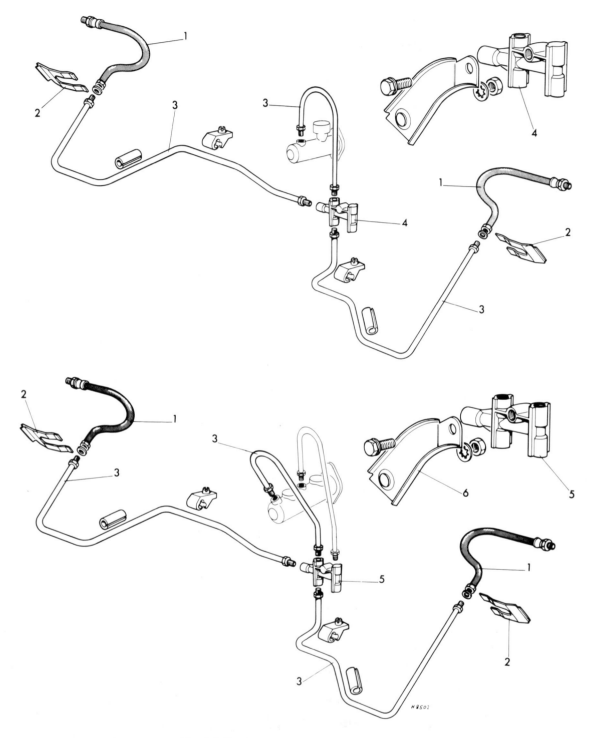

Fig. 8.9 The front brake system piping (Sec 10)

1 Flexible hose
2 Bracket clasp
3 Rigid pipe
4 4-way union
   (single circuit system)
5 5-way union
   (dual circuit system)
6 Union mounting bracket

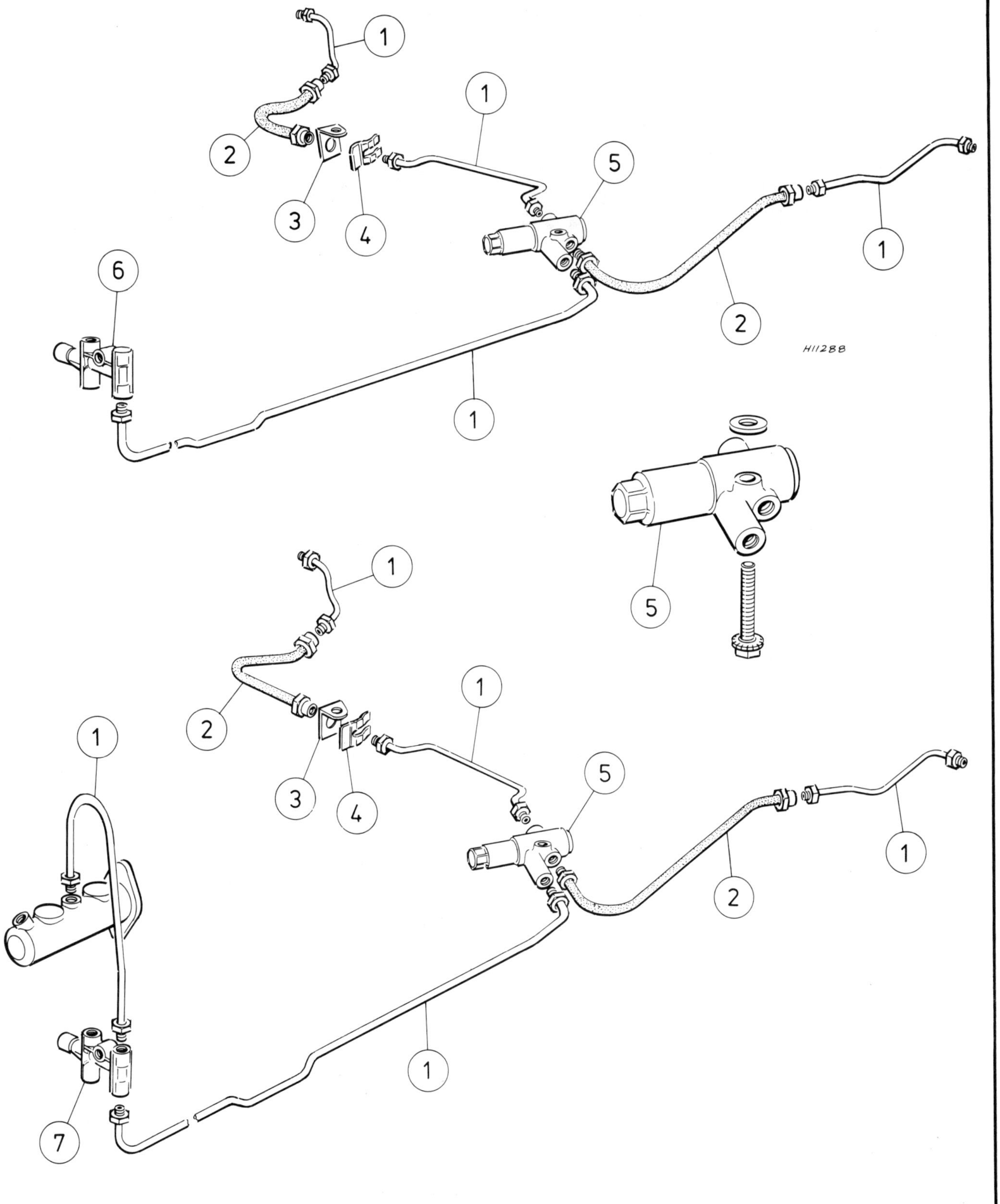

Fig. 8.10 The rear brake system piping (Sec 10)

1 Rigid pipe
2 Flexible hose
3 Bracket
4 Bracket clasp
5 Regulator
6 4-way union
(single circuit system)
7 5-way union
(dual circuit system)

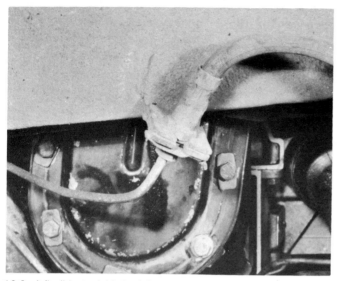

10.6a A flexible-to-rigid pipe joint mounted on a bracket

10.6b A flexible hose joint on a front brake cylinder. Note the dust cap on the bleed screw

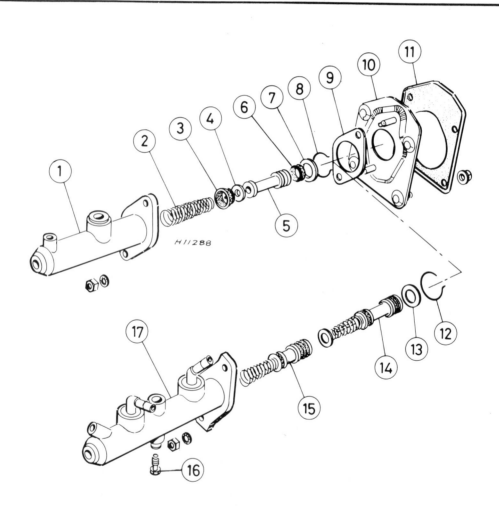

H11288

Fig. 8.11 Exploded view of the two types of master cylinder (Sec 11)

1	Single circuit master cylinder	5	Piston
2	Spring	6	Gasket
3	Cup	7	Washer
4	Safety disc	8	Snap-ring
		9	Gasket

10	Mounting support		assembly
11	Gasket	15	Front brakes piston
12	Snap-ring		assembly
13	Washer	16	Stop screw
14	Rear brakes piston	17	Dual circuit master cylinder

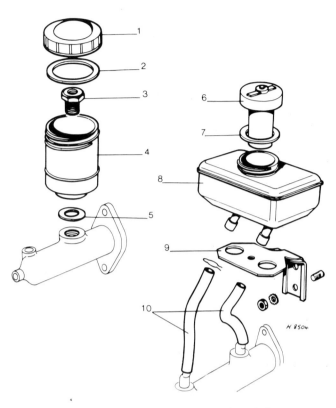

Fig. 8.12 Brake fluid reservoirs (Sec 11)

1 Filler cap
2 Gasket
3 Hollow bolt
4 Fluid container
5 Gasket

6 Filler cap with low level
   indicator switch
7 Gasket
8 Fluid container
9 Mounting bracket
10 Supply pipes

11.3a A single-circuit brake master cylinder with reservoir

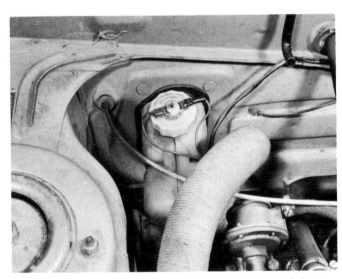

11.3b A brake fluid reservoir cap with a low level warning switch incorporated

carefully push the pipes to one side, just enough to allow removal of the master cylinder. Cover the open pipe ends to prevent dirt getting in.

6 Remove the two nuts and spring washers retaining the master cylinder and remove the unit, wrapped in rag to stop any fluid dripping on the paintwork. Empty any residual fluid when clear of the car.

7 Before dismantling the single circuit master cylinder, remove the reservoir by undoing the hollow bolt in the bottom and separating it from the master cylinder.

8 On the dual circuit master cylinder push the piston inwards using a thin wood dowel and unscrew the stop screw.

9 On either single or dual circuit units remove the snap-ring from the end of the cylinder, restraining the piston spring pressure, and remove the piston assembly. Take careful note of the sequence of assembly of the individual parts and which way round they are fitted. A quick sketch will probably prove more reliable than memory. If necessary, the piston assembly can be blown out with compressed air but hold a piece of rag over the opening in the master cylinder to prevent parts flying out.

10 Clean all metal parts in methylated spirit – never use any abrasive when cleaning hydraulic system fittings, and don't use metal scrapers which could cause scoring of the machined surfaces.

11 Sort out the new seals in the repair kit by matching them carefully with the old ones before discarding the old ones. Immerse the new seals in clean brake fluid before assembly.

12 Closely examine all the metal parts for wear, corrosion and obvious damage. Any sign of scoring in the bore of the master cylinder, however slight, will require renewal and it is clearly sensible to renew the whole master cylinder.

13 Reassembly is the reverse of the dismantling process. Meticulous cleanliness is vital in this work. Wash your hands before starting; wipe all metal components clean, drying them with clean fluff-free rag, and

then freely lubricate with clean hydraulic fluid before assembly. On completion wipe the assembly dry before installing it in the car.

14 Refitting is the reverse of the removal sequence. On models not fitted with a servo unit, locate the footbrake pushrod into the master cylinder through the aperture in the mounting bracket. Again, observe utmost cleanliness at all times. When refitted, and with the pipe connections made, top up the reservoir with new hydraulic fluid and bleed the system as described in Section 3.

15 Test the brakes on the next run out, choosing a quiet, straight stretch or road, and initially, at low speed. Always check that there is nothing behind you before braking.

12 Handbrake system – general

Handbrake lever – removal and refitting

1 Chock the front wheels and engage a gear. Raise the rear of the car and support it on stands or firm blocks. Release the handbrake.

2 Slacken the rear brake cable adjusters where they emerge from the car floor.

3 Working in the car, undo and remove the securing nuts and bolts and release the brake cables from the handbrake equalising bar (photo).

4 Disconnect the handbrake warning light switch, and remove the

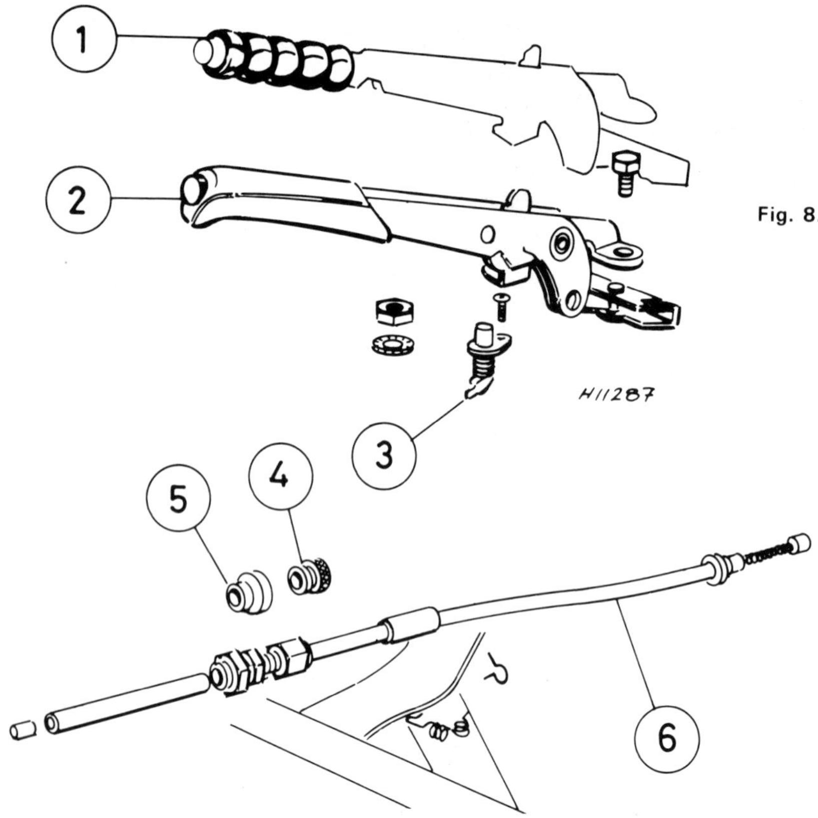

Fig. 8.13 Handbrake system components (Sec 12)

1 Plastic handle
2 Handbrake lever assembly
3 Handbrake indicator switch
4 Cable adjustment nut
5 Rubber sleeve
6 Cable and sheath assembly
   (one of two)

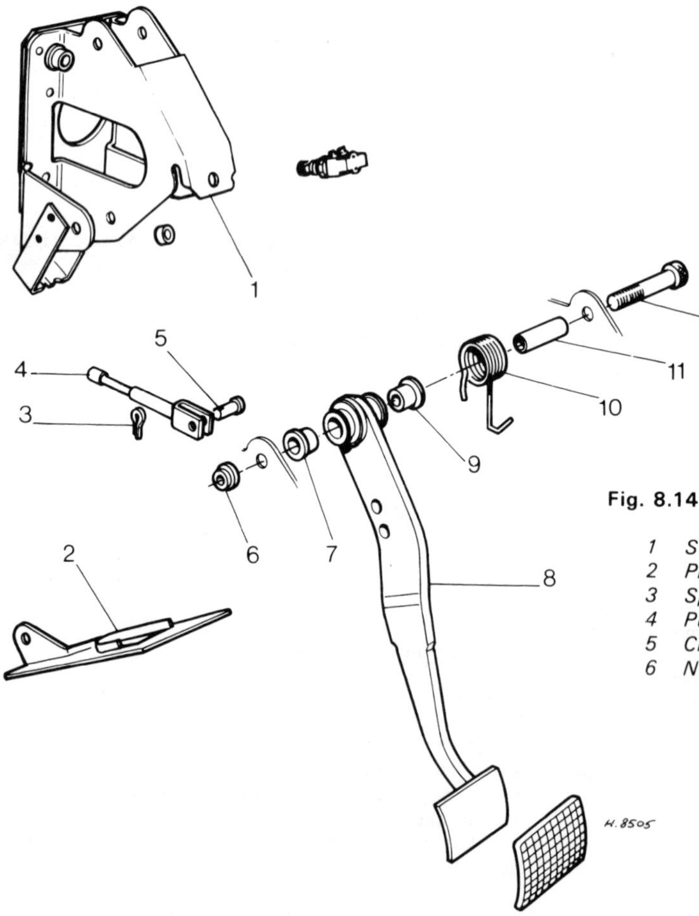

H11287

Fig. 8.14 The foot pedal assembly (left-hand drive shown)

1 Support bracket
2 Plate
3 Split-pin
4 Pushrod
5 Clevis pin
6 Nut
7 Rilsan bushing
8 Pedal lever
9 Rilsan bushing
10 Return spring
11 Spacer tube
12 Bolt

H.8505

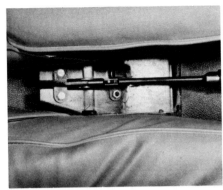

12.3 The handbrake lever mounting bolts

handbrake lever from the car.

5 Refitting is the reverse of the removal sequence. On completion adjust the cables as described in Section 4.

Handbrake cables – removal and refitting

6 Follow the procedures in paragraphs 1 to 3 above and, referring to Section 7, remove the brake drums and disconnect the cables from the

shoe operating levers.

7 Withdraw the cable assemblies from the car by pulling them out of their front end locations and from the rear brake backplates.

8 Refitting is the reverse of the removal procedure but, before refitting a cable assembly, lubricate the inner cable in its sheath with a general purpose grease. Leave the end fitting which fits into the brake shoe lever dry.

9 On completion adjust the cables as described in Section 4.

13 Fault diagnosis – braking system

Before diagnosing faults from the following chart, check that any braking irregularities are not caused by:

(a) Uneven and incorrect tyre pressures
(b) Incorrect mix of radial and crossply tyres
(c) Wear in the steering mechanism
(d) Misalignment of the chassis geometry

Symptom	Reason/s
Pedal travels a long way before the brakes operate	Brake shoes set too far from the drums due to faulty self-adjusting mechanism
Stopping ability poor, even though pedal pressure is firm	Linings/pads and/or drums/disc badly worn or scored One or more wheel hydraulic cylinders or caliper pistons seized resulting in some brake shoes/pads not pressing against the drums/discs Brake linings/pads contaminated with oil Wrong type of linings/pads fitted (too hard) Brake shoes/pads wrongly assembled Faulty servo unit (where fitted)
Car veers to one side when the brakes are applied	Brake linings/pads on one side are contaminated with oil Hydraulic wheel cylinder(s)/caliper on one side partially or fully seized A mixture of lining materials fitted between sides Unequal wear between sides caused by partially seized wheel cylinders/pistons
Pedal feels spongy	Air in the hydraulic system
Pedal feels springy when the brakes are applies	Brake linings/pads not bedded into the drums/discs (after fitting new ones) Master cylinder or brake backplate mounting bolts loose Severe wear in brake drums/discs causing distortion when brakes are applied
Pedal travels right down with little or no resistance and brakes are virtually non-operative	Leak in hydraulic system resulting in lack of pressure for operating wheel cylinders/caliper pistons If no signs of leakage are apparent all the master cylinder internal seals are failing to sustain pressure
Binding, juddering, overheating	One or a combination of causes given in the foregoing sections Handbrake over-adjusted Handbrake cable(s) seized

Chapter 9 Electrical system

Contents

Specifications

Battery

Voltage	12 volt
Polarity	Negative earth
Capacity:	
Europe	28 Ah
Cold climate	36 Ah
Size:	
Europe	178 x 135 x 204 mm (7 x 5.3 x 8.03 in)
Cold climates	219 x 135 x 204 mm (8.62 x 5.3 x 8.03 in)

Alternator

Output:	
Models with heated rear window	500W (Three-phase alternator)
Models without heated rear window	350W (Single-phase alternator)
Type:	
500W	Ducellier 513004A, or Paris-Rhone A12R9, A13R124 A13R143 or A13R143A or Sev-Marchal 71210102 or 71210402
350W	Ducellier 7552 or Paris-Rhone A11M10
Voltage	12 volt
Rotor resistance at 20°C:	
513004A	5.5 ohms
A12R9	5.5 ohms
A13R124	4.7 ohms
A13R143	4.7 ohms
A13R143A	5.5 ohms
7552	7 ohms
A11M10	7 ohms
Regulator	
4.7 ohms rotor	Ducellier 8364, Paris-Rhone AYB21, or Sev-Marchal 72711302
5.5 ohms rotor	Ducellier 8364, Paris-Rhone AYB21 or AYB2119, or Sev-Marchal 72711302
7 ohms rotor	Ducellier 8373, 8380 or 8367C, or Paris-Rhone AYB 2111 or AYB 2120

Starter motor

Europe	Ducellier 6216 or Paris-Rhone D8E107
Cold climate	Ducellier 6220 or Paris-Rhone D8E117

Bulbs

Headlamps	40/45W
Sidelights	5W
Direction indicator	21W
Stoplights	21W
Stoplight/sidelight	21W-5W
Number plate light	5W
Interior light	4W (festoon)

Fuses

Number of fuses	4 to 8 depending on model

Torque wrench settings

	lbf ft	kgf m
Alternator pivot bolt (1)	33	4.5
Alternator, bolts in bracket	13	1.75
Starter motor:		
Bracket engine bolts and nuts	9	1.25
Clutch housing bolts	13	1.75

1 General description

The electrical system is of the 12 volt negative earth type and the major components comprise a 12 volt battery of which the negative terminal is earthed, an alternator which is driven from the crankshaft pulley, and a starter motor.

The battery supplies a steady amount of current for the ignition, lighting and other electrical circuits and provides a reserve of electricity when the current consumed by the electrical equipment exceeds that being produced by the alternator.

The alternator is controlled by a regulator which ensures a high output if the battery is in a low state of charge or the demand from the electrical equipment is high, and a low output if the battery is fully charged and there is little demand for the electrical equipment.

When fitting electrical accessories it is important, if they contain silicone diodes or transistors, that they are connected correctly, otherwise serious damage may result to the components concerned. Items such as radios, tape recorders, electronic ignition systems, electronic tachometer, automatic dipping etc, should all be checked for correct polarity.

It is important that the battery positive lead is always disconnected if the battery is to be boost charged; also if body repairs are to be carried out using electric arc welding equipment the alternator must be disconnected otherwise serious damage can be caused to the more delicate instruments. Whenever the battery has to be disconnected it must always be reconnected with the negative terminal earthed.

2 Battery – removal and refitting

1 The battery is on a carrier fitted to the left-hand wing valance of the engine compartment. It should be removed once every three months for cleaning and testing. Disconnect the positive and then the negative leads from the battery terminals by undoing and removing the terminal nuts and bolts. Note that two cables are attached to the positive terminal.

2 Release the battery clamp and carefully lift the battery from its carrier. Hold it vertically to ensure that none of the electrolyte is spilled.

3 Refitting is a direct reversal of this procedure. **Note:** Reconnect the negative lead before the positive lead and smear the terminals with petroleum jelly to prevent corrosion. **Never** use an ordinary grease.

3 Battery – maintenance and inspection

1 Normal weekly battery maintenance consists of checking the electrolyte level of each cell to ensure that the separators are covered by $\frac{3}{8}$ in (1 cm) of electrolyte. If the level has fallen, top up the battery using distilled water only (photo). Do not overfill. If a battery is overfilled or any electrolyte spilled, immediately wipe away the excess as electrolyte attacks and corrodes any metal it comes into contact with very rapidly.

2 If the battery has the Auto-fill device a special topping up sequence is required. The white balls in the Auto-fill battery are part of the automatic topping up device which ensures correct electrolyte

3.1 Topping up the battery

level. The vent chamber should remain in position at all times except when topping up or taking specific gravity readings. If the electrolyte level in any of the cells is below the bottom of the filling tube, top up as follows:

(a) Lift off the vent chamber cover
(b) With the battery level, pour distilled water into the trough until all the filling tubes and trough are full
(c) Immediately replace the cover to allow the water in the trough and tubes to flow into the cells. Each cell will automatically receive the correct amount of water

3 As well as keeping the terminals clean and covered with petroleum jelly, the top of the battery, and especially the top of the cells, should be kept clean and dry. This helps prevent corrosion and ensures that the battery does not become partially discharged by leakage through dampness and dirt.

4 Once every three months remove the battery and inspect the battery securing bolts, the battery clamp plate, tray and battery leads for corrosion (white fluffy deposits on the metal which are brittle to touch). If any corrosion is found clean off the deposit with ammonia and paint over the clean metal with an anti-rust anti-acid paint.

5 At the same time inspect the battery case for cracks. If a crack is found clean and plug it with one of the proprietary compounds marketed for this purpose. If leakage through the crack has been excessive then it will be necessary to refill the appropriate cell with fresh electrolyte as detailed later. Cracks are frequently caused to the top of the battery case by pouring in distilled water in the middle of winter *after* instead of *before* a run. This gives the water no chance to mix with the electrolyte and so the former freezes and splits the battery case.

6 If topping up the battery becomes excessive and the case has

been inspected for cracks that could cause leakage, but none are found, the battery is being overcharged and the voltage regulator will have to be checked.

7   With the battery on the bench at the three monthly interval check, measure the specific gravity with a hydrometer to determine the state of charge and condition of the electrolyte. There should be very little variation between the different cells and, if a variation in excess of 0·025 is present it will be due to either:

(a) Loss of electrolyte from the battery at some time caused by spillage or a leak, resulting in a drop in the specific gravity of the electrolyte when the deficiency was replaced with distilled water instead of fresh electrolyte

(b) An internal short circuit caused by buckling of the plates or similar malady pointing to the likelihood of total battery failure in the near future

8   The specific gravity of the electrolyte for fully charged conditions, at the electrolyte temperature indicated, is listed in Table A. The specific gravity of a fully discharged battery at different temperatures of the electrolyte is given in Table B.

Table A – Specific gravity – battery fully charged
1.268 at 100°F or 38°C electrolyte temperature
1.272 at 90°F or 32°C electrolyte temperature
1.276 at 80°F or 27°C electrolyte temperature
1.280 at 70°F or 21°C electrolyte temperature
1.284 at 60°F or 16°C electrolyte temperature
1.288 at 50°F or 10°C electrolyte temperature
1.292 at 40°F or 4°C electrolyte temperature
1.296 at 30°F or −1.5°C electrolyte temperature

Table B – Specific gravity – battery fully discharged
1.098 at 100°F or 38°C electrolyte temperature
1.102 at 90°F or 32°C electrolyte temperature
1.106 at 80°F or 27°C electrolyte temperature
1.110 at 70°F or 21°C electrolyte temperature
1.114 at 60°F or 16°C electrolyte temperature
1.118 at 50°F or 10°C electrolyte temperature
1.122 at 40°F or 4°C electrolyte temperature
1.126 at 30°F or −1.5°C electrolyte temperature

4   Battery – electrolyte replenishment

1   If the battery is in a fully charged state and one of the cells maintains a specific gravity reading which is 0·025 or more lower than the others, and a check of each cell has been made with a voltage meter to check for short circuits (a four to seven second test should give a steady reading of between 1·2 and 1·8 volts), then it is likely that electrolyte has been lost from the cell with the low reading at some time.

2   Top the cell up with a solution of 1 part sulphuric acid to 2·5 parts of water. If the cell is already fully topped up, draw some electrolye out of it with a pipette or plastic syringe.

3   When mixing the sulphuric acid and water **never add water to sulphuric acid** – always pour the acid slowly onto the water in a glass container. **If water is added to sulphuric acid it will explode.**

4   Continue to top up the cell with the freshly made electrolyte and then recharge the battery and check the hydrometer readings.

5   Battery – charging

1   In winter time when heavy demand is placed upon the battery, such as when starting from cold and much electrical equipment is continually in use, it is a good idea to occasionally have the battery fully charged from an external source at the rate of 3.5 to 4 amps.

2   Continue to charge the battery at this rate until no further rise in specific gravity is noted over a four hour period.

3   Alternatively, a trickle charger charging a the rate of 1.5 amps can safely be used overnight.

4   Specially rapid 'boost' charges which are claimed to restore the power of the battery in 1 to 2 hours are most dangerous as they can cause serious damage to the battery plates through overheating.

5   While charging the battery note that the temperature of the electrolyte should never exceed 100°F (37.8°C).

6   Alternator – general description

All models covered by this manual are fitted with alternators. The alternator generates alternating current (AC) which is rectified by diodes into direct current (DC) and is the current needed for charging the battery.

The main advantage of the alternator lies in its ability to provide a high charge at low revolutions. Driving slowly in heavy traffic with a dynamo invariably means no charge is reaching the battery. In similar conditions even with the heater, wiper, lights and perhaps radio switched on the alternator will ensure a charge reaches the battery.

The alternator is of the rotating field ventilated design and comprises principally a laminated stator on which is wound the output winding, a rotor carrying the field winding and a diode rectifier. The voltage regulator is separate from the alternator.

The rotor is belt-driven from the engine through a pulley keyed to the rotor shaft. A fan adjacent to the pulley draws air through the unit. Rotation is clockwise when viewed from the drive end.

The voltage regulator is set during manufacture and requires no further attention. However, should its operation be faulty it must be renewed as a complete unit.

7   Alternator – maintenance

1   The equipment has been designed for the minimum amount of maintenance in service, the only items subject to wear being the brushes and bearings.

2   Brushes should be examined after about 75 000 miles (120 000 km) and renewed if necessary. The bearings are pre-packed with grease for life, and should not require further attention.

3   Regularly check the drivebelt tension and if slack adjust as described in Chapter 2.

8   Alternator – special procedures

1   Whenever the electrical system of the car is being attended to or external means of starting the engine is used, there are certain precautions that must be taken otherwise serious and expensive damage can result.

2   Always make sure that the negative terminal of the battery in earthed. If the terminal connections are accidentally reversed or if the battery has been reverse charged the alternator diodes will burn out.

3   The output terminal on the alternator marked 4, BAT or B+ must never be earthed but should always be connected directly to the positive terminal of the battery. Similarly the terminals marked 8, EXC or DF on the alternator and on the regulator must never be earthed.

4   Whenever the alternator is to be removed, or when disconnecting the terminals of the alternator circuit, always disconnect the battery earth terminal first.

5   The alternator must never be operated without the battery to alternator cable connected.

6   If the battery is to be charged by external means always disconnect both battery cables before the external charge is connected.

7   Should it be necessary to use a booster charger or booster battery to start the engine always double check that the negative cable is connected to negative terminal and the positive cable to positive terminal.

9   Alternator – removal and refitting

1   Disconnect the battery leads.

2   Note the terminal connections at the rear of the alternator and disconnect the plug, multi-pin connector or terminals.

3   Undo and remove the alternator adjustment arm bolt, slacken the alternator mounting bolts and push the alternator inwards towards the engine. Lift away the drivebelt from the pulley.

4   Remove the remaining two mounting bolts and carefully lift the alternator away from the car.

5   Take care not to knock or drop the alternator otherwise this can cause irreparable damage.

6   Refitting the alternator is the reverse sequence to removal.

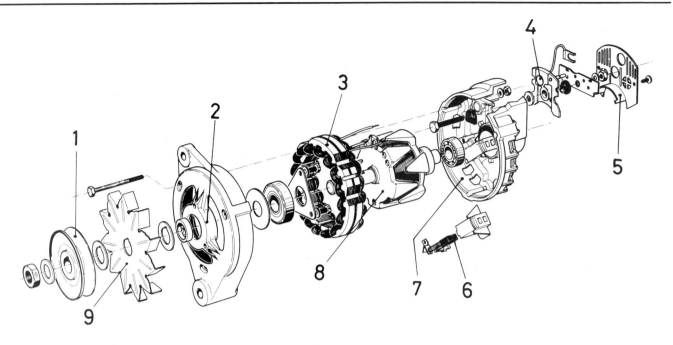

Fig. 9.1 Exploded view of a typical alternator (Sec 6)

1	Drive pulley	3	Stator	6	Brushes	8	Rotor
2	Bearing carrier and drive end bracket	4	Isolating diode	7	Diode holders and end cover	9	Fan
		5	Rear end cover				

10 Alternator – fault diagnosis and repair

1   Due to the specialist knowledge and equipment required to test or service an alternator it is recommended that if the performance is suspect, the car be taken to an automobile electrician who will have the facilities for such work. Because of this recommendation, information is limited to the inspection and renewal of the brushes. Should the alternator not charge or the system be suspect the following points may be checked before seeking further assistance:

(a) Check the drivebelt tension, as described in Chapter 2
(b) Check the battery, as described in Section 3
(c) Check all electrical cable connections for cleanliness and security

2   To change the brushes, unscrew and remove the brush holder retaining screws. The brush holder can then be withdrawn (photo). Fit a replacement unit in reverse sequence and reconnect the terminal.

11 Starter motor – general description

The starter motor is mounted on the front of the engine and is of the pre-engaged type, ie the drive pinion is brought into mesh with the starter ring gear on the flywheel before the main current is applied.

When the starter switch is operated, current flows from the battery to the solenoid which is mounted on the top of the starter motor body. The plunger in the solenoid moves inwards, so causing a centrally pivoted lever to push the drive pinion into mesh with the starter ring gear. When the solenoid plunger reaches the end of its travel, it closes an internal contact and full starting current flows to the starter field coils. The armature is then able to rotate the crankshaft, so starting the engine.

A special freewheel clutch is fitted to the starter drive pinion so that as soon as the engine fires and starts to operate on its own it does not drive the starter motor.

When the starter switch is released, the solenoid is de-energised and a spring moves the plunger back to its rest position. This operates the pivoted lever to withdraw the drive pinion from engagement with the starter ring.

10.2 Removing the alternator brush holder

12 Starter motor – testing on engine

1   If the starter motor fails to turn the engine when the switch is operated there are four possible reasons why:

(a) The battery is discharged or faulty
(b) The electrical connections between switch, solenoid, battery and starter motor are somewhere failing to pass the necessary current from the battery, through the starter to earth
(c) The solenoid has an internal fault
(d) The starter motor is either jammed or electrically defective

2   To check the battery, switch on the headlights. If they go dim after a few seconds the battery is discharged. If the lamp glows brightly next operate the ignition/starter switch and see what happens to the lights.

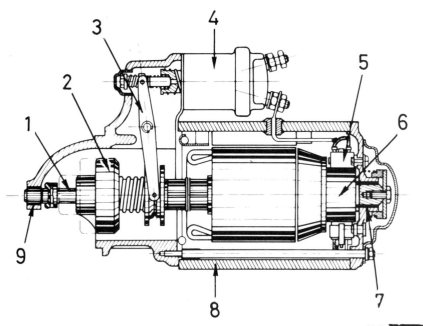

Fig. 9.2 Sectional view of starter motor
(Sec 11)

1   Driveshaft
2   Freewheel
3   Pivot lever
4   Solenoid
5   Brushes
6   Commutator
7   Rear end bearing
8   Body and field coils
9   Front end bearing

If they do dim it is indicative that power is reaching the starter motor but failing to turn it. Therefore check that it is not jammed by placing the car in gear and rocking it to-and-fro. If it is not jammed the starter will have to be removed for examination. If the starter should turn very slowly go on to the next check.

3   If, when the ignition/starter switch is operated the lights stay bright, then the power is not reaching the starter motor. Check all connections from the battery to solenoid for cleanliness and tightness. With a good battery fitted this is the most usual cause of starter motor problems. Check that the earth cable between the engine and chassis is also intact and cleanly connected. This can sometimes be overlooked when the engine is taken out.

4   If no results have yet been achieved turn off the headlights, otherwise the battery will soon be discharged. It may be possible that a clicking noise was heard each time the ignition/starter switch was operated. This is the solenoid switch operating but it does not necessarily follow that the main contact is closing properly. (If no clicking has been heard from the solenoid it is certainly defective). The solenoid contact can be checked by putting a voltmeter or bulb between the main cable connection on the starter side of the solenoid and earth. When the switch is operated there should be a reading or a lighted bulb. If not the switch has a fault.

13 Starter motor – removal and refitting

1   Disconnect the battery earth terminal.
2   The starter motor will have to be removed from underneath the vehicle. Raise the front and support with axle stands or blocks. Alternatively run it onto ramps or over an inspection pit.
3   Disconnect the starter leads from the solenoid.
4   Unscrew and remove the two starter motor mounting bracket-to-engine bolts.
5   Now secure the three mounting bolts from the clutch housing. Use an extension wrench inserted through the aperture in the left-hand side inner wing panel.
6   Withdraw the starter motor from the clutch housing.
7   The starter motor is refitted in the reverse order.

14 Starter motor – dismantling and reassembly

1   Such is the inherent reliability and strength of the starter motor fitted that it is very unlikely that a motor will ever need dismantling until it is totally worn out and in need of replacement. It is not a task for the home mechanic because, although reasonably easy to undertake, the reassembly and adjustment before refitting is beyond his scope because of the need of specialist equipment. It is usually more satisfactory to fit an exchange motor or have an overhaul done

Fig. 9.3 Undo the bolts marked A to remove the starter motor
(Sec 13)

by a specialist auto electrician. However, the more ambitious DIY mechanic can change brushes or renew a solenoid. The dismantling procedure is as follows.

2   Unscrew the two nuts securing the engine mounting bracket to the motor and remove the bracket (photo). Remove the locknuts and retaining nuts and take off the endplate (photo).
3   Hold the shaft from turning by jamming the drive pinion, and undo the end bearing seal retaining bolt. Remove the seal assembly with its spring (photo).
4   To gain access to the brushes, lever the bearing plate from the body. The brushes are mounted on the underside of the plate (photo).
5   Lift the brush spring and remove the brush from its housing to enable the bearing plate to be removed (photo). Note the arrangement of washers on the armature shaft.
6   Disconnect the terminal from the solenoid and carefully slide the body from the armature (photo).
7   To separate the armature from the pinion end bracket, tap out the pivot pin and loosen the solenoid retaining nuts. The armature assembly can be removed by disconnecting the solenoid-operated lever and withdrawing the assembly at the same time (photo).
8   To withdraw the pinion from the armature, tap back the special collar washer and extract the snap-ring from the groove in the shaft. The pinion assembly can then be slid from the shaft.
9   With the starter motor dismantled the various components can be

14.2a Removing the starter-to-engine mounting bracket

14.2b The endplate being removed

14.3 The seal assembly being removed

14.4 The brushes are mounted under the bearing plate

14.5 The bearing plate removed. Note the sequence of washers on the armature shaft

14.6 Removing the starter motor body

14.7 Withdrawing the armature

14.9 The starter motor dismantled

cleaned and inspected for general wear and/or signs of damage (photo). The principle components likely to need attention will be the brushes, the solenoid or possibly the drive pinion unit.

10 The brushes can be removed by unsoldering the connecting wires to the holder and to the field coil unit. Take care not to damage the latter during removal and assembly of the brushes.

11 If the starter motor has shown a tendency to jam or a possible reluctance to disengage then the starter pinion is almost certainly the culprit. Dirt around the pinion and shaft could cause this and when cleaned check the pinion can move freely in a spiral movement along the shaft. If the pinion tends to bind or is defective in any way renew it.

12 Undercut the separators of the commutator using an old hacksaw blade to a depth of about 0.02 to 0.03 in (0.5 to 0.8 mm). The commutator may be further surface cleaned using a strip of very fine glass paper. Do not use emery cloth for this purpose as the carborundum particles will become embedded in the copper surfaces.

13 Testing of the armature is best left to an auto electrician but if an ohmmeter is available it can be done by placing one probe on the armature shaft and the other on each of the commutator segments in turn. If there is a reading indicated at any time during the test, then the armature is defective and must be renewed.

14 The field coil can also be tested using an ohmmeter. Connect one probe to the field coil positive terminal and the other to the positive brush holder. If there is no indication of a reading then the field coil circuit has a break in it.

15 Connect one lead of the meter to the field coil positive lead and the other one to the yoke. If there is a low resistance then the field coil is earthed due to a breakdown in the insulation. If this proves to be the case the field coils must be renewed. As field coil replacement requires special tools and equipment it is a job that should be entrusted to your auto-electrician. In fact it will probably prove more economical and beneficial to exchange the starter motor for a reconditioned unit.

16 Reassembly of the rest of the starter motor is a direct reversal of

14.16a Fitting the pivot lever pin

14.16b Tightening the solenoid retaining nuts

16.2 The fuse box is located under the facia on the right-hand side

17.2 The headlight assembly lowered forward

17.3a Pull off the electrical connector ...

17.3b ... and remove the bulb

17.4 The left-hand or right-hand traffic adjuster in the left-hand position

18.6a The vertical adjustment and ...

18.6b ... the horizontal adjustment for the right-hand headlight

18.7 The load adjuster (early model) for the headlight beam. The bonnet is lifted only for clarity

19.2 Removing a bulb from the front direction indicator/sidelight assembly

20.1 Undoing the screws to remove a rear light lens

the removal procedure (photos), but note the following:

(a) *The snap-ring and collar can be difficult to relocate and to assist in this we used a valve compressor*
(b) *Reassemble the correct number of thrust washers and in the correct sequence namely, fibre, steel, spring, steel fibre*
(c) *Align the key and slot when assembling the body*
(d) *Make sure that the brushes slide freely in their holders*
(e) *Sparingly lubricate the armature shaft with a general purpose grease. Do not lubricate the pinion and splines*

15 Starter motor drive pinion – inspection and repair

1 Persistent jamming or reluctance to disengage may mean that the starter pinion assembly needs attention. The starter motor should be removed first of all for inspection.
2 With the starter motor removed thoroughly remove all grime and grease with a petrol soaked rag, taking care to stop any liquid running into the motor itself. If there is a lot of dirt this could be the trouble and all will now be well. The pinion should move freely in a spiral movement along the shaft against the light spring and return easily on being released. To do this the spiral splines should be completely clean and free of oil. (Oil merely collects dust and grime and gums up the splines). The spring should be intact.
3 If the preceding cleaning and check does not actually remove the fault the starter motor will need to be stripped down to its component parts and a further check made. This has been explained in the preceding Section.

16 Fuses – general

1 All Peugeot 104 models have fuse-protected circuits. As many as eight fuses are fitted to some models, although four is the usual number. The allocation of circuits to fuses varies with individual models and it will be necessary to study the wiring diagrams at the end of this chapter to identify fuses with circuits for any given model.
2 The fuse box is mounted under the front facia on the right hand side in an awkward position (photo). To gain access to the fuses first prise off the cover.
3 Before renewing a blown fuse, trace and rectify the cause and always use a new fuse of the correct value. **Do not** substitute a fuse of a higher rating or wrap tin foil round a blown fuse, or more serious damage or even fire may result.

17 Headlight bulb – removal and refitting

1 Early models had the headlight assemblies mounted on plates which could be removed from the front subframe. Later, the headlight assemblies were mounted direct to the subframe.
2 To remove the early type of headlight, undo the two large headed screws above the lamp and, after pulling the top of the unit forward, remove the assembly by lifting the bottom clips clear of the subframe (photo). To remove the later type of lamp, insert a lever behind the top bracket or side lugs and carefully lever the unit forward until clear of the subframe.
3 Unplug the electrical connector by pulling it off the bulb terminals (photo). Swing back the two spring clips retaining the bulb and remove the bulb (photo).
4 Refitting a bulb is the reverse of the removal procedure. The headlight unit has an adjustment to switch the headlight beams to suit driving on the left or right-hand side of the road. Make sure that this is in the correct position for your location (photo). Also ensure that the locating pip is engaged when the bulb is in position. Check the bulb for operation on completion.
5 After changing a bulb make sure that headlight alignment is satisfactory – see next Section.

18 Headlight beam – adjustment

1 The headlight beam adjustment is most important, not only for your own safety but for that of other road users. Accurate beam alignment can only be obtained using optical beam setting equipment and

you should regard any adjustments made without such equipment as temporary.
2 To make a temporary adjustment, position the car on level grounds about 10 ft (3 metres) in front of a vertical wall or a piece of board secured vertically. The wall or board should be square to the centre-line of the car and the car should be normally laden. Check that the tyre pressures are correct.
3 .Draw a vertical line on the wall or board in line with the centre line of the car.
4 Bounce the car on its suspension several times to ensure correct levelling and then accurately measure the height between the ground and the centre of the headlights.
5 Draw a horizontal line across the wall or board at the same height as the headlight centres and on this line mark a cross on either side of the centreline at the same distance apart as the headlight centres.
6 Now find the adjusters on each headlight. Vertical adjustment of the beam is obtained by adjusting a screw above each headlight unit. Horizontal adjustment is similarly obtained by adjusting a screw, or on some models two screws, at the side (s) of the unit (photos).
7 Before making adjustments make sure that the load selector is in the 'car unloaded' position. At the top of each unit there is a horizontal, centrally pivoted lever (early models) or a vertical lever (later models) which, when operated, rocks the headlamp unit up or down. Position the levers so that each unit points upwards. When the car has a load in the back the tendency for the headlights to shine upwards can be corrected by moving these levers to make the units point down slightly (photo).
8 Switch the headlights on to full beam and adjust each headlamp to align each beam just below the corresponding cross on the wall or board.
9 Bounce the car on its suspension again to check that the beams return to the correct position. At the same time check the operation of the dipswitch to confirm that the beams dip to the nearside. If not, check the adjusters that were mentioned in the previous Section (photo 17.4). Switch off the lights on completion.

19 Front side and direction indicator lights – removal, refitting and bulb renewal

1 To gain access to the sidelight and indicator bulbs unscrew the lens retaining screws and detach the lens.
2 Bayonet fixing bulbs are fitted and these are pushed and twisted anti-clockwise to remove (photo).
3 If the light unit is to be removed, disconnect the battery earth terminal, then detach the wires to the rear of the combination light.
4 Remove the lens and unscrew the retaining screws. Withdraw the combination light unit.
5 Refit in the reverse sequence and check the lights and indicators for correct operation.

20 Rear light clusters – removal, refitting and bulb renewal

1 Access to the rear combination light bulb is obtained by removing the appropriate rear light lens which is retained by screws (photo).
2 Bayonet fixing bulbs are fitted and these are removed by pushing and twisting anti-clockwise (photo).
3 To remove the cluster light unit, first disconnect the battery earth terminal. Remove the lens cover and, working inside the luggage compartment space, disconnect the electric cable terminals from the bulb holders. Unscrew the cluster retaining screws and remove the unit.
4 Refit in the reverse order and check the operation of the lights on completion.

21 Rear number plate light bulbs – renewal

1 On some models the rear number plate light bulb holders are accessible on the inside of the rear door or tailgate. In these cases, remove the bulb holder by pushing it to the rear and then pulling it out of its housing. The bayonet type bulb can then be renewed in the usual way (photo).
2 Where the bulb holders are not accessible from inside, the bright trim covering the two bulbs will have to be removed. Undo and remove the four nuts and washers inside the door on, on ZL and ZS models,

20.2 Removing a rear light bulb

21.1 Removing a rear number plate light bulb (early model)

22.1 Removing the interior light bulb

23.2 Using a feeler gauge to depress the instrument panel retaining catch

23.3 Unplugging a multi-connector

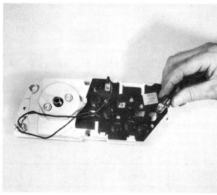
23.5 Removing an indicator lamp from the instrument panel

23.6 The front bezel mouldings removed from the instrument panel

24.1a Easing the tongues open to ...

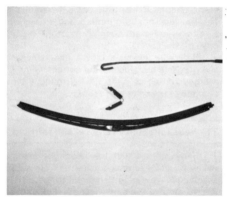
24.1b ... remove the windscreen wiper blade

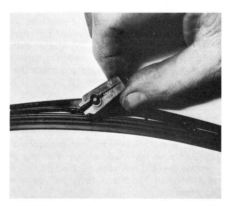
24.2 Fitting the pivot block to the wiper blade

25.3 Make sure that the catch (arrowed) engages under the shaft splines when the arm is assembled to the shaft

remove the four screws and washers in the top of the trim, and then remove the trim. Remove the plastic lens over the bulb and then the bulb can be changed as already described.

3   Check the operation of the lights on completion.

22 Interior light bulb – renewal

1   To renew the interior light bulb, carefully prise the lens from the light unit. The festoon bulb can now be extracted from between the two holders (photo).

2   Fit the new bulb and replace the lens by pushing into position.

3   If the light unit is to be removed, disconnect the battery earth terminal, remove the lens and unscrew the unit retaining screws and withdraw it. Detach the wires.

4   Refit in the reverse order and check operation.

23 Instrument panel – removal and refitting

1   Disconnect the battery earth connection. Remove the steering wheel (see Chapter 10).

2   Using a feeler gauge, depress the retaining catch in the top of the panel and ease the panel forward (photo).

3   Undo the speedometer cable connection at the rear of the panel by reaching up behind the facia. Ease the panel towards you and unplug the multi-connectors from the rear (photo). Where fitted, also disconnect the choke control knob.

4   Remove the panel from the facia.

5   Instrument lamps and warning light bulbs can now be changed if required. Turn the lamps anti-clockwise to remove (photo).

6   Individual instruments can be changed after removing the front bezel mouldings (photo).

7   Refitting is the reverse of the removal procedure.

8   Slight differences exist in the panels for different Peugeot 104 models, but the same principles of removal and refitting will apply.

24 Windscreen wiper blades – removal and refitting

1   To remove a windscreen wiper blade, using a small bladed screwdriver, ease the tongues open on the arm pivot block (photo) and slide the pivot block, together with the blade, out of the U-bend in the end of the arm (photo). The pivot block will open and free itself from the blade assembly.

2   To fit a blade, first fit the pivot block to the blade pivot pin (photo), then slide it into the U-bend on the arm. Make sure that the tongues secure the arm.

25 Windscreen wiper arms – removal and refitting

1   Before removing a wiper arm operate the wipers to ensure that the arms, when at rest, are in their normal parked position with the blades parallel with the bottom of the windscreen.

2   To remove an arm, pivot the arm back as far as it will go and pull the assembly off the splined drive.

3   When refitting an arm place it so that it is in the correct relative parked position. Lift the arm up away from the windscreen, holding the arm socket in alignment with the splined drive and press the socket onto the drive until it is fully home. Lower the arm onto the windscreen and check that the retaining catch engages under the splines on the drive shaft (photo).

26 Windscreen wipers and drive motor – fault diagnosis

1   If the wipers fail to operate first check that current is reaching the motor. This can be done by switching on and using a voltmeter or 12 volt bulb and two wires between the (+) terminal on the motor and earth.

2   If no current is reaching the motor check whether there is any at the switch. If there is then a break has occurred in the wiring between switch and motor.

3   If there is no voltage at the switch go back to the ignition switch and so isolate the area of the fault. The problem may simply be a blown or badly connected fuse.

4   If current is reaching the motor but the wipers do not operate, switch on and give the wiper arm a push – they or the motor could be jammed. Switch off immediately if nothing happens otherwise further damage to the motor may occur. If the wipers now run the reason for them jamming must be found. It will almost certainly be due to wear in either the linkage of the wiper mechanism or the mechanism in the motor gearbox.

5   If the wipers run too slowly it will be due to something restricting the free operation of the linkage or a fault in the motor. In such cases it is well to check the current being used by connecting an ammeter in the circuit. If it exceeds three amps something is restricting free movement. If less, then the commutator and brush gear in the motor are suspect. The shafts to which the wipers are attached run in very long bushes and often suffer from lack of lubrication. Weekly application to each shaft of a few drops of light penetrating oil helps to prevent partial or total seizure.

6   If wear is obviously causing malfunction or there is a fault in the motor it is best to remove the motor or wiper mechanism for further examination and repairs.

27 Windscreen wiper motor and mechanism – removal and refitting

1   To gain access to the windscreen wiper motor and mechanism the bulkhead closure plate must be removed and, on right-hand drive models, the cooling system expansion tank must be moved out of the way.

2   Disconnect the battery earth lead.

3   Undo and remove the expansion tank retaining nuts and bolts. Don't bother to drain any coolant, but carefully move the tank out of the way of the bulkhead closure plate.

4   Undo and remove the closure plate screws and remove the closure plate.

5   Remove the windscreen wiper arms, see previous Section, and remove the driveshaft retaining nuts and spacers (photo).

6   Undo and remove the single nut and washer holding the windscreen wiper motor and mechanism (photo) and then manoeuvre the assembly out of the bulkhead hole, disconnecting the electrical connections as opportunity presents itself. Note the sequence of connections for reassembly (photo).

7   It is unlikely that individual spare parts will be obtainable for the motor or gearbox, but it might be possible to fit new brushes if suitable spares can be obtained. To get to the brushes, undo the two motor cover retaining screws and, being careful not to lose the two screw plates, slide the cover off the motor (photo). This is a permanent magnet type motor and it should not be dismantled where iron filings or ferrous dust are present. The two brushes are mounted at the gearbox end of the armature (photo). After fitting replacements, make sure that they slide freely in their boxes. When refitting the motor cover check that the alignment key fits in the cover groove (photo).

8   If proved unserviceable, the motor and gearbox can be removed for renewal by undoing the three retaining bolts and washers after disconnecting the mechanism drive arm (photo).

9   Refitting is the reverse of the removal procedure. When installing the mechanism, ensure that the weather cover is fitted to the motor assembly (photo). After installation check the wiper operation, but wet the windscreen first to prevent scratching.

28 Windscreen washer unit – general

1   The windscreen washer unit is operated by an electric pump (photo) which draws the cleaning fluid from the reservoir and pressurises the water nozzles.

2   Malfunction is usually due to blocked jets on the screen delivery nozzles. These can be cleared with fine wire. Other causes of failure are blocked, kinked or disconnected pipes. The latter is usually apparent when the pump is operated.

3   Should the pump fail to operate, first check the supply pipes to the nozzles as described above and if they are in order make an inspection of the wiring to the pump.

4   If the pump is found to be defective if must be renewed as a unit as it is not reparable.

Note: *Do not use standard cooling system antifreeze in the washer*

27.5 Removing a wiper driveshaft retaining nut

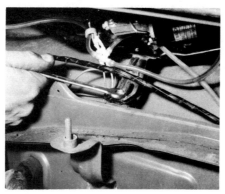
27.6a Undo the retaining nut ...

27.6b ... and manoeuvre the assembly through the bulkhead hole

27.7a Don't lose these loose screw plates

27.7b The wiper motor opened to check the brushes

27.7c Make sure that the alignment key and groove are mated properly

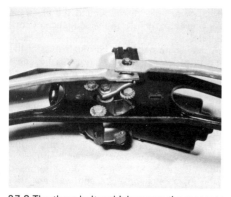
27.8 The three bolts which secure the motor to the assembly

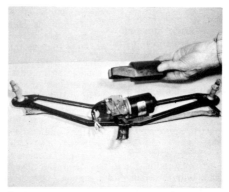
27.9 Refitting the weathershield to the motor assembly

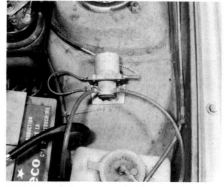
28.1 The windscreen washer pump is located just behind the washer fluid bottle

unit. Special windscreen washer solutions to aid windscreen cleaning and prevent freezing are available from most garages and accessory shops.

29 Horn – fault diagnosis and rectification

1   If the horn works badly or fails completely check the wiring leading to the horn. Make sure that all connections are clean and secure.
2   Using a test light check that current is reaching the horn and then ensure that the horn switch is operating correctly.
3   Check that the horn is secure on its mounting and that there is nothing lying on the horn body.
4   If all appears to be well test the horn and circuit by substitution.

30 Direction indicator circuit – fault diagnosis and rectification

Should the flasher unit fail to operate, or work very slowly or rapidly, check out the circuit as detailed below before assuming that there is a fault in the unit.

(a) *Examine the direction indicator light bulbs, both front and rear, for broken filaments*
(b) *If the external flashers are working, but either of the internal flasher warning lights have ceased to function, check the filaments in the warning light bulb and replace with a new bulb if necessary*
(c) *If a flasher bulb is sound but does not work, check all the flasher circuit connections with the aid of the relevant wiring diagram at the end of the Chapter*

(d) With the ignition switched on check that the correct voltage is reaching the flasher unit

(e) Should all appear to be well then check the flasher unit by substitution

31 Radios and tape players – fitting (general)

A radio or tape player is an expensive item to buy and will only give its best performance if fitted properly. It is useless to expect concert hall performance from a unit that is suspended from the dash panel on string with its speaker resting on the back seat or parcel shelf! If you do not wish to do the installation yourself there are many in-car entertainment specialists who can do the fitting for you.

Make sure the unit purchased is of the same polarity as the car, and ensure that units with adjustable polarity are correctly set before commencing installation.

It is difficult to give specific information with regard to fitting, as final positioning of the radio/tape player, speakers and aerial is entirely a matter of personal preference. However, the following paragraphs give guidelines to follow, which are relevant to all installations.

Radios

Most radios are a standardised size of 7 inches wide, by 2 inches deep – this ensures that they will fit into the radio aperture provided in most cars. If your car does not have such an aperture, then the radio must be fitted in a suitable position either in, or beneath, the dash-panel. Alternatively, a special console can be purchased which will fit between the dashpanel and the floor, or on the transmission tunnel. These consoles can also be used for additional switches and instrumentation if required. Where no radio aperture is provided, the following points should be borne in mind before deciding exactly where to fit the unit:

(a) The unit must be within easy reach of the driver wearing a seat belt

(b) The unit must not be mounted in close proximity to an electric tachometer, the ignition switch and its wiring, or the flasher unit and associated wiring

(c) The unit must be mounted within reach of the aerial lead, and in such a place that the aerial lead will not have to be routed near the components detailed in the preceding paragraph

(d) The unit should not be positioned in a place where it might cause injury to the car occupants in an accident; for instance, under the dashpanel above the driver's or passenger's legs

(e) The unit must be fitted really securely

Some radios will have mounting brackets provided together with instructions: others will need to be fitted using drilled and slotted metal strips, bent to form mounting brackets – these strips are available from most accessory shops. The unit must be properly earthed, by fitting a separate earthing lead between the casing of the radio and the vehicle frame.

Use the radio manufacturer's instructions when wiring the radio into the vehicle's electrical system. If no instructions are available refer to the relevant wiring diagram to find the location of the radio 'feed' connection in the vehicle's wiring circuit. A 1-2 amp 'in-line' fuse must be fitted in the radio's 'feed' wire – a choke may also be necessary (see next Section).

The type of aerial used, and its fitted position, is a matter of personal preference. In general the taller the aerial, the better the reception. It is best to fit a fully retractable aerial – especially if a mechanical car wash is used or if you live in an area where cars tend to be vandalised. In this respect electric aerials which are raised and lowered automatically when switching the radio on or off are convenient, but are more likely to give trouble than the manual type.

When choosing a site for the aerial the following points should be considered:

(a) The aerial lead should be as short as possible – this means that the aerial should be mounted at the front of the car

(b) The aerial must be mounted as far away from the distributor and HT leads as possible

(c) The part of the aerial which protrudes beneath the mounting point must not foul the roadwheels, or anything else

(d) If possible the aerial should be positioned so that the coaxial lead does not have to be routed through the engine compartment

(e) The plane of the panel on which the aerial is mounted should not be so steeply angled that the aerial cannot be mounted vertically (in relation to the 'end-on' aspect of the car). Most aerials have a small amount of adjustment available

Having decided on a mounting position, a relatively large hole will have to be made in the panel. The exact size of the hole will depent upon the specific aerial being fitted, although, generally, the hole required is of ¾ inch (19 mm) diameter. On metal bodied cars, a 'tank-cutter' of the relevant diameter is the best tool to use for making the hole. This tool needs a small diameter pilot hole drilled through the panel, through which, the tool clamping bolt is inserted. On GRP bodied cars, a 'hole-saw' is the best tool to use. Again, this tool will require the drilling of a small pilot hole. When the hole has been made the raw edges should be de-burred with a file and then painted, to prevent corrosion.

Fit the aerial according to the manufacturer's instructions. If the aerial is very tall, or if it protrudes beneath the mounting panel for a considerable distance it is a good idea to fit a stay between the aerial and the vehicle frame. This stay can be manufactured from the slotted and drilled metal strips previously mentioned. The stay should be securely screwed or bolted in place. For best reception it is advisable to fit an earth lead between the aerial and the vehlcle frame – this is essential for GRP bodied cars.

It will probably be necessary to drill one or two holes through bodywork panels in order to feed the aerial lead into the interior of the car. Where this is the case ensure that the holes are fitted with rubber grommets to protect the cable, and to stop possible entry of water.

Positioning and fitting of the speaker depends mainly on its type. Generally, the speaker is designed to fit directly into the aperture already provided in the car (usually in the shelf behind the rear seats, or in the top of the dashpanel). Where this is the case, fitting the speaker is just a matter of removing the protective grille from the aperture and screwing or bolting the speaker in place. Take great care not to damage the speaker diaphragm whilst doing this. It is a good idea to fit a 'gasket' between the speaker frame and the mounting panel, in order to prevent vibration – some speakers will already have such a gasket fitted.

If a 'pod' type speaker was supplied with the radio, the best acoustic results will normally be obtained by mounting it on the shelf behind the rear seat. The pod can be secured to the mounting panel with self-tapping screws.

When connecting a rear mounted speaker to the radio, the wires should be routed through the vehicle beneath the carpets or floor mats – preferably the middle, or along the side of the floorpan, where they will not be trodden on by passengers. Make the relevant connections as directed by the radio manufacturer.

By now you will have several yards of additional wiring in the car, use PVC tape to secure this wiring out of harms way. Do not leave electrical leads dangling. Ensure that all new electrical connections are properly made (wires twisted together will not do) and completely secure.

The radio should now be working, but before you pack away your tools it will be necessary to 'trim' the radio to the aerial. If specific instructions are not provided by the radio manufacturer, proceed as follows. Find a station with a low signal strength on the medium waveband, slowly, turn the trim screw of the radio in, or out, until the loudest reception of the selected station is obtained – the set is then trimmed to the aerial.

Tape players

Fitting instructions for both cartridge and cassette stereo tape players are the same and in general the same rules apply as when fitting a radio. Tape players are not usually prone to electrical interference like radio – although it can occur – so positioning is not so critical. If possible the player should be mounted on an 'even-keel'. Also it must be possible for a driver wearing a seatbelt to reach the unit in order to change or turn over tapes.

For the best results from speakers designed to be recessed into a panel, mount them so that the back of the speaker protrudes into an enclosed chamber within the car (eg door interiors or the boot cavity).

To fit recessed type speakers on the front doors first check that there is sufficient room to mount the speakers in each door without it fouling the latch or window winding mechanism. Hold the speaker against the skin of the door, and draw a line around the periphery of the speaker. With the speaker removed draw a second 'cutting' line, within the first, to allow enough room for the entry of the speaker back, but at the same time providing a broad seat for the speaker flange. When you are sure that the cutting line is correct, drill a series of holes around its periphery. Pass a hacksaw blade through one of the holes and then cut through the metal between the holes until the centre section of the panel falls out.

De-burr the edges of the hole and then paint the raw metal to prevent corrosion. Cut a corresponding hole in the door trim panel – ensuring that it will be completely covered by the speaker grille. Now drill a hole in the door edge and a corresponding hole in the door surround. These holes are to feed the speaker leads through – so fit grommets. Pass the speaker leads through the door trim, door skin and out through the holes in ther side of the door and door surround. Refit the door trim panel and then secure the speaker to the door using self-tapping screws. Note: If the speaker is fitted with a shield to prevent water dripping on it, ensure that this shield is at the top.

Pod type speakers can be fastened to the shelf behind the rear seat, or anywhere else offering a corresponding mounting point on each side of the car. If the pod speakers are mounted on each side of the shelf behind the rear seat, it is a good idea to drill several large diameter holes through to the boot cavity beneath each speaker – this will improve the sound reproduction. Pod speakers sometimes offer a better reproduction quality if they face the rear window – which then acts as a reflector – so it is worthwhile to do a little experimenting before finally fixing the speaker.

32 Radios and tape players – suppression of interference (general)

To eliminate buzzes and other unwanted noises costs very little and is not as difficult as sometimes thought. With a modicum of common sense and patience and following the instructions in the following paragraphs, interference can be virtually eliminated.

The first cause for concern is the generator. The noise this makes over the radio is like an electric mixer and the noise speeds up when you rev up (if you wish to prove the point, you can remove the drivebelt and try it). The remedy for this is simple; connect a 1.0 μf-3.0 μf capacitor between earth, probably the bolt that holds down the generator base, and the output (B+) terminal on the alternator. This is most important for if you connect it to the wrong terminal, you will probably damage the generator permanently (see Fig. 9.4).

A second common cause of electrical interference is the ignition system. Here a 1.0 μf capacitor must be connected between earth and the 'SW' or '+' terminal on the coil (See Fig. 9.5). This may stop the tick-tick-tick sound that comes over the speaker. Next comes the spark itself.

There are several ways of curing interference from the ignition HT system. One is to use carbon film HT lead but these have a tendency to 'snap' inside and you don't know then, why you are firing on only half your cylinders. So the second, and more successful method is to use resistive spark plug caps (see Fig. 9.6) of about 10,000 to 15,000 ohm resistance. If, due to lack of room, these cannot be used, an alternative is to use 'in-line' suppressors (Fig. 9.6). If the interference is not too bad, you may get away with only one suppressor in the coil to distributor line. If the interference does continue (a 'clacking' noise) then doctor all HT leads.

At this stage it is advisable to check that the radio is well earthed, also the aerial, and to see that the aerial plug is pushed well into the set and that the radio is properly trimmed (see preceding Section). In addition, check that the wire which supplies the power to the set is as short as possible and does not wander all over the car. At this stage it is a good idea to check that the fuse is of the correct rating. For most sets this will be about 1 to 2 amps.

At this point the more usual causes of interference have been suppressed. If the problem still exists, a look at the causes of interference may help to pinpoint the component generating the stray electrical discharges.

The radio picks up the electromagnetic waves in the air; now some are made by radio stations and other broadcasters and some, not wanted, are made by the car. The home made signals are produced by stray electrical discharges floating around the car. Common producers of these signals are electric motors; ie, the windscreen wipers, electric

screen washers, electric window winders, heater fan or an electric aerial if fitted. Other sources of interference are electric fuel pumps, flashing turn signals, and instruments. The remedy for these cases is shown in Fig. 9.7 for an electric motor whose interference is not too bad and Fig. 9.8 for instrument suppression. Turn signals are not normally suppressed. In recent years, radio manufacturers have included in the line (live) of the radio, in addition to the fuse, an 'in-line' choke. If your installation lacks one of these, put one in as shown in Fig. 9.9.

All the foregoing components are available from radio shops or accessory shops. For a transistor radio a 2A choke should be adequate. If you have an electric clock fitted this should be suppressed by connecting a 0.5 μf capacitor directly across it as shown for a motor in Fig. 9.7.

If, after all this, you are still experiencing radio interference, first assess how bad it is, for the human ear can filter out unobtrusive unwanted noise quite easily. But if you are still adamant about eradicating the noise, then continue.

As a first step, a few 'experts' seem to favour a screen between the radio and the engine. This is OK as far as it goes, literally! – for the whole set is screened and if interference can get past that then a small piece of aluminium is not going to stop it.

A more sensible way of screening is to discover if interference is coming down the wires. First, take the live lead; interference can get between the set and the choke (hence the reason for keeping the wires short). One remedy here is to screen the wire and this is done by buying screened wire and fitting that. The loudspeaker lead could be screened also to prevent 'pick-up' getting back to the radio – although this is unlikely.

Without doubt, the worst source of radio interference comes from the ignition HT leads, even if they have been suppressed. The ideal way of suppressing these is to slide screening tubes over the leads themselves. As this is impractical, we can place an aluminium shield over the majority of the lead areas. In a vee – or twin-cam engine, this is relatively easy but for a straight engine the results are not particularly good.

Now for the really impossible cases, here are a few tips to try out. Where metal comes into contact with metal, an electrical disturbance is caused which is why good clean connections are essential. To remove interference due to overlapping or butting panels you must bridge the join with a wide braided earth strap (like that from the frame to the engine/transmission). The most common moving parts that could create noise and should be strapped are, in order of importance:

(a) Silencer to frame
(b) Exhaust pipe to engine block and frame
(c) Air cleaner to frame
(d) Front and rear bumpers to frame
(e) Steering column to frame
(f) Bonnet and boot lids to frame

These faults are most pronounced when (1) the engine is idling, (2) labouring under load. Although the moving parts are already connected with nuts, bolts etc, these do tend to rust and corrode, thus creating a high resistance interference source.

If you have a 'ragged' sounding pulse when mobile, this could be wheel or tyre static. This can be cured by buying some anti-static powder and sprinkling it liberally inside the tyres.

If the interference takes the shape of a high pitched screeching noise that changes its note when the car is in motion and only comes now and then, this could be related to the aerial, especially if it is of the telescopic or whip type. This source can be cured quite simply by pushing a small rubber ball on top of the aerial as this breaks the electric field before it can form; but it would be much better to buy yourself a new aerial of a reputable brand. If, on the other hand, you are getting a loud rushing sound every time you brake, then this is brake static. This effect is most prominent on hot dry days and is cured only by fitting a special kit, which is quite expensive.

In conclusion, it is pointed out that it is relatively easy, and therefore cheap to eliminate 95 per cent of all noises, but to eliminate the final 5 per cent is time and money consuming. It is up to the individual to decide if it is worth it. Please remember also, that you will not get concert hall performance from a cheap radio.

Finally at the beginning of this Section are mentioned tape players; these are not usually affected by interference but in a very bad case, the best remedies are the first three suggestions plus using a 3-5 amp choke in the 'live' line and in incurable cases screen the live and

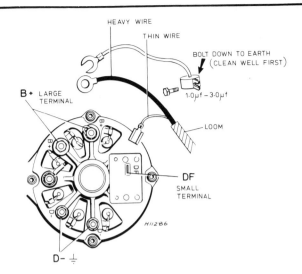

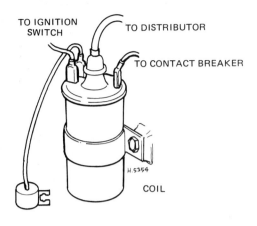

Fig. 9.5 The capacitor must be connected to the ignition switch side of the coil (Sec 32)

Fig. 9.4 The correct way to connect a capacitor to the generator (Sec 32)

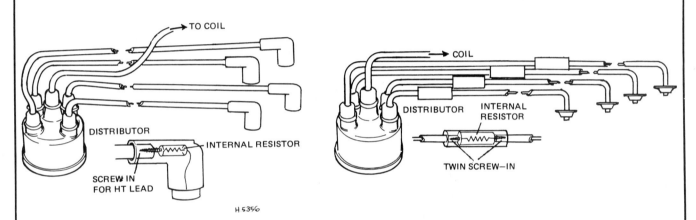

Fig. 9.6 Ignition HT lead suppressors (Sec 32)

Resistive spark plug caps (left)   In-line suppressors (right)

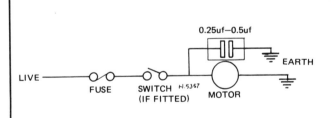

Fig. 9.7 Correct method of suppressing electric motors (Sec 32)

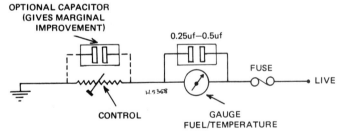

Fig. 9.8 Method of suppressing gauges and their control units (Sec 32)

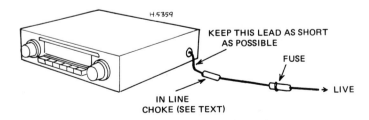

Fig. 9.9 An in-line choke should be fitted into the live supply lead as close to the unit as possible (Sec 32)

speaker wires.

Note: If your car is fitted with electronic ignition, then it is not recommended that either the spark plug resistors or the ignition coil capacitor be fitted as these may damage the system. Most electronic ignition units have built-in suppression and should, therefore, not cause interference.

33 Fault diagnosis – electrical system (general)

Symptom	Reason/s
Starter fails to turn engine	Battery discharged Battery defective internally Battery terminal leads loose or earth lead not securely attached to body Loose or broken connections in starter motor circuit Starter motor switch or solenoid faulty Starter motor pinion jammed in mesh with flywheel gear ring Starter brushes badly worn, sticking, or brush wires loose Commutator dirty, worn or burnt Starter motor armature faulty Field coils earthed
Starter turns engine very slowly	Battery in discharged condition Starter brushes badly worn, sticking or brush wires loose Loose wires in starter motor circuit
Starter spins but does not turn engine	Starter motor pinion sticking on the screwed sleeve Pinion or flywheel gear teeth broken or worn
Starter motor noisy or excessively rough engagement	Pinion or flywheel gear teeth broken or worn Starter motor retaining bolts loose
Battery will not hold charge for more than a few days	Battery defective internally Electrolyte level too low or electrolyte too weak due to leakage Plate separators no longer fully effective Battery plates severely sulphated Drivebelt slipping Battery terminal connections loose or corroded Alternator not charging Short in lighting circuit causing continual battery drain Regulator unit not working correctly
Ignition light fails to go out, battery runs flat in a few days	Drivebelt loose and slipping or broken Alternator brushes worn, sticking, broken or dirty Alternator brush springs weak or broken Internal fault in alternator Regulator faulty

Failure of individual electrical equipment to function correctly is dealt with alphabetically, item-by-item, under the headings below
Horn

Horn operates all the time	Horn push either earthed or stuck down Horn cable to horn push earthed
Horn fails to operate	Cable or cable connection loose, broken or disconnected Horn has an internal fault Blown fuse
Horn emits intermittent or unsatisfactory noise	Cable connections loose

Lights

Lights do not come on	If engine not running, battery discharged Wire connections loose, disconnected or broken Light switch shorting or otherwise faulty
Lights come on but fade out	If engine not running, battery discharged Wire connections loose Light switch shorting or otherwise faulty
Lights work erratically – flashing on and off, especially over bumps	Battery terminals or earth connections loose Lights not earthing properly Contacts in light switch faulty

Symptom	Reason/s

Wipers

Wiper motor fails to work

Blown fuse
Wire connections loose, disconnected or broken
Brushes badly worn
Armature worn or faulty

Wiper motor works very slowly and takes excessive current

Commutator dirty, greasy or burnt
Armature bearings dirty or unaligned
Armature badly worn or faulty

Wiper motor works slowly and takes little current

Brushes badly worn
Commutator dirty, greasy or burnt
Armature badly worn or faulty

Wiper motor works but wiper blades remain static

Wiper motor gearbox parts badly worn

Key to wiring diagrams on pages 132 to 165

1	Headlight	42	Sidelights tell-tale
2	Front direction indicators	43	Brake warning light
3	Front sidelights	43A	Brake warning light control diode
4	Direction indicators relay	44	Water temperature tell-tale or water temperature gauge
5	Starter relay	45	Oil pressure tell-tale
6	Alternator	47	Oil and water tell-tale
7	Oil pressure switch	49	Charge indicator
8	Electro-magnetic or motor driven fan	50	Facia lighting
8A	Motor driven fan relay	50B	Facia lighting rheostat
9	Thermal switch for electro-magnetic fan or motor driven fan	50C	Switch lighting
9A	Thermal switch in water circuit for electro-magnetic fan	51A	Console lighting
10	Horn	53	Front door light switch
11	Headlight relay	53A	Rear door light switch
12	Battery	54	Vehicle interior lights
12A	Battery cut-out terminal	55	Handbrake tell-tale switch
13	Starter	56	Hazard warning switch
15	Water temperature transmitter	57	Sliding roof panel switch
15A	Water temperature thermostat	57A	Sliding roof panel motor
15B	Water temperature tell-tale switch or water temperature tell-tale	57B	Sliding roof panel max travel cut-out
		57C	Sliding roof panel safety cut-out
16	Brake fluid reservoir	58	Ignition/anti-theft lock
17	Stoplight switch	63	Direction indicator/horn dual purpose switch
18	Reversing light switch	64	Boot or tailgate light
21	Regulator	64A	Boot or tailgate light switch
22	Ignition coil	65	Fuel tank unit, with or without reserve fuel tell-tale switch
22A	Coil relay	65A	Fuel tank unit external resistor
22B	Coil resistor	66	Rear number plate light
23	Distributor	67	Reversing lights
24	Front screen wiper	68	Stoplights
24A	Screen wiper relay	68B	Stop and sidelights (twin filament)
24B	Screen wiper timer	69	Rear direction indicators
24C	Rear window wiper	70	Rear lights
25	Front screen washer pump	71	Tailgate light switch
25A	Rear window washer pump	90	Rear foglights
26	Car heater blower	90A	Rear foglights
26B	Car heater blower switch	90B	Rear foglights tell-tale
27	Heater blow switch, or rheostat	91	Relay
27A	Rheostat resistors or heater blower resistor	92	Terminal
29	Heated rear window switch	93	Multiple junction box
29A	Heated rear window	94	Conductive tailgate stay
30	Screen wash/wipe switch	95	Brake pressure switch
30A	Rear window wash/wipe switch	96	Brake pedal travel switch
31	Direction indicator unit	100	Oil pressure drop warning light
32	Lights-screen wash/wipe dual purpose switch	104	Main feed tell-tale
33	Headlight flasher relay	104A	Main feed tell-tale switch
34	Sidelights	105	Ventilation fan
35	Cigarette lighter	105A	Ventilation fan switch
36	Clock	107	Socket
37	Direction indicators tell-tale	109	Thermostat
38	Fuel gauge	110	Pressure switch
39	Headlights tell-tale	+P	Continuous feed
40	Hazard warning tell-tale	+aa	Feed to accessories
41	Tachometer	+ac	Feed after switch-on

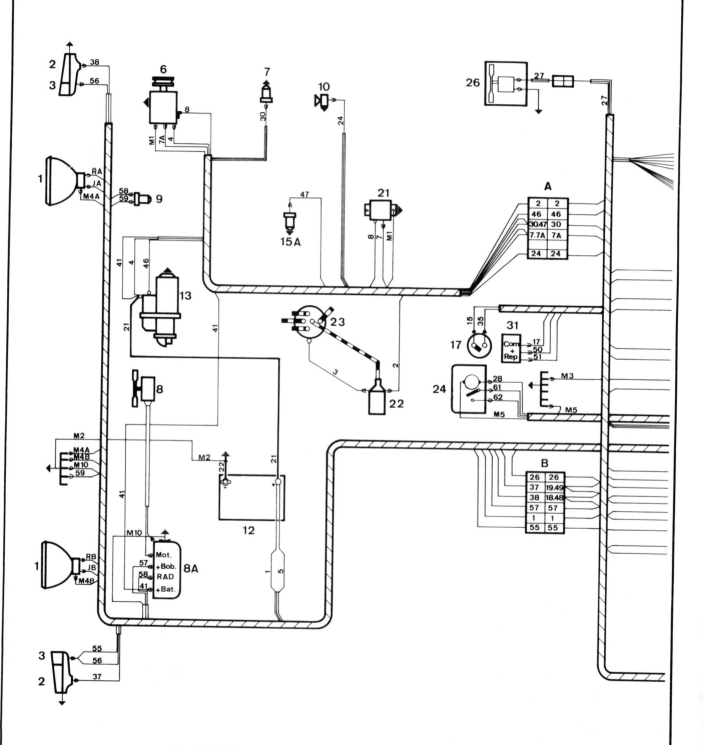

Fig. 9.10 Wiring diagram for 104 Saloon from start to 5 066 973

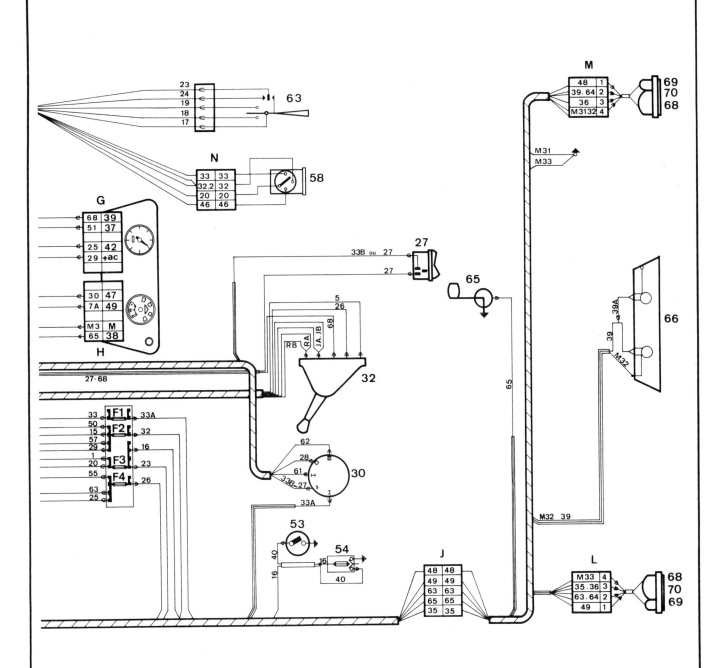

Fig. 9.10 Wiring diagram for 104 Saloon from start to 5 066 973 (continued)

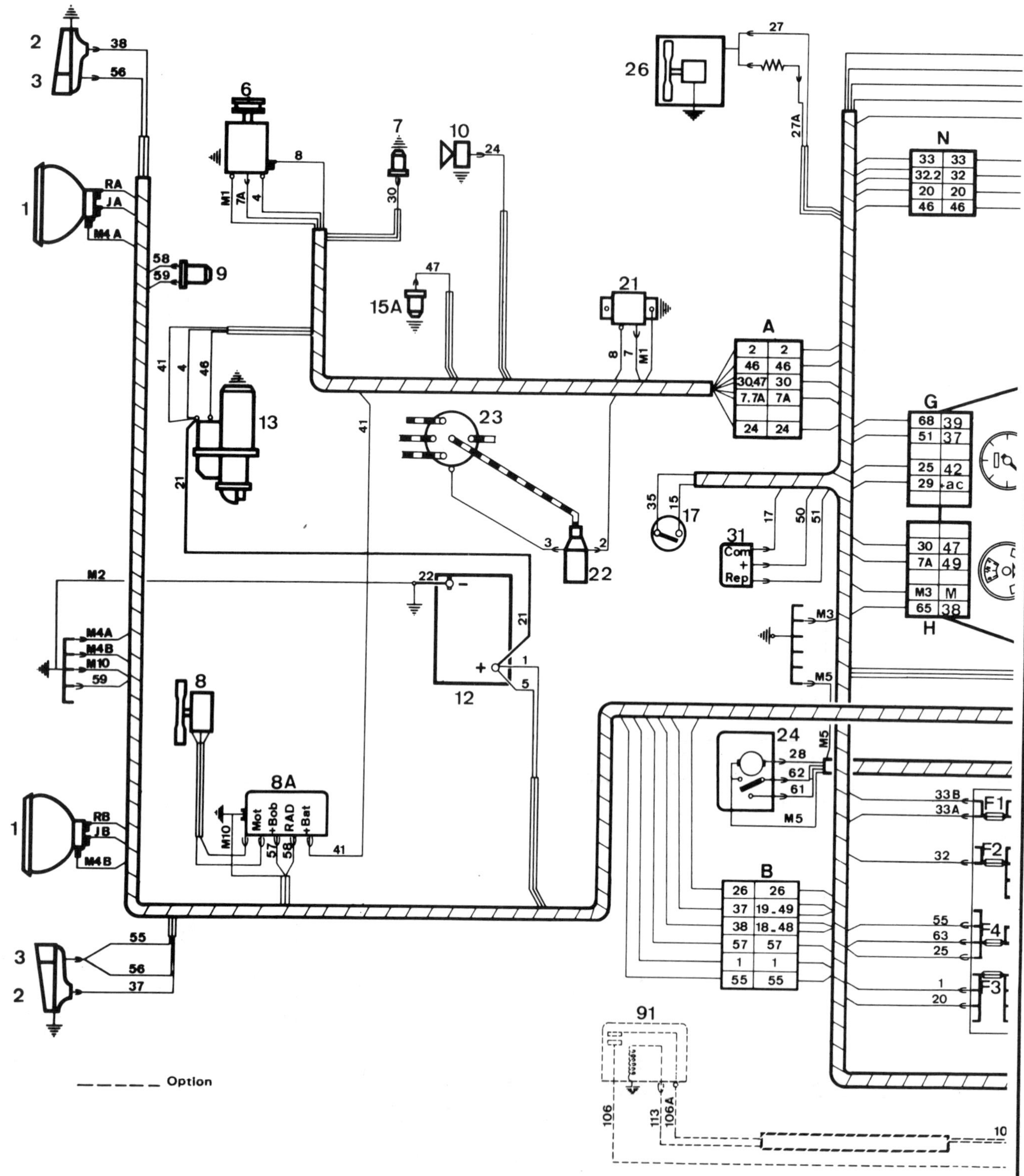

N

33	33
32.2	32
20	20
46	46

A

2	2
46	46
30,47	30
7,7A	7A
24	24

G

68	39
51	37
25	42
29	ac

H

30	47
7A	49
M3	M
65	38

B

26	26
37	19.49
38	18.48
57	57
1	1
55	55

— — — — Option

Fig. 9.11 Wiring diagram for 104 Saloon from 5 066 974 to 5 200 500

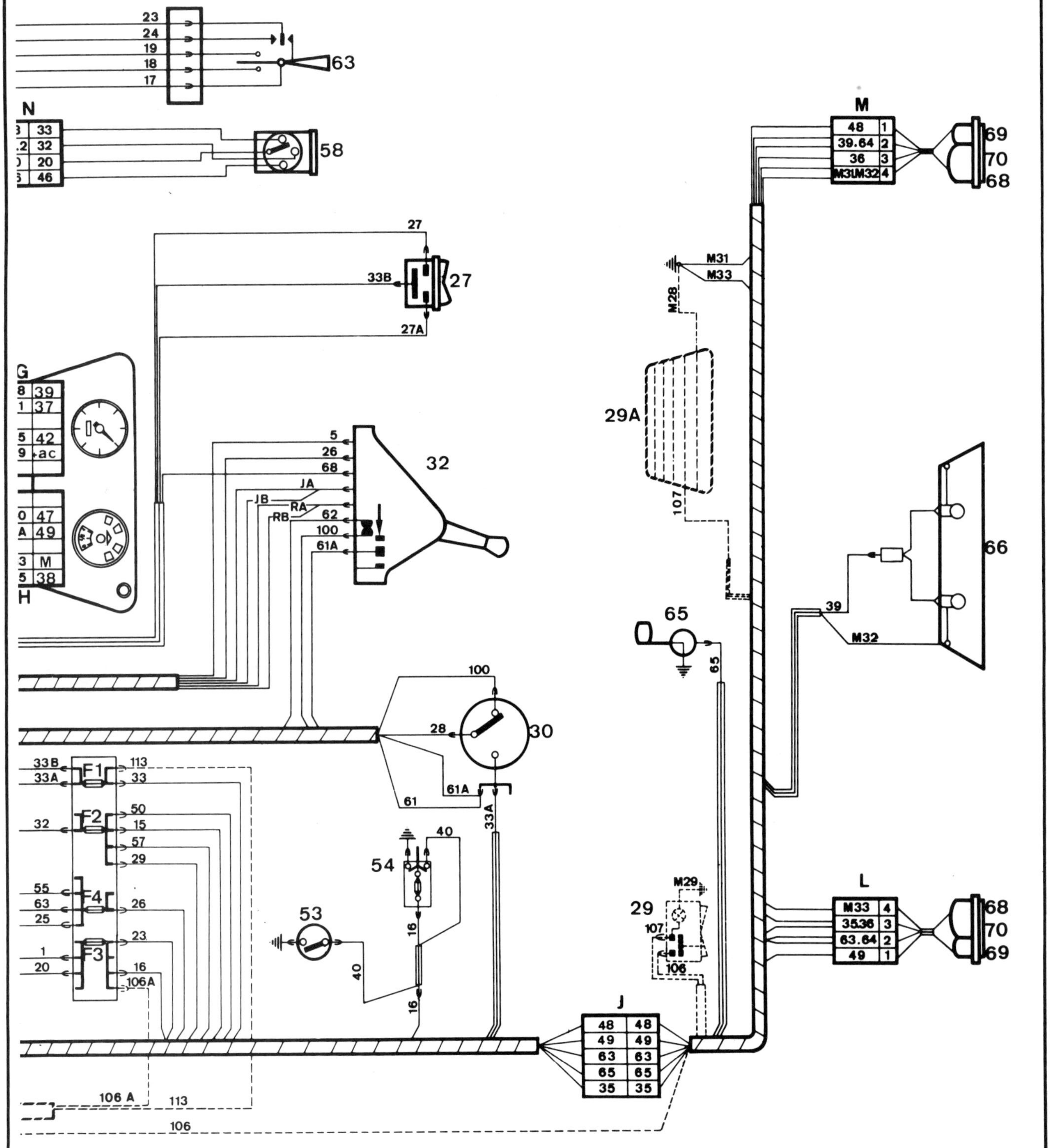

Fig. 9.11 Wiring diagram for 104 Saloon from 5 066 974 to 5 200 500 (continued)

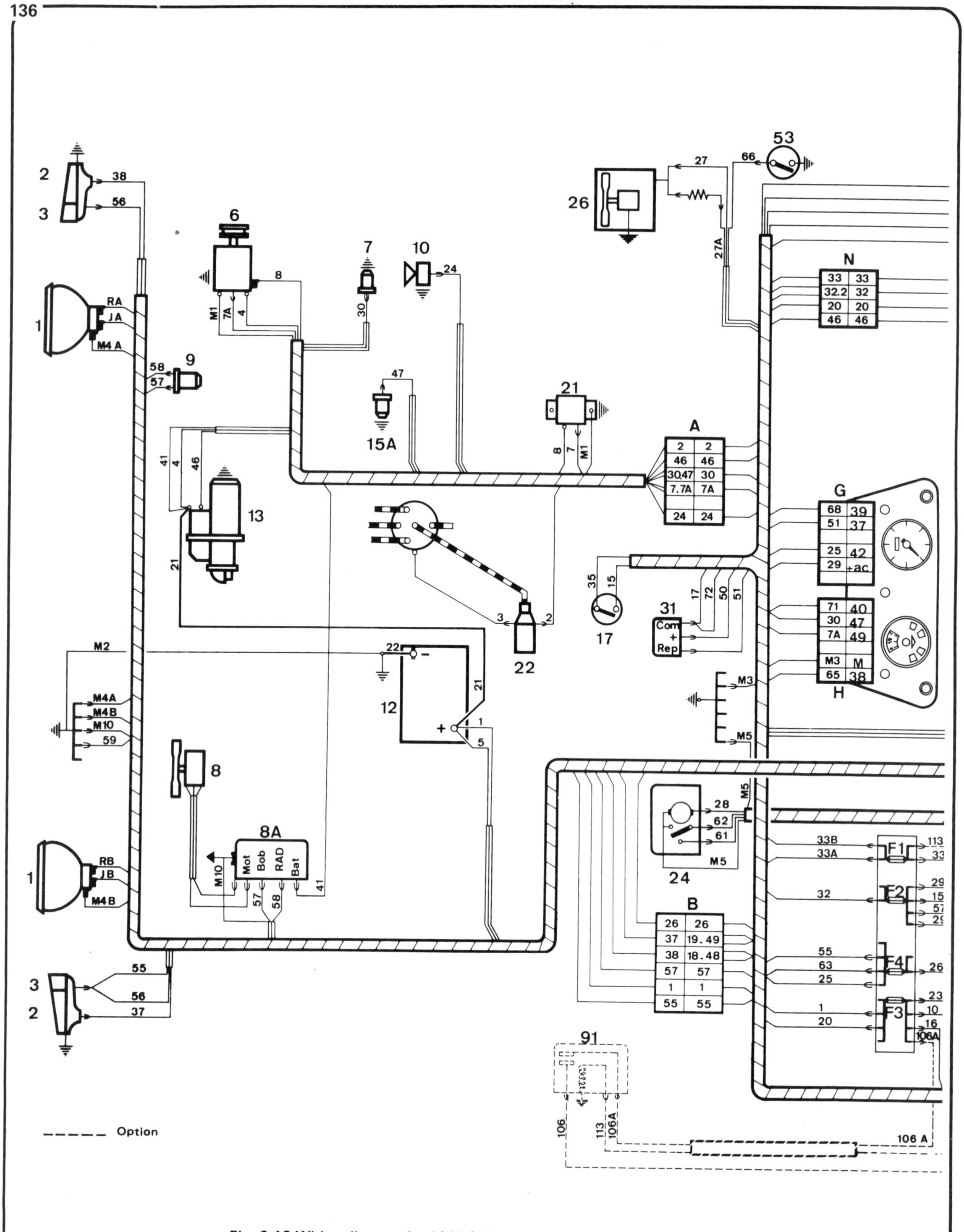

Fig. 9.12 Wiring diagram for 104L Saloon from 5 200 501 to 5 330 000

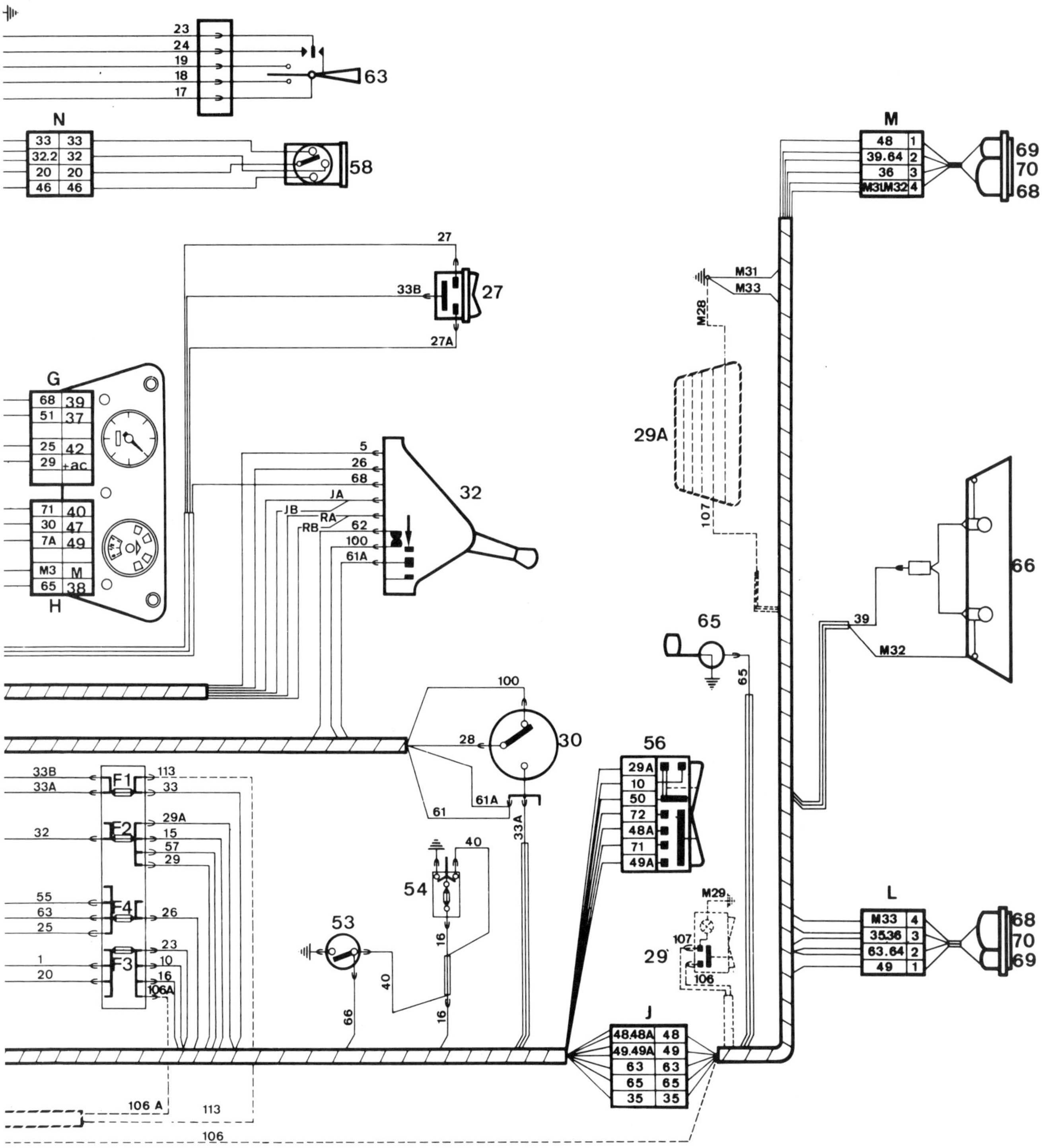

Fig. 9.12 Wiring diagram for 104L Saloon from 5 200 501 to 5 330 000 (continued)

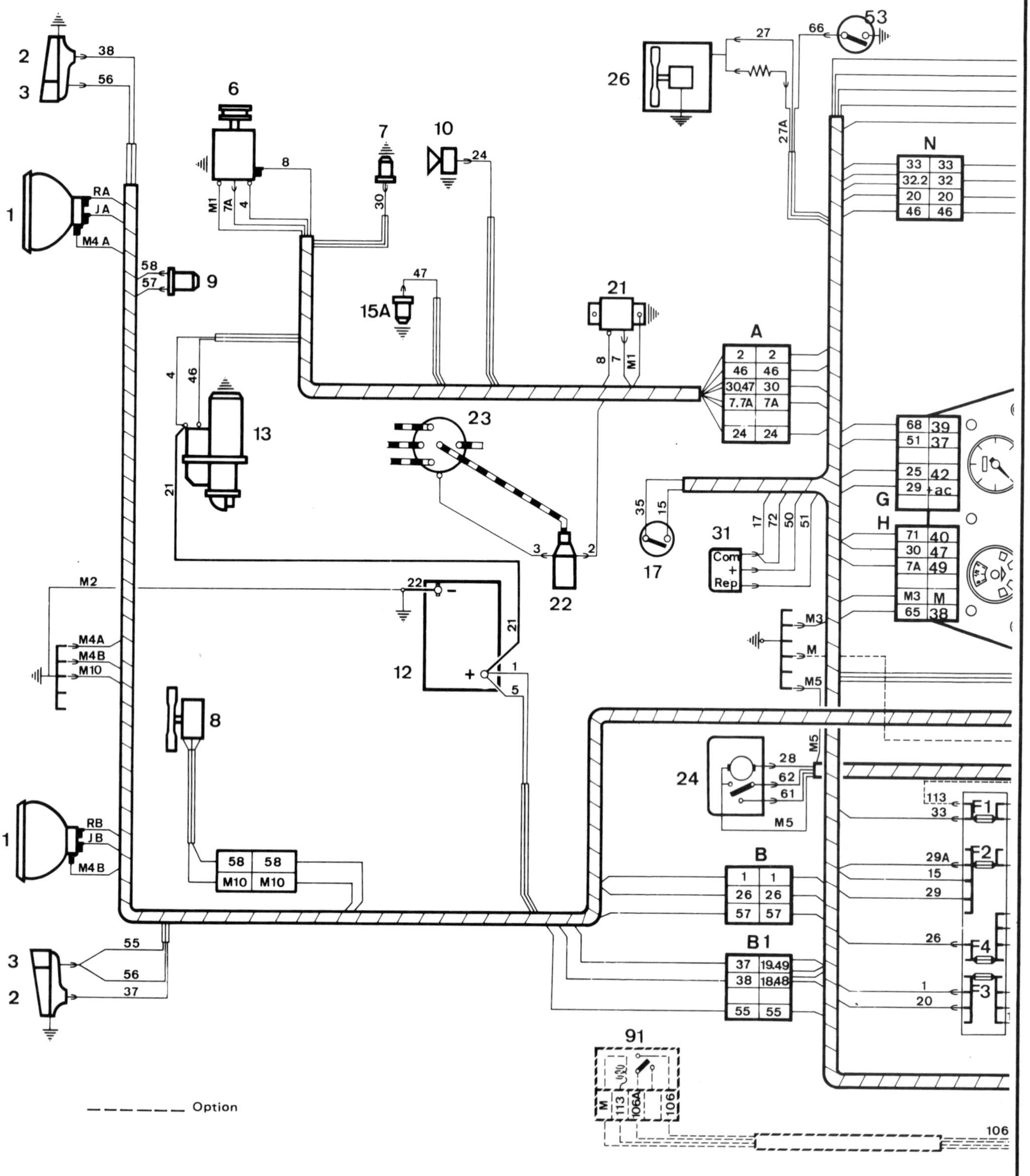

138

Fig. 9.13 Wiring diagram for 104L Saloon from 5 330 001 to 5 465 000

- - - - - Option

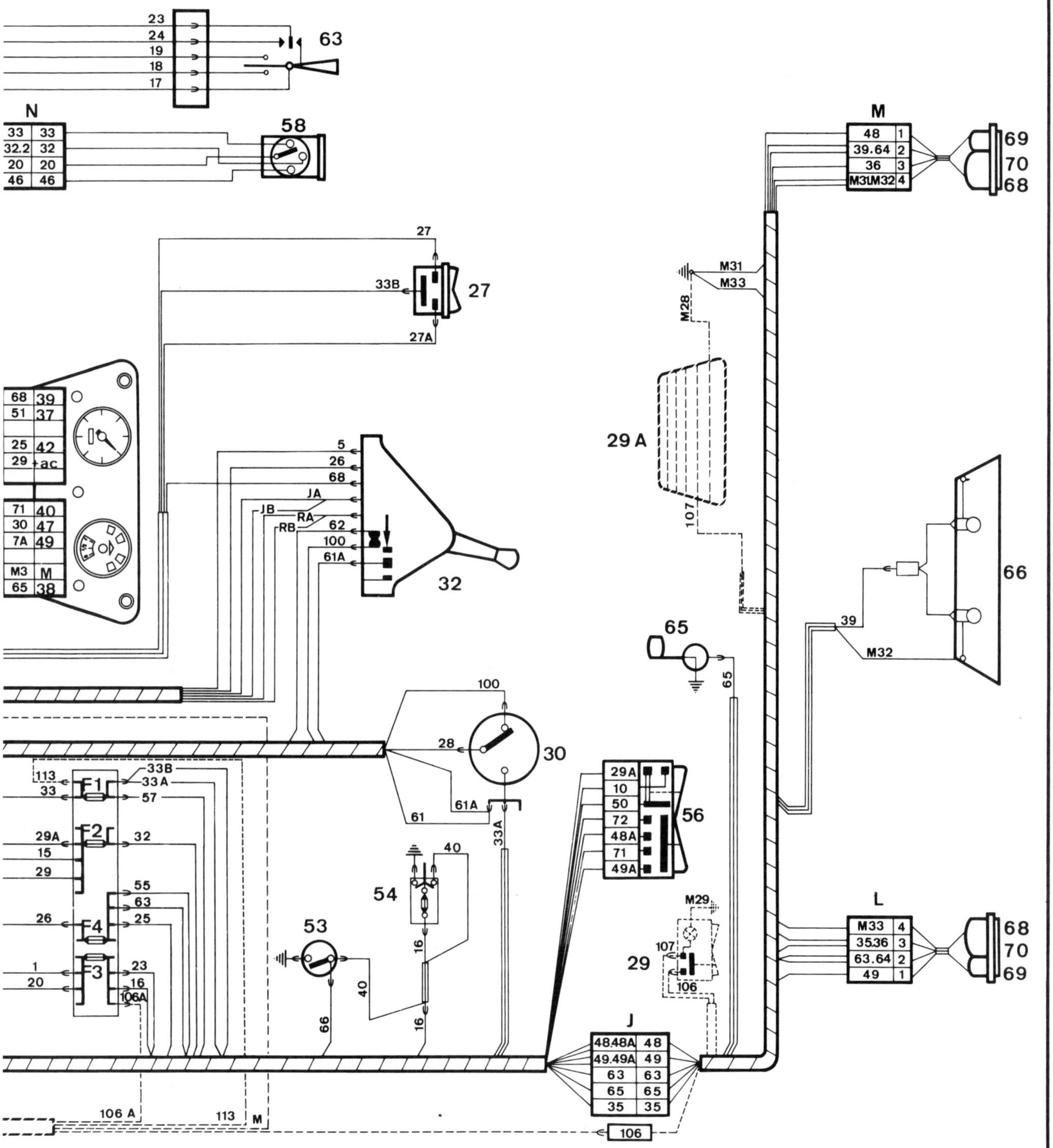

Fig. 9.13 Wiring diagram for 104L Saloon from 5 330 001 to 5 465 000 (continued)

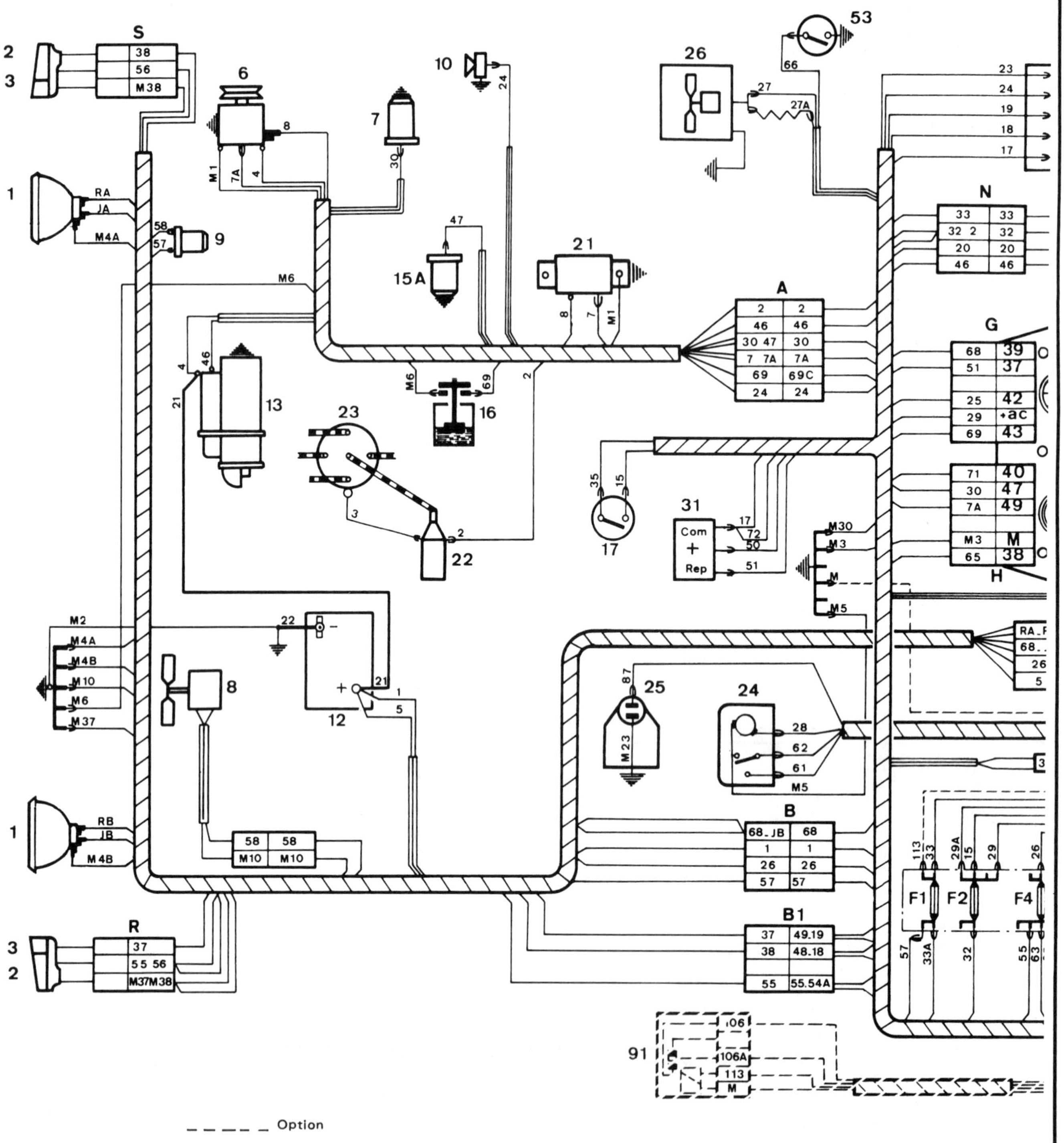

Fig. 9.14 Wiring diagram for 104GL/GL6 Saloon from 5 465 001 and from 7 000 001

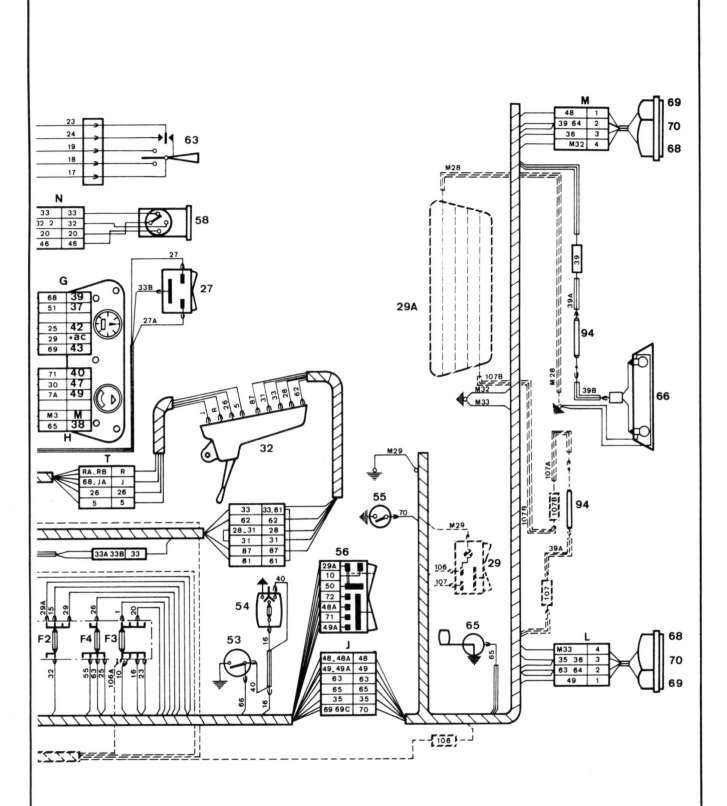

Fig. 9.14 Wiring diagram for 104GL/GL6 Saloon from 5 465 001 and from 7 000 001 (continued)

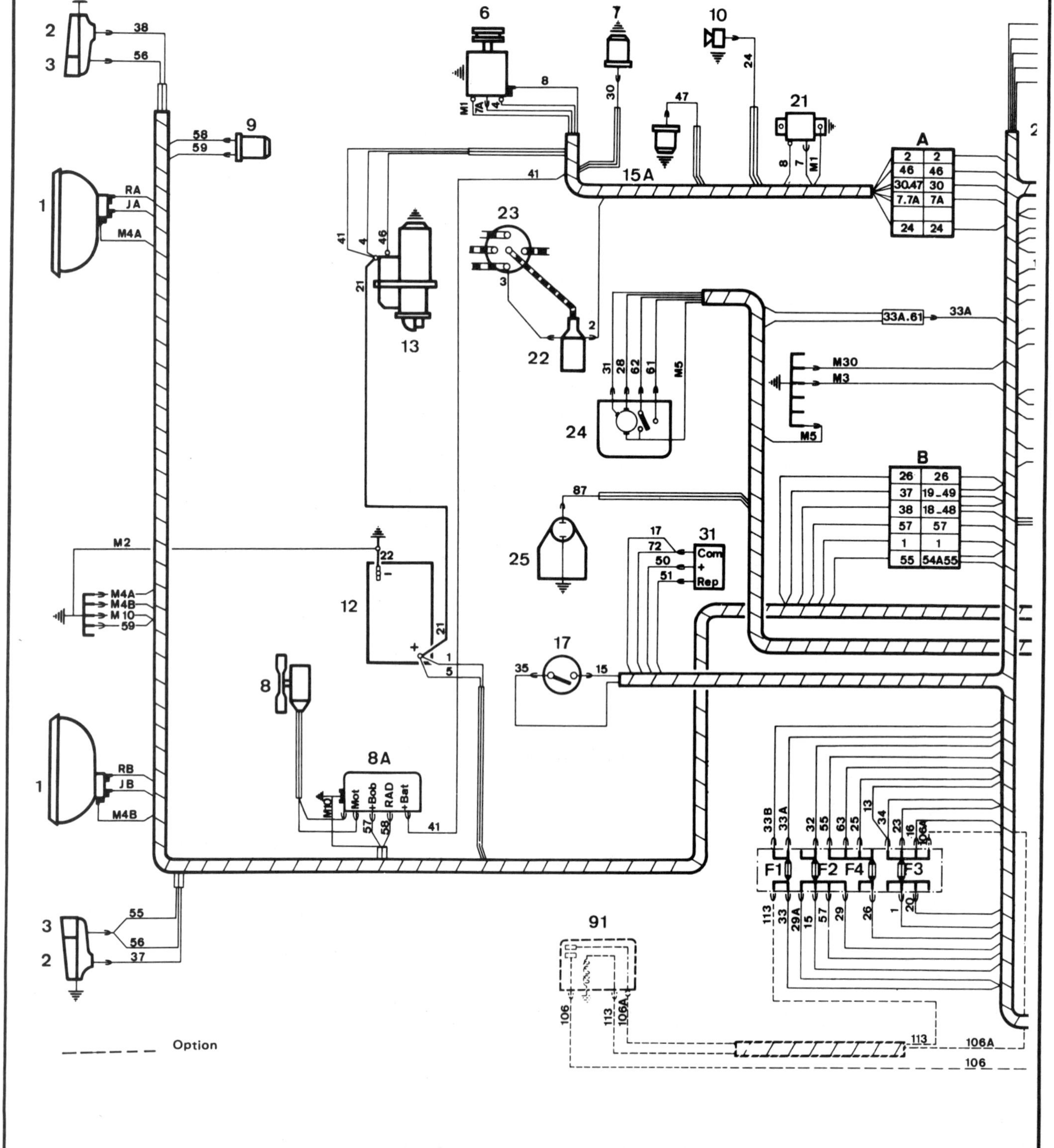

Fig. 9.15 Wiring diagram for 104GL Saloon from 5 200 501 to 5 330 000

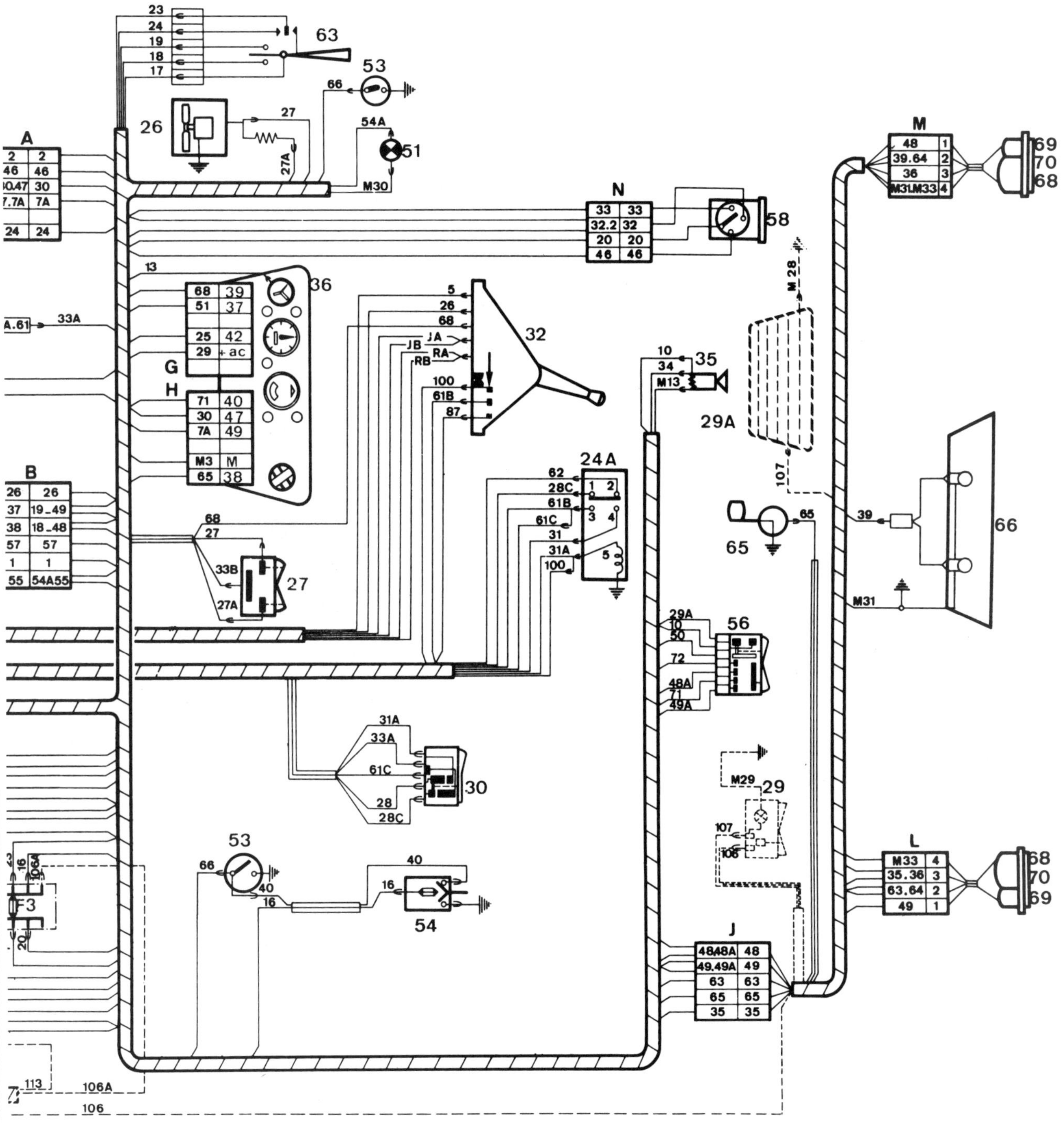

Fig. 9.15 Wiring diagram for 104GL Saloon from 5 200 501 to 5 330 000 (continued)

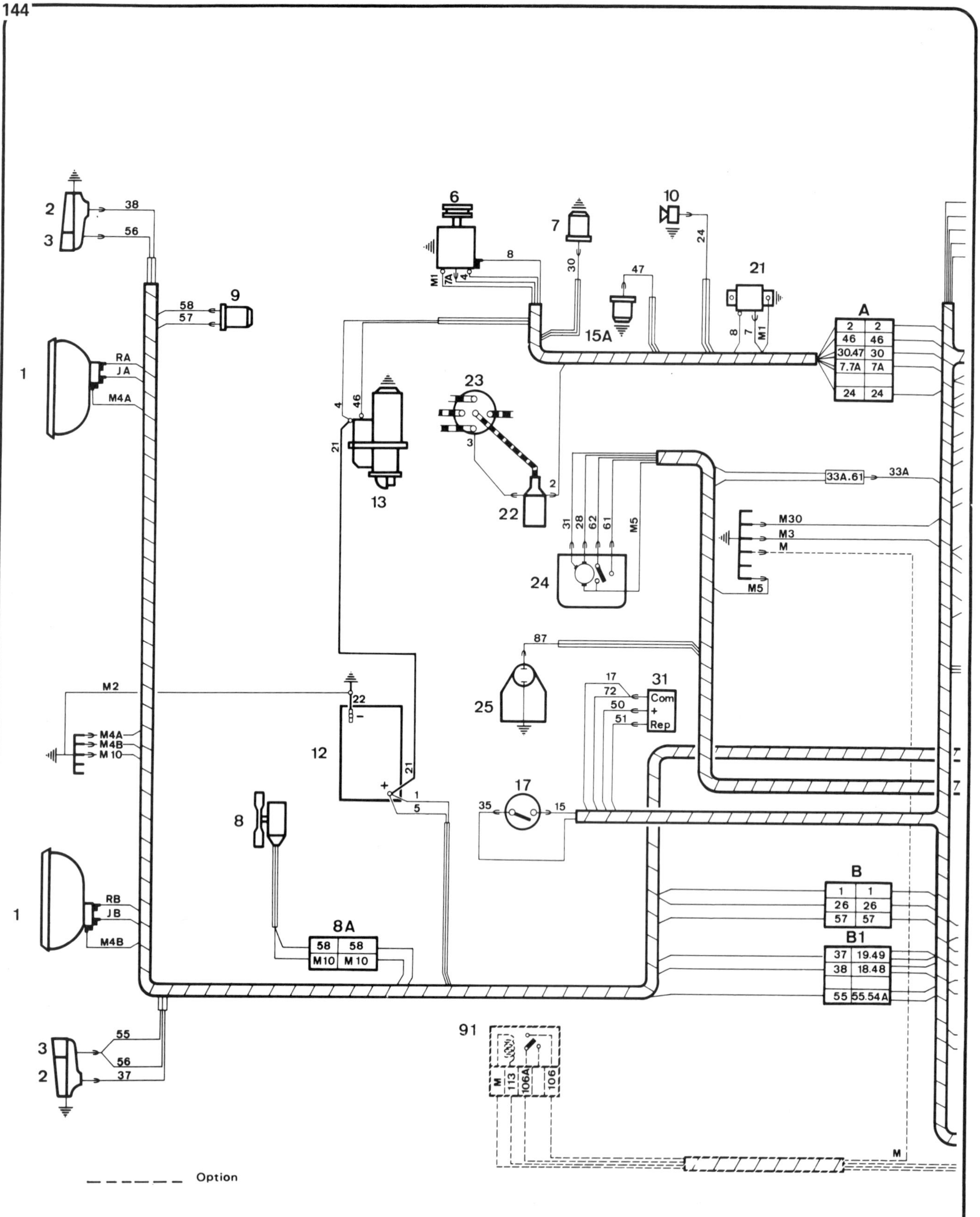

Fig. 9.16 Wiring diagram for 104GL Saloon from 5 330 001 to 5 465 000

145

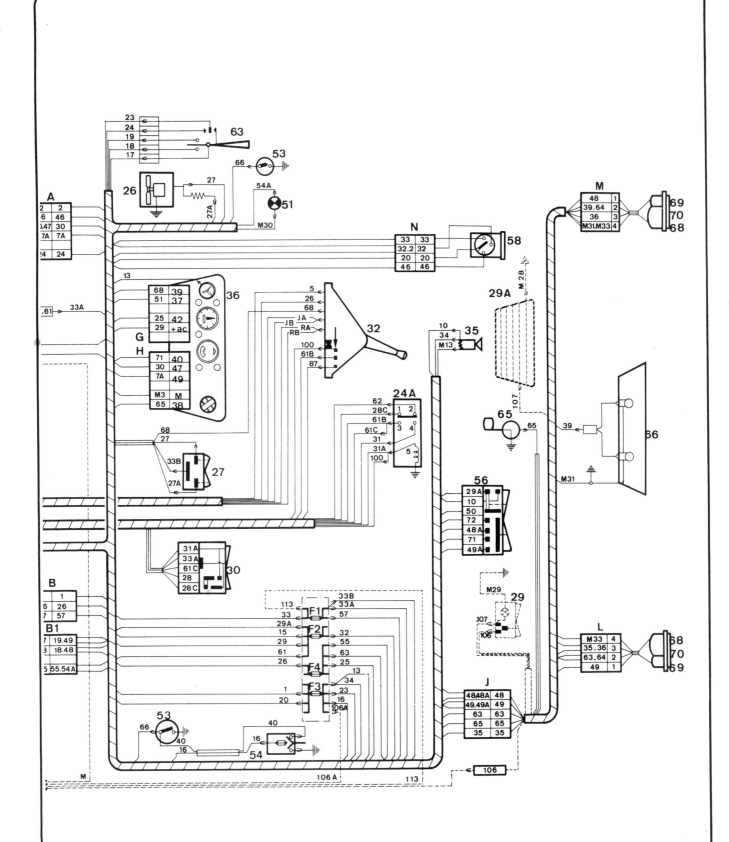

Fig. 9.16 Wiring diagram for 104GL Saloon from 5 330 001 to 5 465 000 (continued)

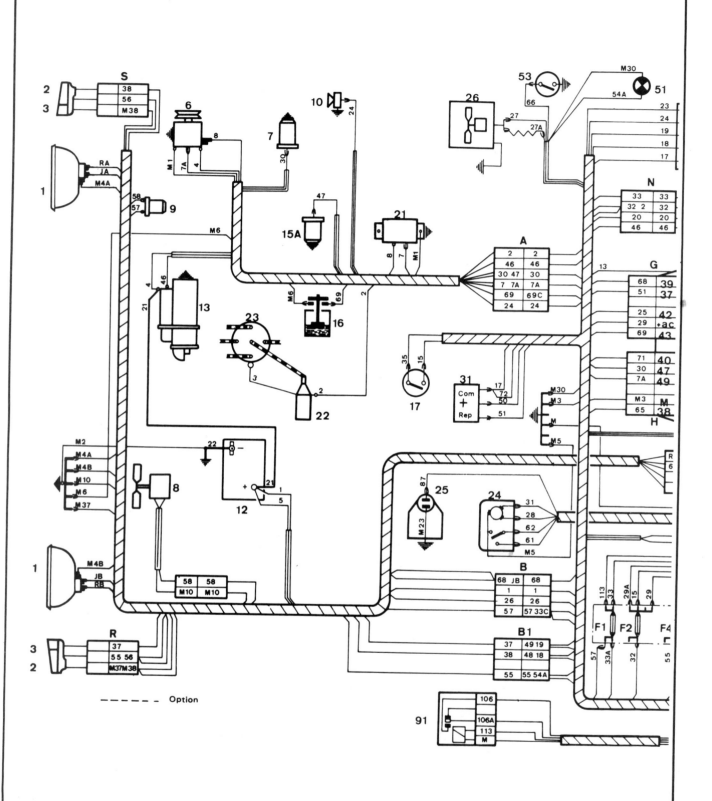

Fig. 9.17 Wiring diagram for 104SL Saloon from 7 000 001

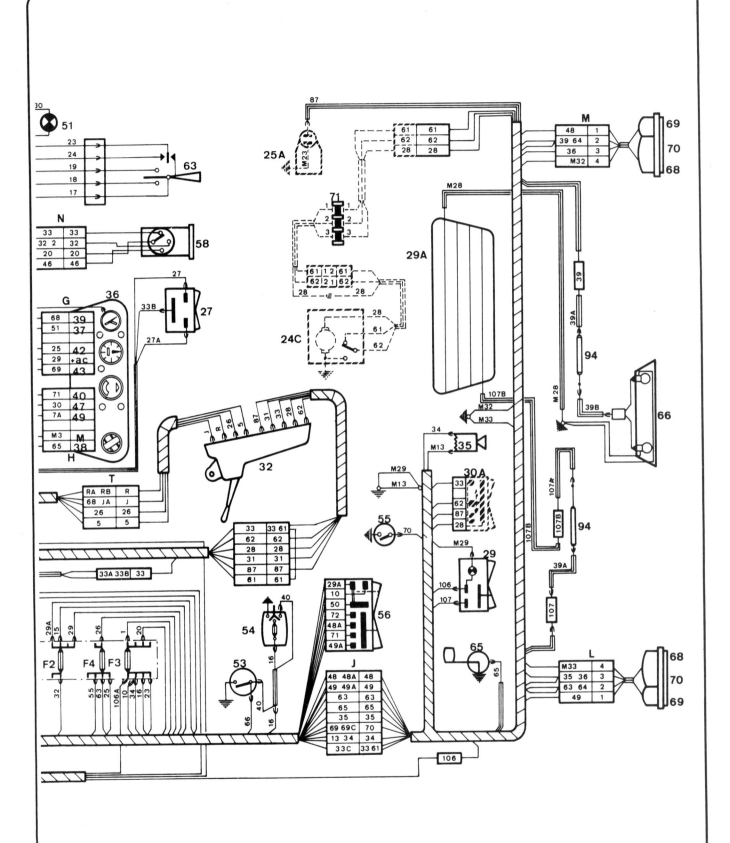

Fig. 9.17 Wiring diagram for 104SL Saloon from 7 000 001 (continued)

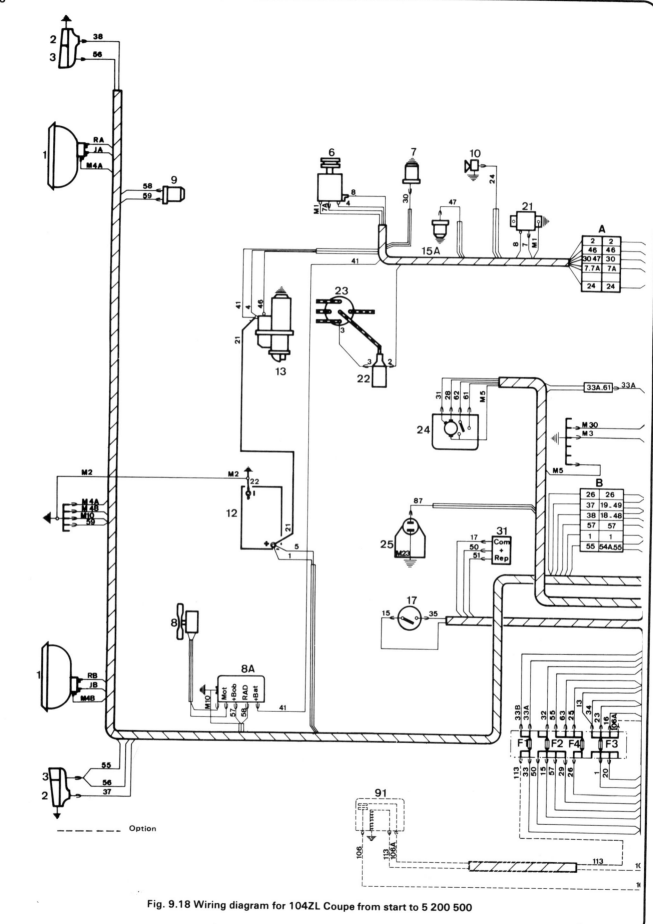

Fig. 9.18 Wiring diagram for 104ZL Coupe from start to 5 200 500

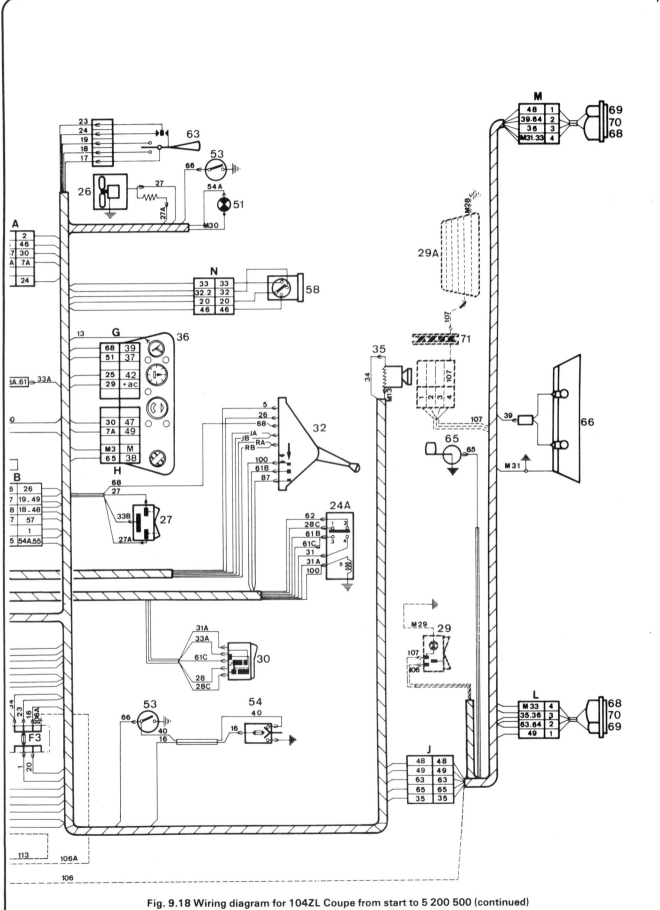

Fig. 9.18 Wiring diagram for 104ZL Coupe from start to 5 200 500 (continued)

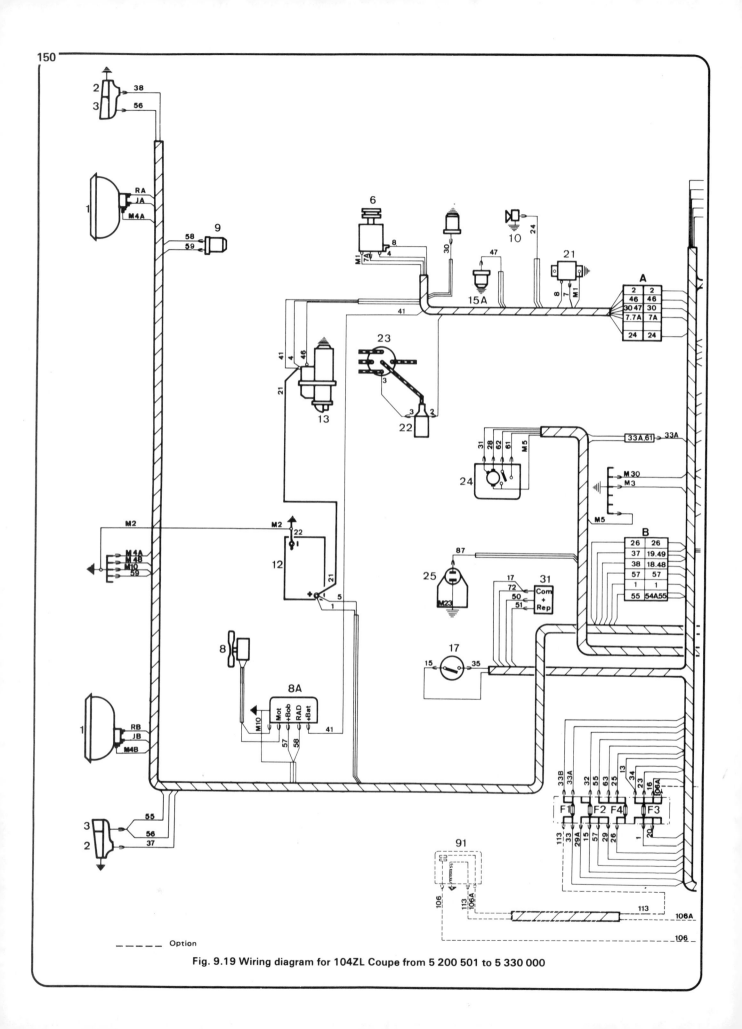

Fig. 9.19 Wiring diagram for 104ZL Coupe from 5 200 501 to 5 330 000

151

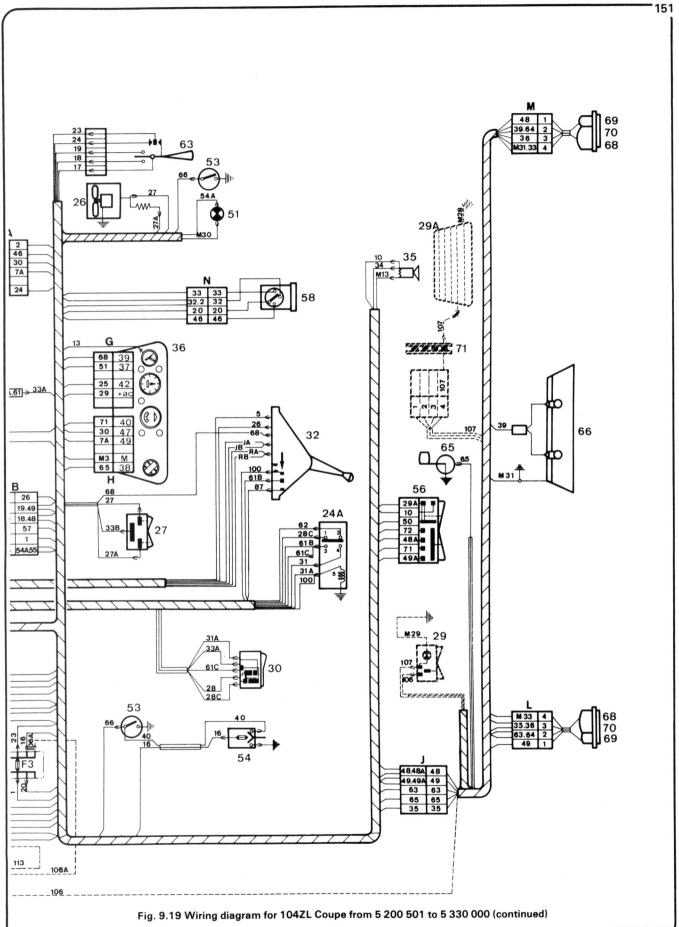

Fig. 9.19 Wiring diagram for 104ZL Coupe from 5 200 501 to 5 330 000 (continued)

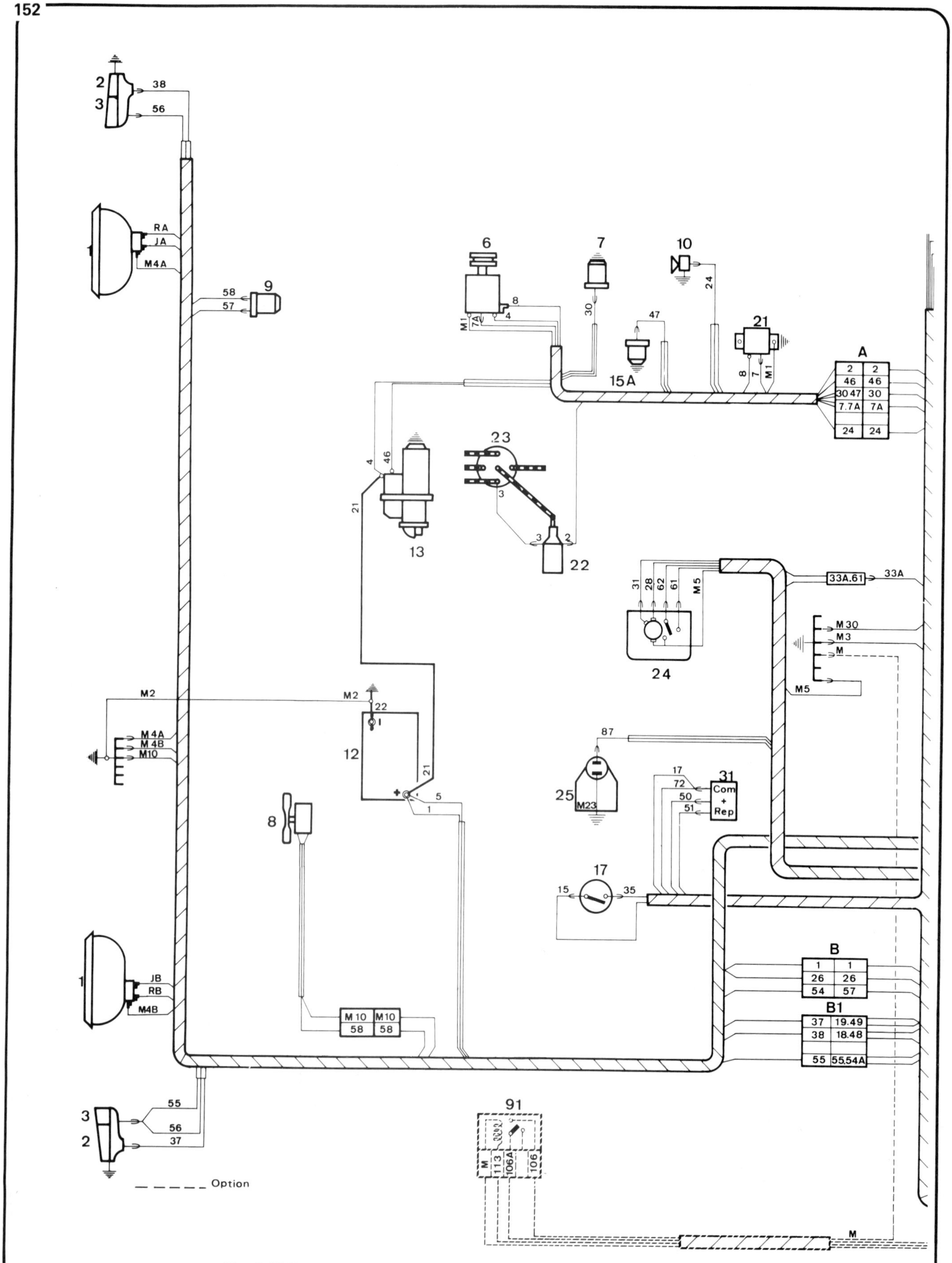

2
3
38
56

RA
JA
M4A

58
57
9

6
7
10

24

M1
7A
4
8

30

47

8
7
M1

21

A

2	2
46	46
30 47	30
7.7A	7A
24	24

15A

4
46

21

13

23

3

3 2

22

31 28 62 61 M5

24

33A.61 33A

M30
M3
M

M5

M2

M2
22

M4A
M4B
M10

12

I

21

8

+
1
5

87

25 M23

17
72
50
51

31
Com
+
Rep

17
15 35

B

1	1
26	26
54	57

B1

37	19.49
38	18.48
55	55.54A

JB
RB
M4B

1

M10 M10
58 58

3
2
55
56
37

91

M
113
106A
106

M

— — — — Option

Fig. 9.20 Wiring diagram for 104ZL Coupe from 5 330 001 to 5 465 000

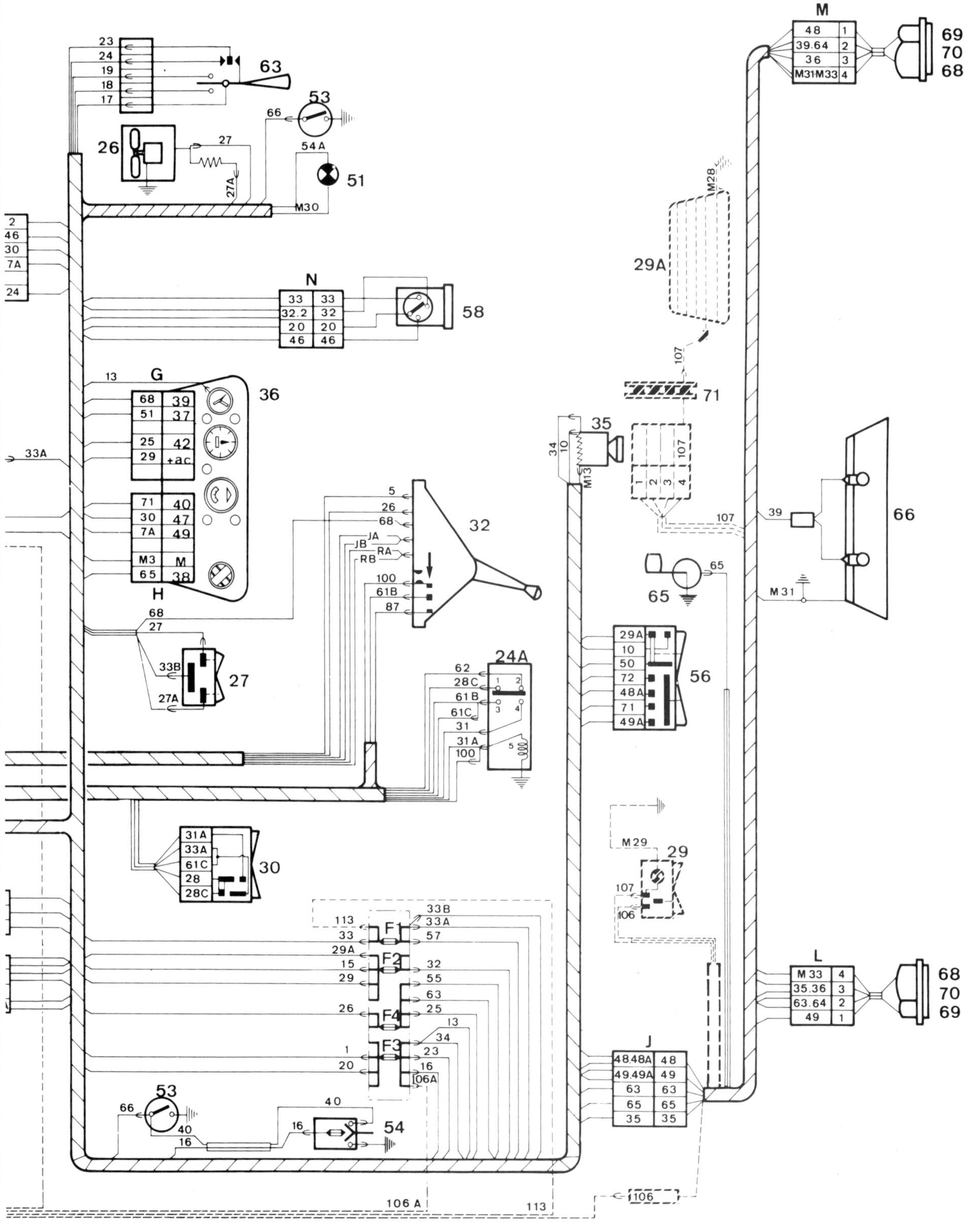

Fig. 9.20 Wiring diagram for 104ZL Coupe from 5 330 001 to 5 465 000 (continued)

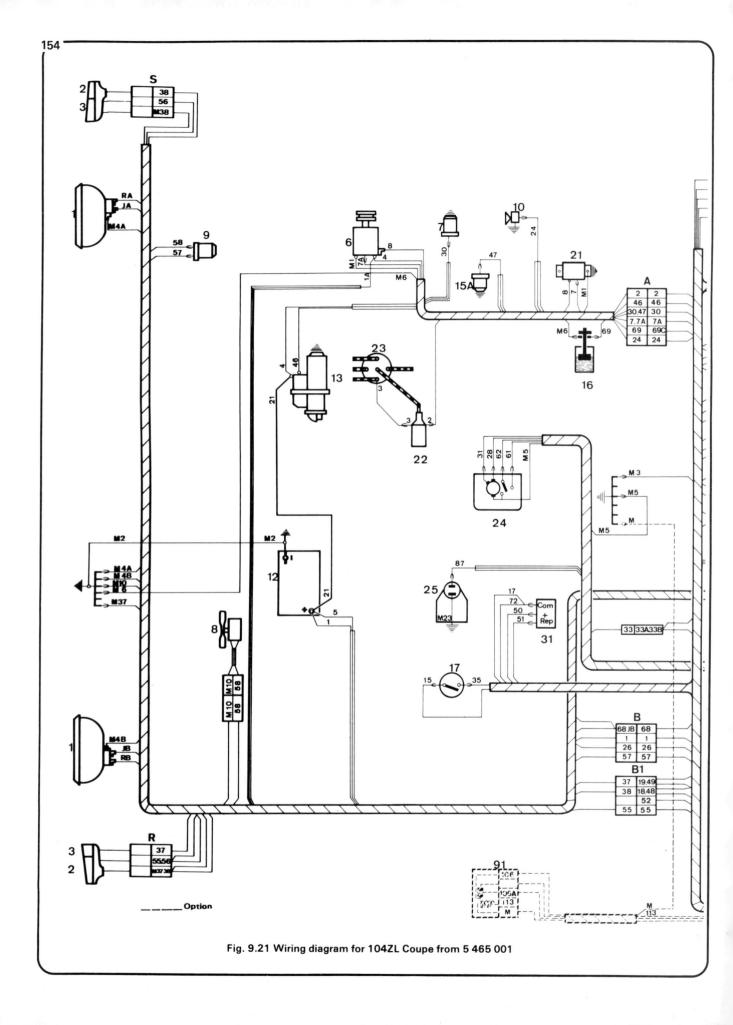

Fig. 9.21 Wiring diagram for 104ZL Coupe from 5 465 001

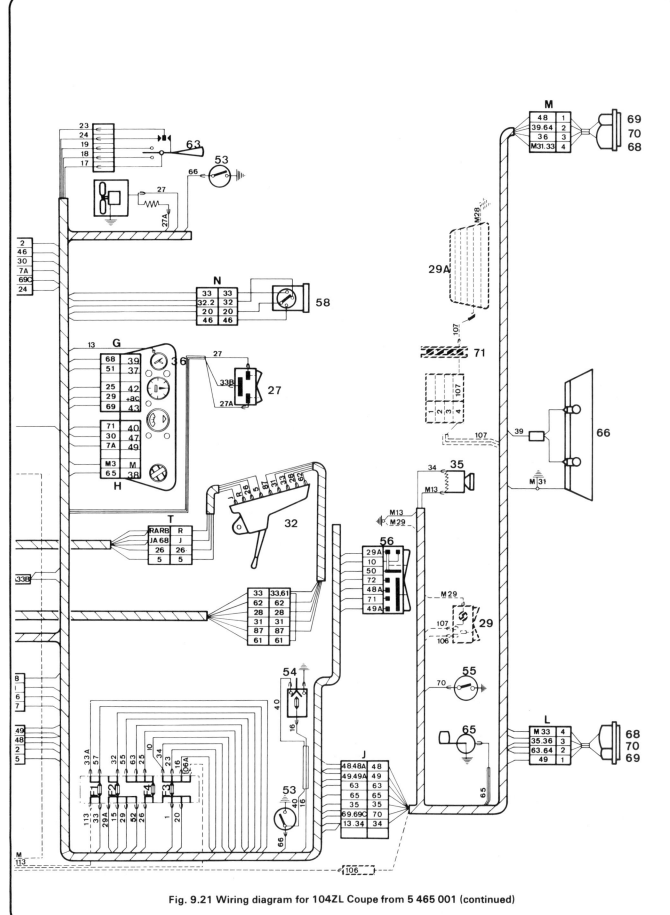

Fig. 9.21 Wiring diagram for 104ZL Coupe from 5 465 001 (continued)

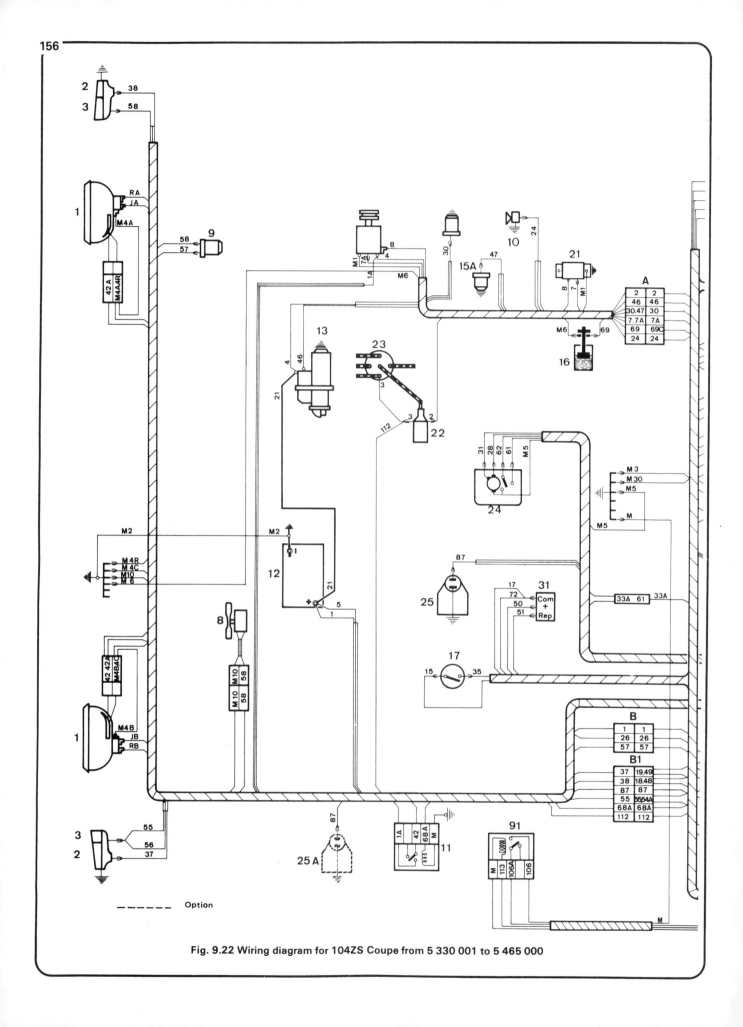

Fig. 9.22 Wiring diagram for 104ZS Coupe from 5 330 001 to 5 465 000

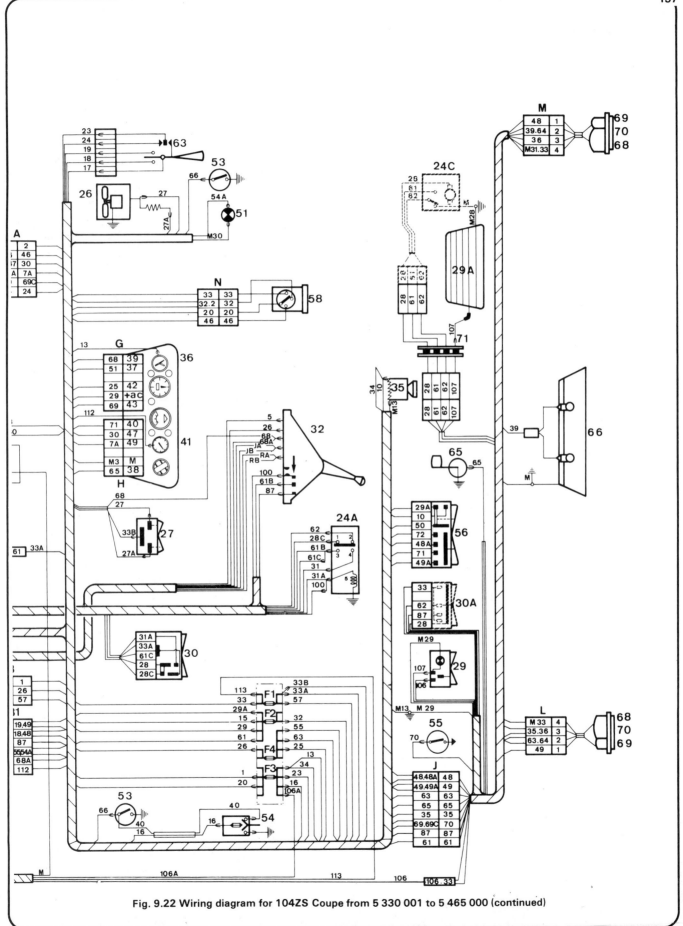

Fig. 9.22 Wiring diagram for 104ZS Coupe from 5 330 001 to 5 465 000 (continued)

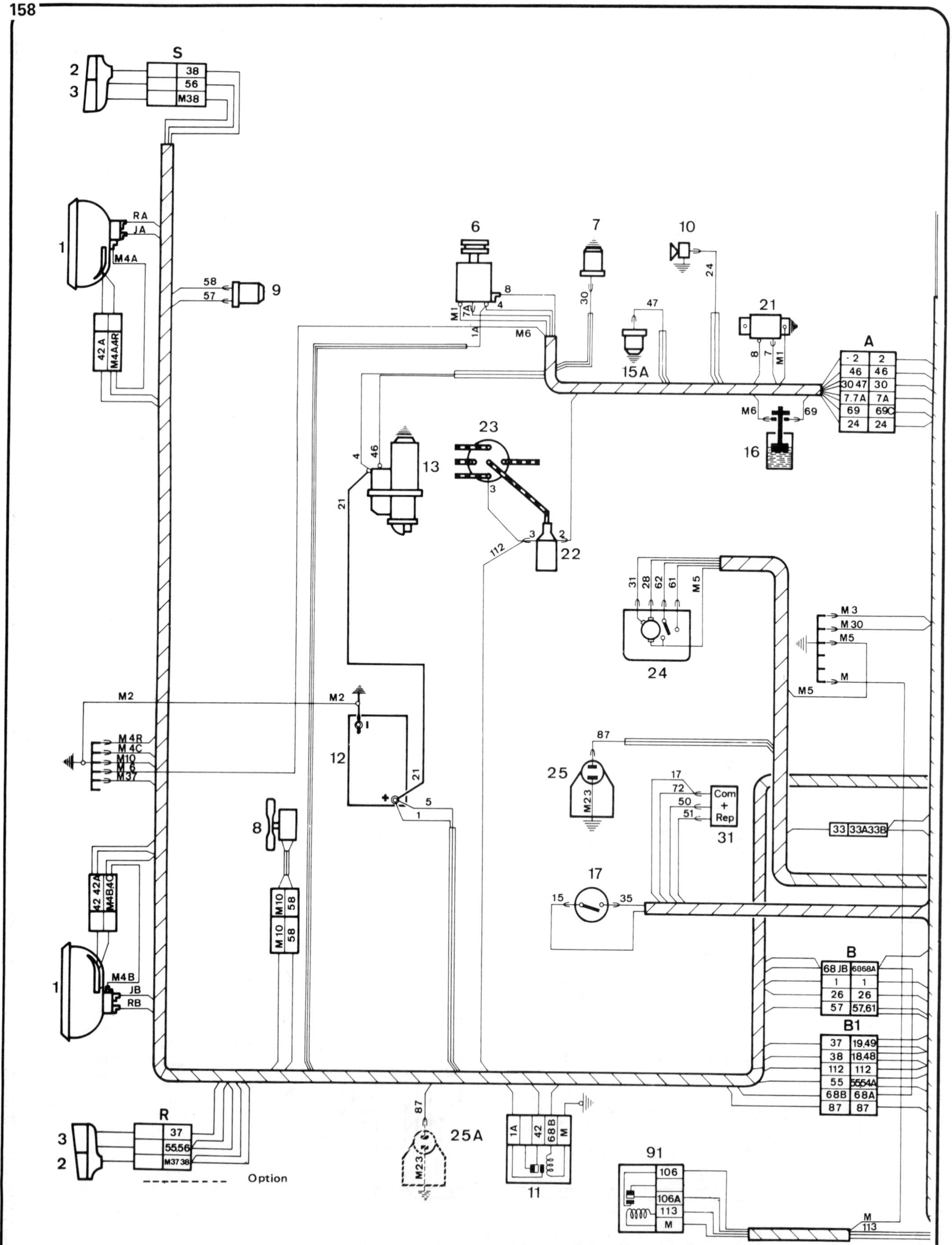

Fig. 9.23 Wiring diagram for 104ZS Coupe from 5 465 001 to 5 554 000

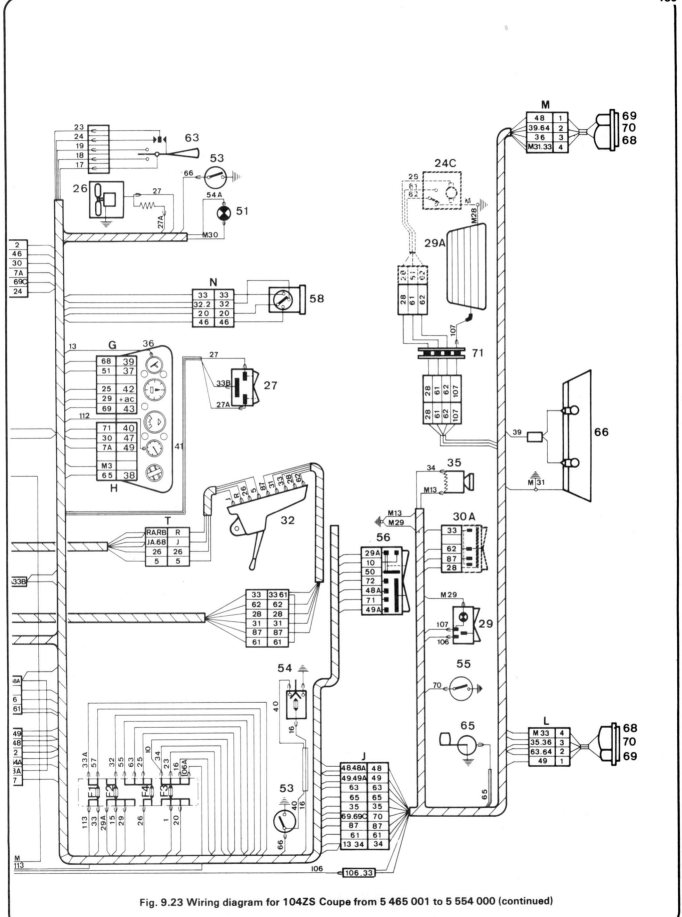

Fig. 9.23 Wiring diagram for 104ZS Coupe from 5 465 001 to 5 554 000 (continued)

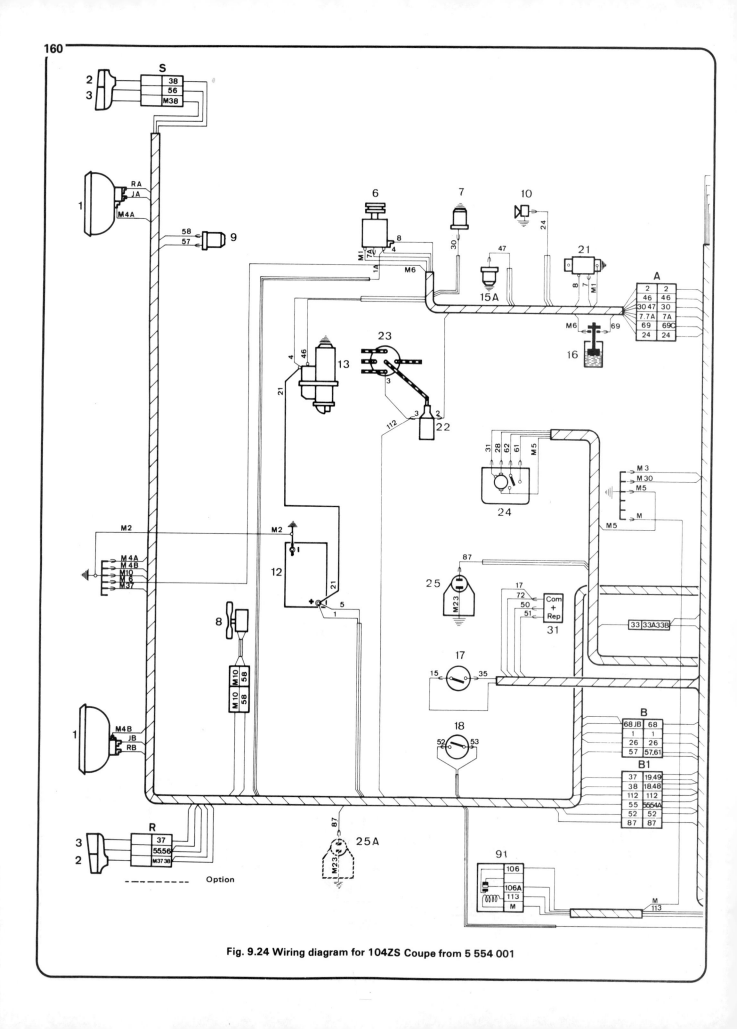

Fig. 9.24 Wiring diagram for 104ZS Coupe from 5 554 001

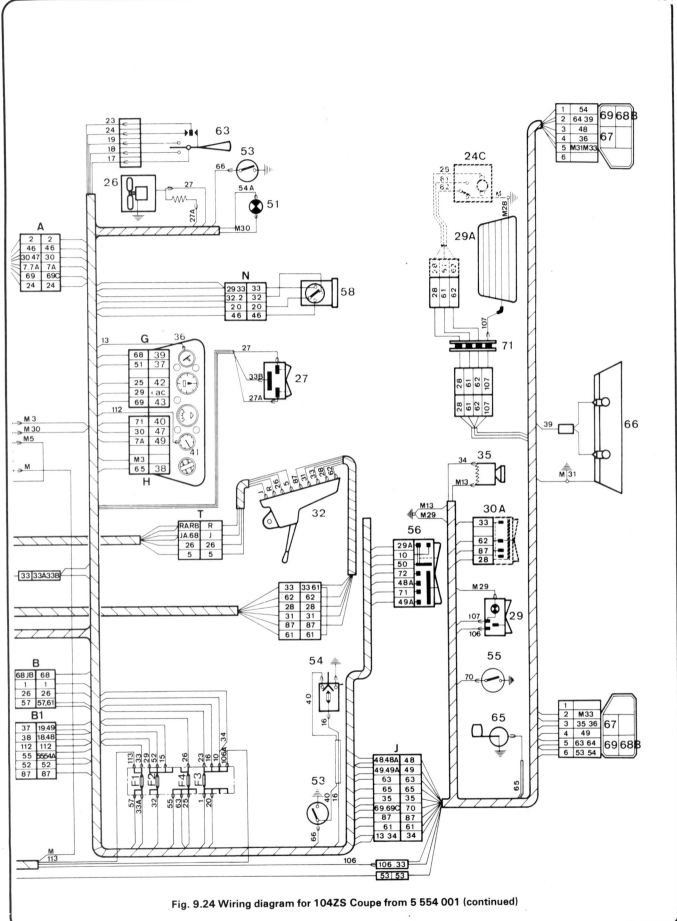

Fig. 9.24 Wiring diagram for 104ZS Coupe from 5 554 001 (continued)

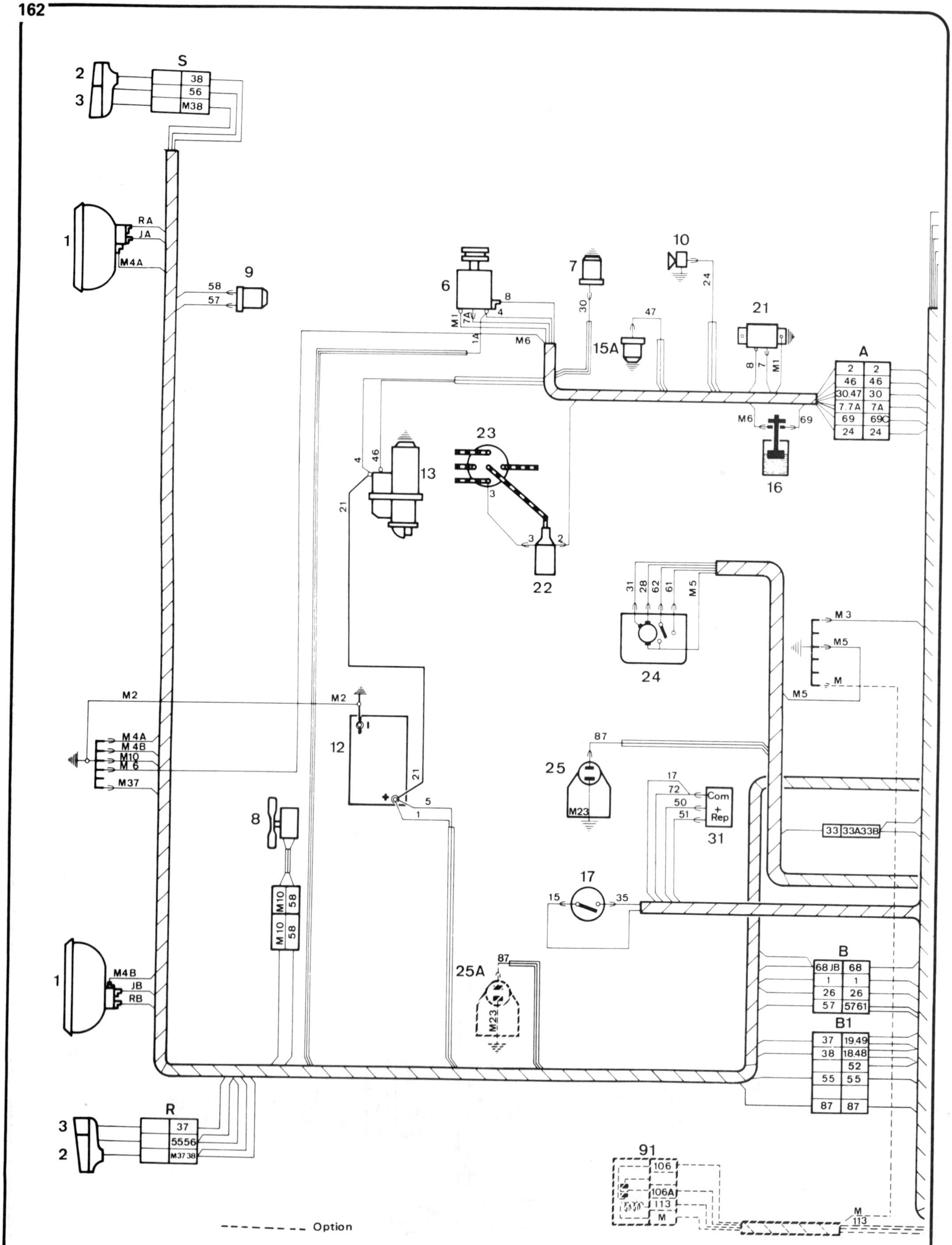

Fig. 9.25 Wiring diagram for 104ZA from start (5 554 008)

- - - - - - Option

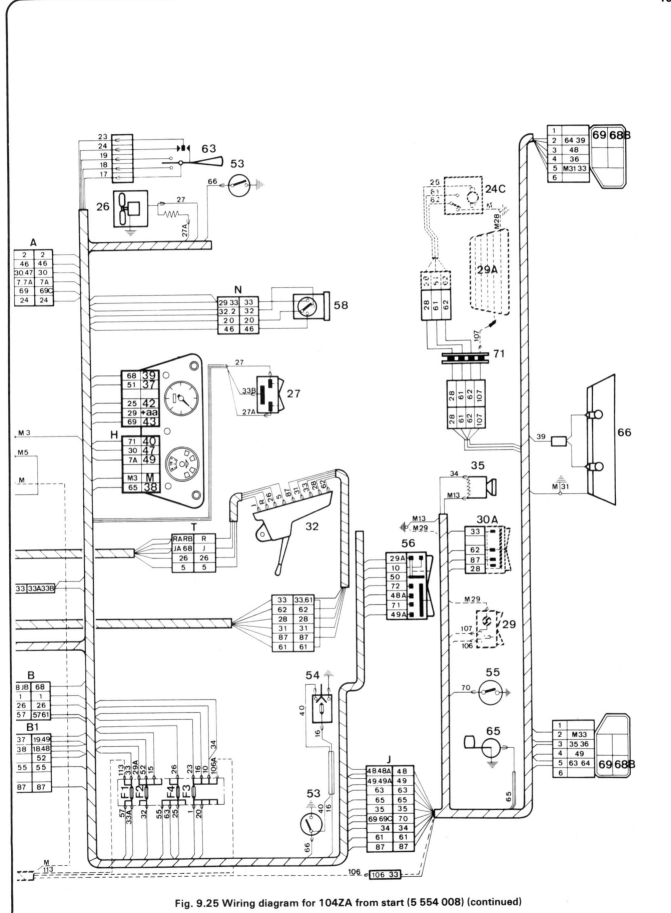

Fig. 9.25 Wiring diagram for 104ZA from start (5 554 008) (continued)

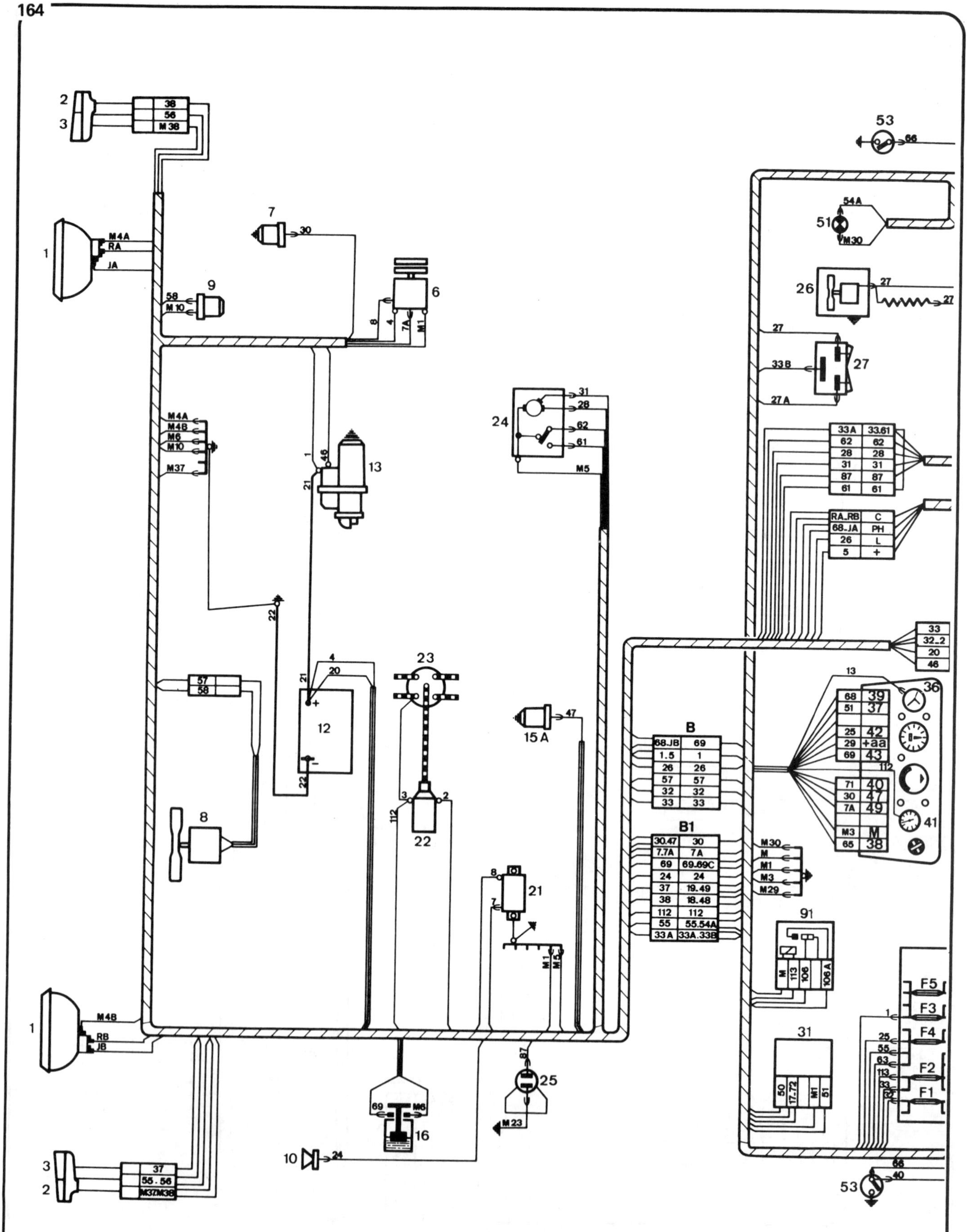

2
3
38
56
M 38

53
66

54A
51
M30

1
M 4A
RA
JA

7
30

6
8
4
7A
M1

26
27
27

9
58
M 10

27
33 B
27 A
27

M 4A
M 4B
M 6
M 10
M 37

1
46
21
13

24
31
28
62
61
M 5

33 A   33.61
62   62
28   28
31   31
87   87
61   61

RA..RB   C
68..JA   PH
26   L
5   +

22

33
32.2
20
46

57
58

4
20
21
12
22

23
23

112   3   2
22

15 A
47

13
36
68   39
51   37
25   42
29   +aa
69   43
112
71   40
30   47
7A   49
M3   M
65   38

8

B
68.JB   69
1.5   1
26   26
57   57
32   32
33   33

B1
30.47   30
7.7A   7A
69   69.69C
24   24
37   19.49
38   18.48
112   112
55   55.54A
33 A   33A.33B

M30
M
M1
M3
M29

91
M   113   106   106 A

31
50
17.72   M1   51

F5
F3
F4
F2
F1

1
25
55
63
113
33
62

8   21
7
M 1
M 5

87
25
M 23

69   M6
16
10   24

66
53   40

3
2
37
55 . 56
M37M38

1
M 4B
RB
JB

Fig. 9.26 Wiring diagram for 104S from start in 1978

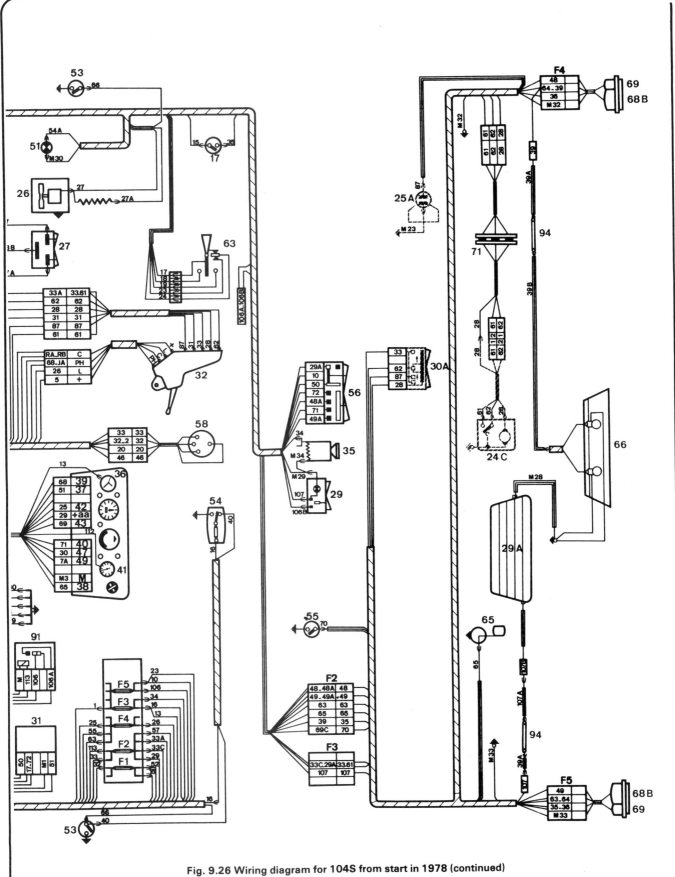

Fig. 9.26 Wiring diagram for 104S from start in 1978 (continued)

Chapter 10 Suspension and steering

Contents

Specifications

Front suspension
Type . . . . Independent, coil springs and MacPherson struts, with anti-roll bar

Rear suspension
Type . . . . Independent trailing arms, coil springs and MacPherson struts. Anti-roll bar on ZS models

Rear wheel toe-in:
    Saloon . . . . 1.5 to 3.5 mm (0.059 to 0.138 in)
    Coupe . . . . 0.5 to 2.5 mm (0.020 to 0.099 in)
Camber . . . . -0° 30' to -1° 30'

Shock absorbers
Type (front and rear) . . . . Peugeot double-acting telescopic hydraulic. Removable front shock absorbers from 1979 on

Steering
Type . . . . Rack-and-pinion
Reduction ratio 18.38:1
Turning radius (between kerbs) . . . . 4.82 m (15 ft 9¾ in)
Toe-in:
    GL, GL6, S and SL . . . . 1.5 to 3.5 mm (0.059 to 0.138 in)
    ZL, ZS and ZA . . . . 0 to 2 mm (0 to 0.079 in)

Dimensions
Wheelbase:
    GL, GL6, S and SL . . . . 2.42 m (7ft 11.28 in)
    ZL, ZS and ZA . . . . 2.23 m (7 ft 3.79 in)
Track:
    Front . . . . 1.29 in (4ft 2.78 in)
    Rear . . . . 1.24 m (4ft 0.82 in)

Torque wrench settings

	lbf ft	kgf m
Front suspension unit upper attachment nuts	8	1.15
Steering track rod balljoint/suspension unit	25	3.5
Driveshaft/wheel hub nut	180	25
Brake caliper securing bolts	51	7
Wheel retaining nuts	43.5	6
Front anti-roll bar bracket bolts:		
8 mm (early cars)	9	1.25
10 mm (later cars)	33	4.5
Track control arm pivot bolt nut	25	3.5
Anti-roll bar/track control arm nut	40	5.5
Anti-roll bar/track control arm locknut (if fitted)	7	1.0
Rear suspension unit:		
Upper attachment nuts	7	1.0
Lower attachment nut	27	3.75
Lower attachment lockbolt	27	3.75

	lbf ft	kgf m
Rear subframe/chassis nuts	25	3.5
Rear suspension arm pivot nuts	40	5.5
Rear suspension support attachment bolts	23.5	3.25
Steering rack retaining bolts	25	3.5
Track rod balljoint nuts	25	3.5
Track rod clamp bolts (early cars)	12.7	1.75
Track rod locknuts (later cars)	32.5	4.5
Track rod flexible joint bolt (early cars)	25	3.5
Track rod/steering rack balljoint (later cars)	32.5	4.5
Gear lever/steering rack unit pivot bolt	9	1.25
Steering column flexible coupling bolts	10.8	1.5

1 General description

The Peugeot 104 has independent suspension at the front and rear. At the front, MacPherson struts incorporate telescopic double-acting hydraulic shock absorbers and coil springs. The struts are located at the top end within the inner wing panel. At their bottom end the struts are located by the track control arms and the anti-roll bar. The front wheel bearings, steering arm and track control arm mountings, and the brake mountings, are all located in the lower portion of the MacPherson strut.

Single trailing suspension arms are used for each rear wheel, with separate double-acting shock absorbers to control coil spring movement. ZS models also have an anti-roll bar on the rear suspension.

A rack-and-pinion steering unit is fitted, together with a two-piece safety steering column connected by a flexible coupling.

Some of the necessary repair and maintenance work can be undertaken on the suspension and steering by the home mechanic although some special tools, which may possibly be home made, will be necessary. Before starting any such work, read through the instructions and be absolutely sure that you have the knowledge and facilities to finish and have the correct replacement parts for your model. There have been detail changes during production, so ensure that you have the correct replacement part before fitting it. Do not start a job you cannot finish – asking the local Peugeot garage to come out and replace a part which you have removed and find you cannot refit will be very expensive!

All work undertaken on the steering mechanism must be to the highest standard. Always use the right fasteners with the correct locking devices where appropriate. Adjustment must be within

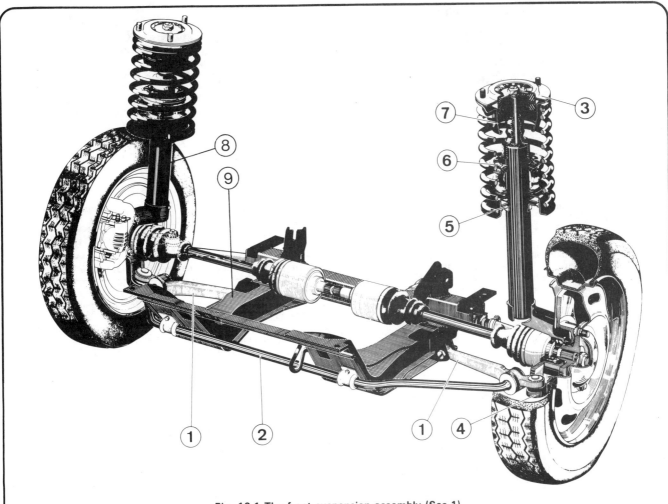

Fig. 10.1 The front suspension assembly (Sec 1)

1	Track control arm	3	Upper mounting	5	Friction ring
2	Anti-roll bar	4	Lower mounting balljoint	6	Rebound stop
				7	Thrust cup

8 Shock absorber/
  suspension unit
9 Subframe

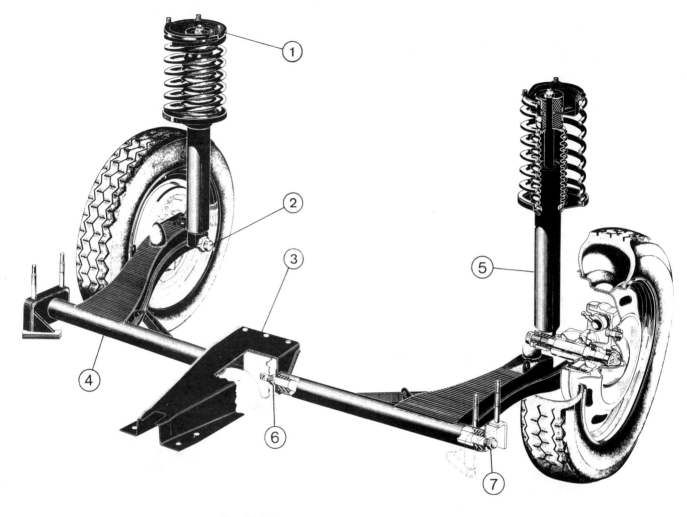

Fig. 10.2 The rear suspension assembly (Sec 1)

1	Upper mounting cup	3	Centre support	5	Shock absorber	7	Outer pivot nut
2	Stub axle	4	Rear suspension arm	6	Inner pivot nut		

specified limits where these apply and spare parts must be new or in faultless condition. Your life, and perhaps the lives of others, could depend on these points and if you are in any doubt at all concerning what to do or how to do it you should get professional advice or have the job done by an expert.

2   Routine maintenance

1   Whilst the maintenance to the steering and suspension components has been reduced to the minimum, it does not mean that it can be ignored completely! A periodic manual and visual inspection should be made.
2   Inspect the suspension joints and their fixings for security and excessive play.
3   Check the steering components and connections for signs of wear and security.
4   Inspect the shock absorbers for looseness in their mountings – look at the top and bottom rubber bushes and check for leakage of the unit itself. If it leaks renew it and the one on the opposite side also.
5   Check the tightness of the steering rack mountings. Check the steering joints for signs of excessive wear and the rack gaiters for splits and leakage. Check the flexible coupling and the column universal joints and replace as and when necessary.

3   Front anti-roll bar and bushes – removal and refitting

1   Remove the retaining bolts and washers securing the two anti-roll bar brackets to the front subframe. Remove the brackets and retrieve the packing plate from each mounting (photo).
2   Remove the pin from each end of the anti-roll bar, or if applicable remove the thin locknuts which are fitted instead to early models, and then undo and remove the two retaining nuts with their steel and rubber washers. Note the order of assembly (photo).
3   To remove the anti-roll bar it is necessary to load the front suspension so that the anti-roll bar mounting holes in the track control arms are brought horizontally in line with the bottom of the front sub frame. Coil spring compressors applied to the front suspension springs could be employed to achieve this; Peugeot use a special tool, but the car needs to be on a car lift for it to be fitted. With the suspension compressed, remove the anti-roll bar and retrieve the washers from each end fitting. Note the location of each of the washers, and that the chamfered washer has its chamfer adjacent to the face on the bar.
4   If the bushes in the track control arms are defective they can be removed using a long bolt, washers, nut and a piece of appropriate sized tubing. It is important that only the correct type replacement parts are fitted; check with your Peugeot agent if in doubt.
5   *Do not drive the car without the anti-roll bar fitted.*
6   Refitting of the anti-roll bar is the reverse of the removal procedure. Ensure that the bushes and washers are fitted in their correct order and lightly smear the bearing areas with general purpose grease.

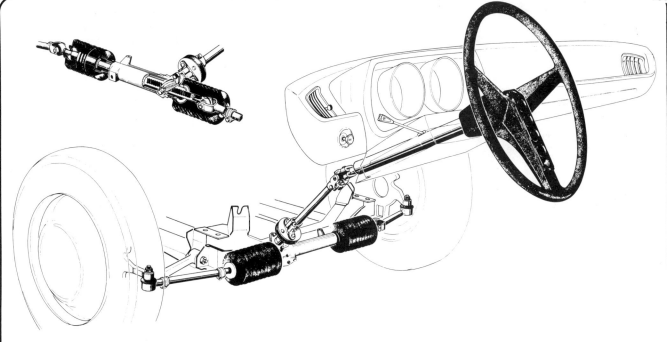

Fig. 10.3 The steering assembly (Sec 1). Inset, part sectioned view of the steering rack-and-pinion

Fig. 10.4 The correct bush and washer locations on the ends of the anti-roll bar (Sec 3)

3.1 The anti-roll bar left-hand bracket

3.2 The anti-roll bar attachment to the track control arm

Release the suspension compression and have the weight of the car on its wheels before tightening the fasteners to their specified torques. Do not forget to refit the packing plates between the mounting brackets and the subframe.

4 Track control arms – removal and refitting

1   Excessive wear in the steering track rod balljoint in the track control arms will require renewal of the track control arms as the balljoint cannot be dismantled from the arms.
2   Refer to Section 3 and disconnect the anti-roll bar from the track control arms.
3   Raise the vehicle until the front wheels are hanging free and support the chassis on stands or blocks. Make sure that the handbrake is on and preferably chock the rear wheels as well.
4   Turn the steering wheel in the opposite direction to the side being worked on and engage the lock after removing the ignition key.
5   Undo and remove the track control arm inner pivot bolt nut (photo) and then remove the pivot bolt. If your car has a 76 mm diameter driveshaft joint you can then pull the front wheel to one side to free the track control arm from its location in the subframe. However, if your car has an 86 mm diameter driveshaft joint you will need to remove the wheel, undo the driveshaft-to-wheel hub retaining nut, and then pull the hub sideways to release the driveshaft. Ensure that the

4.5 The track control arm inner pivot bolt nut (arrowed)

Fig. 10.5 Removing the track control arm inner pivot bolt (1) (Sec 4)

driveshaft is not pulled out of the differential case or you will lose engine oil. Refer to Chapter 7 for details concerning the removal and refitting of the driveshaft in the wheel hub.
6   To remove the track control arm from the suspension assembly you will require a balljoint separator. Remove the retaining nut and separate the balljoint pin from the hub. One type of separator uses the retaining nut as a screw jack to separate the balljoint pin.
7   If the track control arm inner pivot bush is worn it can be renewed. Use suitable sized socket spanners in a vice to press the old bush out and the new one in or, if a large vice is not available, use a long bolt, nut, washers and a piece of tube. Renewal of either the bush or the track control arm requires considerable care in making sure that the correct replacement parts are fitted. With at least six types of arm and four types of bush used on Peugeot 104 cars it is easy to go wrong and the help of your Peugeot agent is imperative. One particular point to watch is that there are two different tapers used in the balljoint pin-to-hub joint. They are *not* interchangeable as a 20% taper pin in a 10% taper hole will result in a sloppy fit.
8   Refitting a track control arm is the reverse of the removal sequence. Lightly smear pivot pins, bushes and driveshaft splines, if disconnected, with a general purpose grease. Tighten the fasteners to the specified torque loads with the weight of the car on the wheels.

5 Front suspension unit – removal and refitting

1   Refer to Section 3 and disconnect the anti-roll bar from the track control arm on the suspension unit to be removed.
2   Remove the nut, then using a balljoint separator, disconnect the steering track rod from the steering knuckle, taking care not to damage the rubber boot.
3   Raise the front end of the car until the wheels hang free and support the chassis firmly on stands or blocks. Apply the handbrake and chock the rear wheels.
4   Remove the roadwheel. Undo the two bolts securing the brake caliper to the wheel hub. Remove the caliper, taking care not to put any tension on the brake hose, and suspend the caliper from the chassis; there is no need to undo the brake hose from the caliper. Insert a piece of wood or rubber hose between the brake disc pads to keep them in position.
5   Undo the driveshaft-to-hub retaining nut, using a padded bar between two wheel studs to prevent the hub turning. This nut is done up to a very high torque.
6   Undo the track control arm inner pivot bolt nut and remove the pivot bolt.

Fig. 10.6 Removing the brake caliper (Sec 5)

1   Inner pivot bolt   2   Caliper retaining bolts

7   Disconnect the hub from the driveshaft. Make sure that the driveshaft is not withdrawn from the differential case or you will lose engine oil. Suspend the driveshaft from the chassis and ensure that the seal bearing surface at the hub end is protected from possible damage.
8   Support the suspension unit at the bottom and undo the three upper retaining nuts (photo). Lower the suspension unit and remove it from the car.
9   Before refitting a suspension unit examine all the rubber boots and gaiters in the front steering/suspension assembly for splits, deterioration, leaking lubricant and general condition. Check the condition of the balljoints in the track control arm and in the steering track rod. Examine the composite bushes in the track control arm for wear and deterioration. Where necessary new parts should be fitted. Note that on pre-1979 models the shock absorber unit can be overhauled, although this work is best entrusted to your Peugeot garage. On models manufactured from 1979 on, the shock absorber can be removed from the suspension strut as one unit.
10 Refitting a suspension unit is the reverse of the removal procedure, but the following points should be noted:

   (a) Use a new tab washer to lock the three retaining nuts at the top of the suspension unit if your car has tab locked nuts
   (b) Lightly smear pivot pins, bushes and driveshaft splines with a general purpose grease
   (c) Remove all traces of grease from the brake disc before assembling the caliper
   (d) Smear the threads of the two caliper securing bolts with thread locking compound and don't forget the lockwashers
   (e) Tighten the suspension fasteners only when the weight of the car is on the wheels
   (f) Where specified, tighten all fasteners to the appropriate torques

6   Front coil springs – removal and refitting

1   Refer to Section 5 and remove the suspension unit.
2   A suitable coil spring compressor will be required to enable the spring to be removed from the strut.
3   Unscrew and free the bellows from between spring coils and slide up the strut (Fig. 10.7).
4   Position the spring compressor to relieve the expansion pressure of the spring between the strut lower flange and the upper mounting flange. Ensure that the spring compressor is fully and securely located on the spring bottom cup, and through the coils of the spring near the top. Compress the spring sufficiently to enable the top mounting to be removed.
5   Use a box spanner or socket and unscrew the strut rod nut at the top end. The nut will have been staked to lock it and the indent must be relieved if the nut is reluctant to unscrew.
6   Now remove the top mounting flange, cup and rubber cone. The spring can be withdrawn together with the bottom cup and bump stop rubber.
7   If a new spring is being fitted make sure that it is the correct type for your car; alternative types are not interchangeable. Both front springs must have the same rating; check with your Peugeot agent if in doubt. The new spring will need to be compressed using the spring compressor prior to assembly.
8   The anti-friction washer must always be renewed.
9   Renew the top cup rubber and bottom cup unit if the originals are worn or defective in any way.
10 Fitting the spring into position on the strut is a reversal of the removal procedure. Remember to lubricate and reposition the rubber bellows over the shock absorber. Always use a new retaining nut and stake the nut to the rod when tightened to the specified torque (Fig. 10.9).

7   Rear suspension unit – removal and refitting

1   Chock the front wheels. Remove the falsework in the car covering the top attachment nuts of the rear suspension unit to be removed. Raise the rear end of the car and support it on stands so that the rear wheels hang free. Using blocks support the rear wheel on the suspension unit to be removed but do not compress the suspension unit.
2   Undo and remove the locking bolt in the lower attachment of the suspension unit and then undo and remove the retaining nut (Fig. 10.10).

5.8 The front suspension unit upper retaining nuts (arrowed)

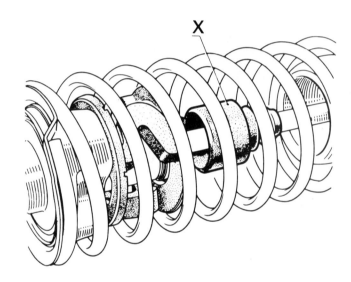

Fig. 10.7 Free the bellows (X) and slide them up the strut (Sec 6)

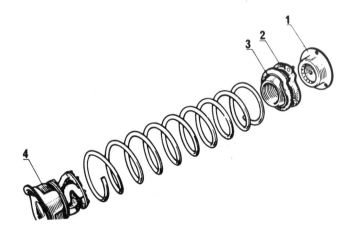

Fig. 10.8 The front suspension coil spring assembly (Sec 6)

1 Top mounting flange	4 Bottom cup and bump
2 Top cup	stop
3 Top rubber	

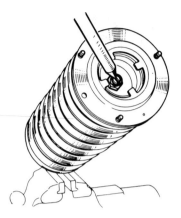

Fig. 10.9 Stake punch the retaining nut to secure it (Sec 6)

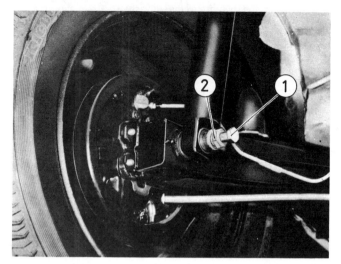

Fig. 10.10 Rear suspension lower attachment (Sec 7)

1   Lockbolt   2   Retaining nut

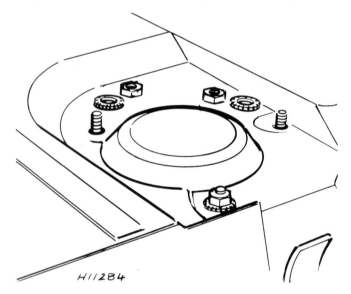

Fig. 10.11 Rear suspension unit upper attachment nuts (Sec 7)

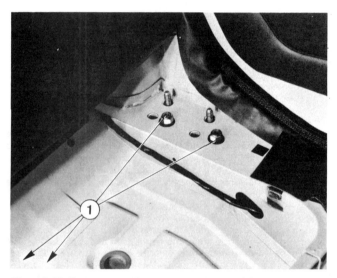

Fig. 10.12 Rear suspension arm attachment (1) nuts removed
(Sec 8)

3   Undo and remove the three upper attachment nuts and washers. Disengage the bottom end of the suspension unit from its spindle on the rear suspension arm and remove the suspension unit from the car. Renewal of the coil spring is similar to the procedure described for the front coil springs (see Section 6).

4   To refit the suspension unit follow the reverse procedure to removal. Locate the suspension unit in its upper mounting and then fit the lower end on the spindle, having made sure that the plain washer is in position on the spindle. Fit the other plain washer and the nut but do not tighten it at this stage.

5   Fit the three upper attachment nuts and washers and tighten to the specified torque. Lower the vehicle onto its wheels.

6   It is now necessary to load the rear of the car before tightening the bottom retaining nut and its locking bolt. The car must be loaded so that, with the tyres at correct pressure, the centre point of the hub cap retaining bolt is 245 mm (9.65 in) from the ground directly beneath it. If possible, also obtain the two blocks (Peugeot No 8.0908H) to fit beneath the underframe.

7   With the rear suspension compressed, tighten the suspension unit lower attachment nut to the specified torque. Fit the lockbolt and tighten it to its specified torque.

8   Rear suspension arm – removal and refitting

1   Removal and refitting of either the rear suspension arms or the complete subframe is not particularly difficult, but any work of this nature will upset the rear wheel alignment. The rear wheels on the

Peugeot 104 are set to a specific toe-in and unless equipment is available to measure and set toe-in accurately, it is recommended that the job be left for your local agent.

2   For the more ambitious D-I-Y mechanic a brief outline of the work involved is as follows.

3   Remove the attachment nuts of the suspension arm to be changed. These are located inside the car under the rear seat at either side. If only one suspension arm is being removed, loosen the nuts on the other side.

4   Remove the handbrake lever and disconnect the appropriate cable. Seal the brake system reservoir with a piece of clean polythene film under the cap. Raise the rear end of the car and support on stands with wheels hanging. Withdraw the handbrake cable, and disconnect the brake line at the pipe/hose connection. Disconnect the exhaust system from its rear mountings.

5   Remove the suspension arm inner pivot nut and loosen the other pivot nuts (photos). Disconnect the suspension unit from the arm, see Section 7. Remove the four bolts retaining the centre support to the car underfloor (photo) lower the outer attachment bolts out of the car floor and remove the suspension arm from the car.

8.5a A suspension arm inner pivot nut and ...

8.5b ... an outer pivot nut

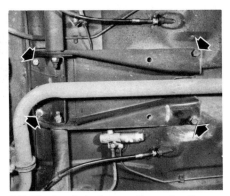

8.5c The four bolts (arrowed) securing the centre support

6   Follow the reverse procedure for refitting. Leave the tightening of the four suspension arm pivot nuts and the suspension unit retaining nut and lockbolt until the car can be loaded to compress the rear suspension, see Section 7. After connecting the handbrake and the brake pipeline, remove the polythene seal from the brake system reservoir. Then bleed and adjust the brakes, see Chapter 8.
7   Rear wheel alignment is carried out with the vehicle at kerb weight by moving the centre support, bolted by four bolts to the bottom of the car, forwards or backwards until correct toe-in is achieved. On completion tighten the four bolts to the correct torque.

9   Steering rack – removal and refitting

1   Apply the handbrake and raise the front of the vehicle, supporting it firmly on stands. Centralise the steering wheel.
2   Undo and remove the pivot bolt securing the gearchange lever to the steering rack. Retrieve the washers, noting the sequence of assembly.
3   Undo and remove the steering flexible coupling upper bolt. Remove the two bolts securing the bottom end of the exhaust pipe support strut to the gearcase, loosen the U-bolt nuts at the upper end, undo the clips holding the clutch cable and move the strut out of the way.
4   The steering assembly fitted to early models has one adjustable track rod on the right-hand side, and the other is of fixed length. Later assemblies have adjustable track rods on both sides. With an early type assembly disconnect the track rods by first removing the gaiter outer rings, sliding them on to the track rods, then sliding the gaiter outer ends back and removing the rack eye pivot pins. On later assemblies, loosen the track rod locknuts and unscrew the track rods from their balljoints at the outer ends (Figs. 10.13, 10.15 and 10.16).
5   Undo and remove the two bolts securing the rack to the subframe and remove the rack from the car. Retrieve the two spacers in the subframe (Fig. 10.14).
6   Before refitting the steering rack check that the rubber gaiters are in good condition and renew the lockwashers, locking plates, gaiter retaining rings and the flexible coupling bolt. With the steering rack in the mid-stroke position and the steering column in the straight-ahead position, engage the flexible coupling on the rack with the lower end of the steering column, Locate the two spacers in the subframe and insert the rack retaining bolts. Tighten the securing nuts to the specified torque. Tighten the steering column flexible coupling bolt and nut to the specified torque. Position the gaiter retaining rings.
7   On the early type steering rack insert the track rod rack eye pivot bolts with new lockwashers. Tighten to the specified torque and bend up the locking tabs. On the later steering rack, screw the balljoint into the track rod on each side and adjust to a length of 59 mm (2.32 in) from the end of the track rod to the centre of the balljoint pivot pin (Fig. 10.17).
8   Position the rubber gaiters in the grooves on the track rod end fittings and locate the retainer rings or clips.
9   Refit the gearchange lever pivot bolt. Make sure that all the washers are fitted and in the correct sequence. Tighten the bolt to the specified torque. Refit the exhaust pipe support strut and secure the clutch cable retaining clips.

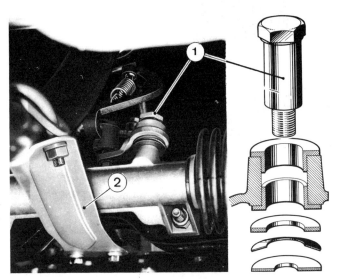

Fig. 10.13 Removing the steering rack-and-pinion (Sec 9)

1   The gearchange lever pivot bolt and washers
2   The exhaust pipe stay

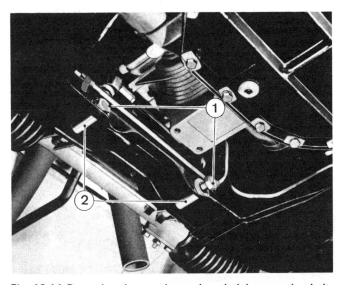

Fig. 10.14 Removing the steering rack and pinion securing bolts (Sec 9)

1   Securing bolts   2   Spacers in subframe

174

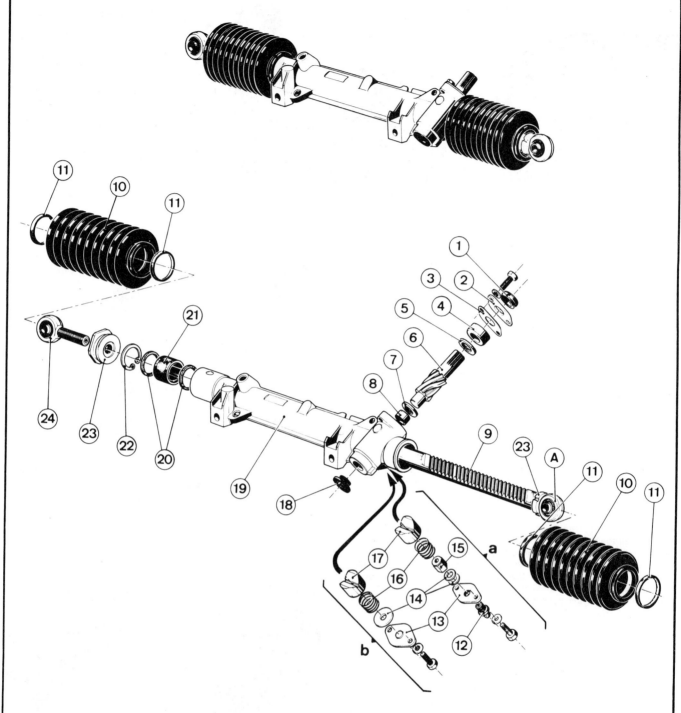

Fig. 10.15 The steering rack-and-pinion (early version) (Sec 9) (Left-hand drive shown – RHD similar)

A   The original adjustment setting of this rack eye must never be
     altered
a   Original rack plunger assembly
b   Later rack plunger assembly (no grease nipple)

1 Seal	7 Pinion lower thrust washer	13 Plunger retaining plate	19 Housing
2 Pinion retaining plate	8 Pinion lower bush	14 Shims	20 Flexible bushing shim
3 Shims	9 Rack	15 Plunger spacer	washers
4 Pinion upper bush	10 Rack end protectors	16 Plunger spring	21 Flexible bush
5 Pinion upper thrust washer	11 Flexible clips	17 Plunger	22 Circlips
6 Pinion	12 Grease nipple	18 Plug	23 Steering lock stop
			24 Rack eye

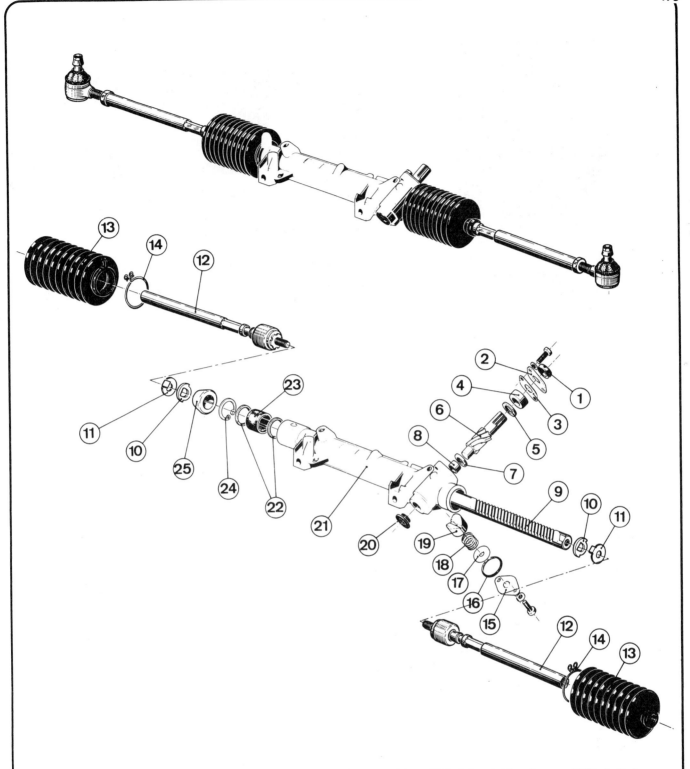

Fig. 10.16 The steering rack-and-pinion (both track rods adjustable) (Sec 9) (Left-hand drive shown – RHD similar)

1 Seal	7 Pinion lower thrust washer	12 Track rods	19 Plunger
2 Pinion retaining plate	8 Pinion lower bush	13 Rack gaiters	20 Plug
3 Adjustment shim	9 Rack	14 Hautrifil clips	21 Steering box
4 Pinion upper bush	10 Turning lock stop washer	15 Rack plunger plate	22 Flexible bush retaining collars
5 Pinion upper thrust washer	11 Locking washer	16 O-ring	23 Flexible bush
6 Pinion		17 Adjustment shims	24 Circlip
		18 Plunger spring	25 Turning lock stop

Fig. 10.17 Assembling the ball-joint to the later type track rods (Sec 9)

1 Balljoint
2 Track rod with loosened locknut

10.3 The adjustable track rod on the right-hand side in the early steering arrangement

Fig. 10.18 Track rod assemblies (Sec 12)

A Early type, with clamp bolts on one side only
B Later type, with locknuts, both sides similar

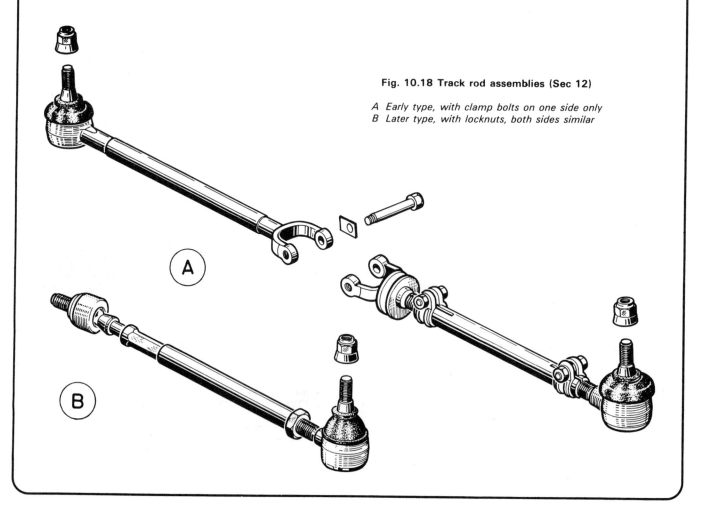

10 Adjust the front wheel alignment, see Section 10, and tighten the track rod clamp bolts or locknuts to their respective torques.

10 Front wheel alignment

1   Correct front wheel alignment is achieved when the wheels toe-in by the amount quoted in the Specifications. The measurement of this small dimension requires the use of special equipment. If the wheels are not correctly aligned, tyre wear will be heavy and uneven and the steering will be stiff and unresponsive. In the absence of the special tools the job is best left to the local Peugeot garage. However, if the tools can be borrowed, the adjustment is made as follows.

2   Check that the car is at normal kerb weight and that the tyre pressures are normal. Centralise the steering and measure the toe-in. If necessary adjust as follows.

3   On early steering racks with a right-hand side track rod adjustment, slacken the two clamp bolts on the track rod and rotate the rod to increase or decrease its length as necessary (photo). On later steering racks with both track rods adjustable, slacken both locknuts and rotate the rods to increase or decrease their lengths. Note that, if it is necessary to give more than 2 turns on a rod, the adjustment must be digided between the two track rods evenly.

4   After adjustment, position the balljoints at the ends of the track rods with the axis of each pivot vertical and tighten the clamp bolts (early cars) or the locknuts (later models) to their respective torques.

11 Steering rack – overhaul

1   Although the Peugeot 104 steering rack is a fairly simple component and a straightforward dismantling procedure, a number of special tools including a dial test indicator are required to assemble it and some degree of precision is essential. In particular, setting the pinion preload and the rack plunger preload needs very careful measurement and any error in these respects would adversely affect the steering rack performance. For these reasons it is considered that overhaul of the steering rack should be left to your Peugeot agent. Some points which should be noted however are:

(a)   *The eye fitting in the pinion end of the steering rack in early cars is preset in manufacture and must not subsequently be disturbed*

(b)   *Early steering racks have a grease nipple mounted in a plate on the lower side of the steering rack. These racks are lubricated with general purpose grease. Later steering racks, although they have the plate fitted, have no grease nipple in the plate. These racks are lubricated with a special grease designed to last for life. This special grease is not miscible with general purpose grease and it is the only grease to be used in these racks*

(c)   *Although individual parts may not be interchangeable between steering racks, complete steering racks, regardless of standard, are interchangeable*

12 Track rods and balljoints – removal and refitting

1   Individual track rods may be renewed in the event of damage or severe corrosion. Proceed as follows.

Early type track rods (with clamp bolts)

2   Loosen the retaining nut and, using a universal balljoint separator, remove the track rod balljoint from the strut bottom fitting (photo).

3   Remove the gaiter retaining ring and slide the steering rack gaiter back to reveal the track rod inboard pivot bolt. Undo the locking tab then undo and remove the pivot bolt to release the track rod.

4   The balljoint in the adjustable rod can be renewed by undoing the clamp bolt and removing the old balljoint. Fit a new balljoint and adjust the length of the rod to 250 mm (9.84 in) from the axis of the joint pivot pin to the near face of the gaiter mounting collar. Ensure that an equal amount of thread protrudes at each end of the rod (Fig. 10.19).

5   The balljoint fitted to the non-adjustable rod cannot be renewed and the rod assembly has to be changed if the balljoint is defective.

6   It is a sensible precaution to renew both balljoints together. This will avoid possible steering problems and also avoid the need for

12.2 The left-hand track rod balljoint (early model)

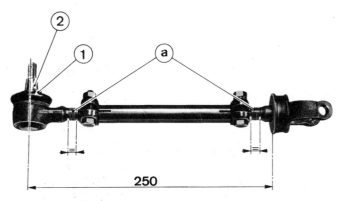

Fig. 10.19 Presetting the early type adjustable track rod (Sec 12)

1   *Gaiter*
2   *Balljoint tapered pin*
a   *Ensure equal thread each side*

renewing the other balljoint shortly afterwards. Note that balljoints are available with either 10° or 20° tapers – they are not interchangeable and it would be dangerous to attempt to fit the wrong one.

7   To refit the track rod, using a new tab washer assemble the inner pivot bolt with the rod and rack end fitting and tighten the bolt to the specified torque. Bend up the tab to lock the bolt head.

8   Locate the steering rack gaiter on the collar on the track rod and fit the retaining ring, making sure that the ring is not twisted.

9   Degrease the taper shank of the balljoint and its seat in the strut bottom fitting. Fit the balljoint to the fitting. Use a new Nylstop skirted nut and tighten to the specified torque.

10   Check and, if necessary, adjust the front wheel alignment, see Section 10.

Later type track rods (with locknuts)

11   Loosen the retaining nut and, using a universal balljoint separator, remove the track rod balljoint from the strut bottom fitting.

12   Disengage the gaiter by opening the Hautrifil clip at the rack end and moving the gaiter back to reveal the balljoint. Unscrew the balljoint from the rack and recover the lockwasher, the thrust washer and, from the side opposite to the pinion only, the turning lock stop.

13   Refitting a track rod is the reverse of the removal procedure. Tighten the ball socket onto the rack to the specified torque. A special spanner is available for this and should be borrowed or hired from your Peugeot agent. The part number is 8.0707. Lock the socket by bending up the lockwasher.

14   Reposition the rack gaiter and secure the Hautrifil clip. Note that

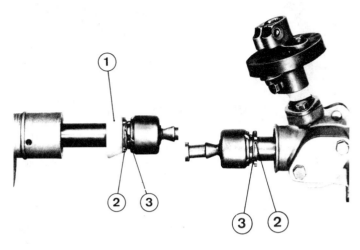

Fig. 10.20 Track rod/steering rack joints on later type track rods (Sec 12)

1   Steering lock stop
2   Thrust washer

3   Lockwasher (renew on reassembly)

Fig. 10.21 Wrong and right ways of fitting the Hautrifil clip (Sec 12)

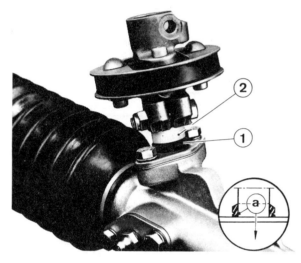

Fig. 10.22 Fitting the steering flexible coupling (Sec 13)

1   Seal
2   Spacer
a   Fit seal, lightly greased, with lip down

13.2 The steering shaft lower flexible coupling

there is a wrong and a right way to secure this clip, see Fig. 10.21.

15 Fit the balljoint to the track rod and adjust it to a length of 59 mm (2.32 in) from the near end of the track rod to the centre-line of the balljoint pivot pin. Fit the balljoint to the strut bottom fitting, see paragraphs 6 and 9 for details.

16 Check and, if necessary, adjust the front wheel alignment as explained in Section 10.

13 Steering shaft lower flexible coupling – removal and refitting

1 Raise the vehicle at the front and support on axle stands, or position the vehicle over an inspection pit.

2 Unscrew and remove the gear selector quadrant retaining bolt from the steering box. Loosen the clamp-bolt holding the coupling to the pinion shaft (photo).

3 Unscrew and remove the bolts holding the intermediate shaft to the flexible coupling.

4 Unscrew and remove the two bolts securing the steering rack to the crossmember, then lower the steering rack and remove the coupling.

5 Before refitting a coupling, change the seal on the steering rack pinion. Slightly grease the new seal and fit it with the lip facing the steering rack. Fit the spacer followed by the flexible coupling. Complete the refitting by following the removal sequence in reverse (Fig. 10.22).

6 Tighten the clamp bolts to the specified torque.

14 Steering wheel – removal and refitting

1 Using a knife carefully prise out the central plastic panel in the steering wheel.

2 Undo and remove the nut securing the wheel to the steering column.

3 With a long punch, or similar tool, mark the relative positions of the steering wheel hub and the steering column so that they may be refitted in the same positions.

4 With the palms of the hands behind the spokes and near to the centre hub, thump the steering wheel up from the splines on the column.

5 Refitting the steering wheel is the reverse of the removal sequence.

15 Fault diagnosis – suspension and steering

Before diagnosing faults from the following chart, check that any irregularities are not caused by:
  (a) Binding brakes
  (b) Incorrect tyres
  (c) Incorrect tyre pressures
  (d) Misalignment of the bodyframe or rear suspension

Symptom	Reason/s
Steering wheel can be moved considerably before any sign of movement of the wheels is apparent	Wear in the steering linkage, rack-and-pinion or column coupling
Vehicle difficult to steer in a consistent straight line – wandering	As above Wheel alignment incorrect (indicated by excessive or uneven tyre wear) Front wheel hub bearings loose or worn Worn balljoints or track control arm bushes
Steering stiff and heavy	Incorrect wheel alignment (indicated by excessive or uneven tyre wear) Excessive wear or seizure in one or more of the joints in the steering linkage or track control arm balljoints Excessive wear in the steering rack-and-pinion Defective driveshaft joints
Wheel wobble and vibration	Roadwheels out of balance Roadwheels buckled/damaged Wheel alignment incorrect Wear in steering linkage, track control arm balljoint or track control arm inner bushes
Excessive pitching and rolling on corners and during braking	Defective shock absorbers Incorrect tyre pressures Anti-roll bar broken away

Chapter 11 Bodywork and fittings

Contents

1 General description

The models in the Peugeot 104 range have a very substantial body structure which is built up of a number of steel pressings welded to form a rigid shell. Extensive use is made of stiffening in the shaping of the pressings which are made of steel sheet in a thicker gauge than is usual in this type of car. The shell is specially designed to have a non-deformable passenger compartment with the front and rear progressively collapsible to absorb impact.

Apart from the hinged components (doors, bonnet and tailgate) which are straightforward to renew, the two front wings are bolt-on panels and can be renewed without welding or jigging if the need arises.

The cavities of the lower bodyshell sections have been injected with special anti-corrosive sealants to prevent rusting in and around the respective structural joints and panels. The paint colour code is stencilled on the crossmember at the front of the engine compartment (photo). Always quote the number to ensure getting the correct colour match when ordering the paint.

2 Maintenance – body exterior

1 The general condition of your car's bodywork is the one thing that significantly affects its value. Maintenance is easy but needs to be regular and particular. Neglect – particularly after minor damage – can quickly lead to further deterioration and costly repair bills. It is important also to keep watch on those parts of the bodywork not immediately visible, for example the underside, inside all the wheel arches and the lower part of the engine compartment.

2 The basic maintenance routine for the bodywork is washing – preferably with a lot of water from a hose. This will remove all the loose solids which may have stuck to the car. It is important to flush these off in such a way as to prevent grit from scratching the finish. The wheel arches and underbody need washing in the same way to remove any accumulated mud which will retain moisture and tend to encourage rust.

3 Paradoxically enough, the best time to clean the underbody and wheel arches is in wet weather when the mud is thoroughly wet and soft. In very wet weather the underbody is usually cleaned of large accumulations automatically and this is a good time for inspection.

4 If you have the energy, jack-up the car, remove all the road wheels and clean their inner sides. The wheel offset keeps mud captive for a long time and could unbalance the wheel! **Do not** hose excessive quantities of water at the windows, heater vents etc.

5 Periodically have the whole of the underside steam cleaned, engine compartment as well so that a thorough inspection can be carried out to see what minor repairs and renovations are necessary.

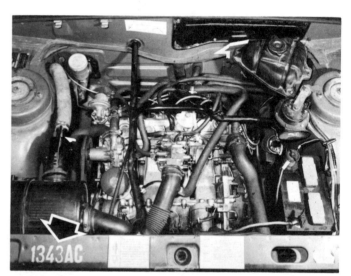

1.1 The paint colour code is stencilled on the front crossmember (arrowed)

Steam cleaning is available at some garages and is necessary for removal of the accumulation of oily grime which sometimes collects thickly in areas near the engine and gearbox. If steam facilites are not available there are one or two grease solvent available which can be brush applied. The dirt can then be simply hosed off. Any signs of rust on the underside panels must be attended to immediately. Thoroughly wire brushing followed by treatment with an anti-rust compound primer and underbody sealer will prevent continued deterioration. If not dealt with the car could eventually become structurally unsound and therefore unsafe.

6 After washing the paintwork wipe off with a chamois leather to give a clear unspotted finish. A coat of clear wax polish will give added protection against chemical pollutants in the air and will survive several subsequent washings. If the paintwork sheen has dulled or oxidised use a cleaner/polisher combination to restore the brilliance of the shine. This requires a little effort but is usually because regular washing has been neglected! Always check that door and drain holes and pipes are completely clear so that water can drain out (photo). Brightwork should be treated the same way as paintwork. Windscreens and windows can be kept clear of the smeary film which often appears if a little ammonia is added to the water. If glasswork is scratched a good rub with a proprietary metal polish will often clean it. Never use any form of wax or other paint/chromium polish on glass.

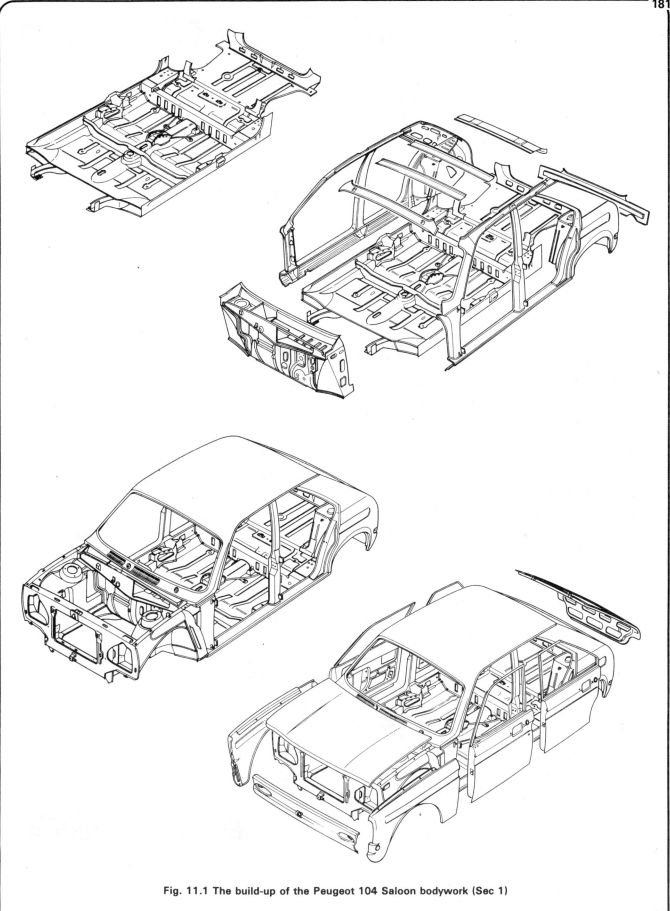

Fig. 11.1 The build-up of the Peugeot 104 Saloon bodywork (Sec 1)

This sequence of photographs deals with the repair of the dent and paintwork damage shown in this photo. The procedure will be similar for the repair of a hole. It should be noted that the procedures given here are simplified — more explicit instructions will be found in the text

In the case of a dent the first job — after removing surrounding trim — is to hammer out the dent where access is possible. This will minimise filling. Here, the large dent having been hammered out, the damaged area is being made slightly concave

Now all paint must be removed from the damaged area, by rubbing with coarse abrasive paper. Alternatively, a wire brush or abrasive pad can be used in a power drill. Where the repair area meets good paintwork, the edge of the paintwork should be 'feathered', using a finer grade of abrasive paper

In the case of a hole caused by rusting, all damaged sheet-metal should be cut away before proceeding to this stage. Here, the damaged area is being treated with rust remover and inhibitor before being filled

Mix the body filler according to its manufacturer's instructions. In the case of corrosion damage, it will be necessary to block off any large holes before filling — this can be done with aluminium or plastic mesh, or aluminium tape. Make sure the area is absolutely clean before ...

... applying the filler. Filler should be applied with a flexible applicator, as shown, for best results; the wooden spatula being used for confined areas. Apply thin layers of filler at 20-minute intervals, until the surface of the filler is slightly proud of the surrounding bodywork

Initial shaping can be done with a Surform plane or Dreadnought file. Then, using progressively finer grades of wet-and-dry paper, wrapped around a sanding block, and copious amounts of clean water, rub down the filler until really smooth and flat. Again, feather the edges of adjoining paintwork

Again, using plenty of water, rub down the primer with a fine grade wet-and-dry paper (400 grade is probably best) until it is really smooth and well blended into the surrounding paintwork. Any remaining imperfections can now be filled by carefully applied knifing stopper paste

The top coat can now be applied. When working out of doors, pick a dry, warm and wind-free day. Ensure surrounding areas are protected from over-spray. Agitate the aerosol thoroughly, then spray the centre of the repair area, working outwards with a circular motion. Apply the paint as several thin coats

The whole repair area can now be sprayed or brush-painted with primer. If spraying, ensure adjoining areas are protected from over-spray. Note that at least one inch of the surrounding sound paintwork should be coated with primer. Primer has a 'thick' consistency, so will find small imperfections

When the stopper has hardened, rub down the repair area again before applying the final coat of primer. Before rubbing down this last coat of primer, ensure the repair area is blemish-free — use more stopper if necessary. To ensure that the surface of the primer is really smooth use some finishing compound

After a period of about two weeks, which the paint needs to harden fully, the surface of the repaired area can be 'cut' with a mild cutting compound prior to wax polishing. When carrying out bodywork repairs, remember that the quality of the finished job is proportional to the time and effort expended

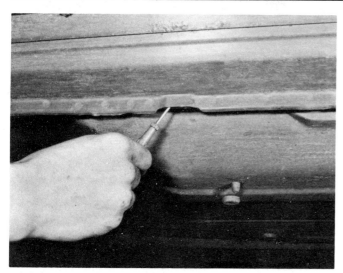

2.6 Checking a drain hole with a screwdriver

3   Maintenance – interior

The floor cover should be brushed or vacuum cleaned regularly to keep it free of grit. If badly stained, remove it from the car for scrubbing or sponging and make quite sure that it is dry before replacement. Seat and interior trim panels can be kept clean with a wipe over with a damp cloth. If they do become stained (which can be more apparent on light coloured upholstery especially when the nylon 'cloth' type) use a little liquid detergent and a soft nail-brush to scour the grime out of the grain of the material. Do not forget to keep the headlining clean in the same way as the upholstery. When using liquid cleaners inside the car do not over-wet the surface being cleaned. Excessive damp could get into the upholstery seams and padded interior, causing stains, offensive odours or even rot. If the inside of the car gets wet accidentally it is worthwhile taking some trouble to dry it out properly. **Do not** leave oil or electric heaters inside the car for this purpose. If, when removing mats for cleaning, there are signs of damp underneath, all the interior of the car floor should be uncovered and the point of water entry found. It may only be a missing grommet, but it could be a rusted through floor panel and this demands immediate attention as described in the next Section. More often than not both sides of the panel will require treatment.

4   Minor body damage – repair

The photographic sequences on pages 182 and 183 illustrate the operations detailed in the following sub-sections.

Repair of minor scratches in the car's bodywork

If the scratch is very superficial, and does not penetrate to the metal of the bodywork, repair is very simple. Lightly rub the area of the scratch with a paintwork renovator, or a very fine cutting paste, to remove loose paint from the scratch and to clear the surrounding bodywork of wax polish. Rinse the area with clean water.

Apply touch-up paint to the scratch using a fine paint brush; continue to apply thin layers of paint until the surface of the paint in the scratch is level with the surrounding paintwork. Allow the new paint at least two weeks to harden: then blend it into the surrounding paintwork by rubbing the scratch area with a paintwork renovator or a very fine cutting paste. Finally, apply wax polish.

Where the scratch has penetrated right through to the metal of the bodywork, causing the metal to rust, a different repair technique is required. Remove any loose rust from the bottom of the scratch with a penknife, then apply rust inhibiting paint to prevent the formation of rust in the future. Using a rubber or nylon applicator fill the scratch with bodystopper paste. If required, this paste can be mixed with cellulose thinners to provide a very thin paste which is ideal for filling narrow scratches. Before the stopper-paste in the scratch hardens,

wrap a piece of smooth cotton rag around the top of a finger. Dip the finger in cellulose thinners and then quickly sweep it across the surface of the stopper-paste in the scratch; this will ensure that the surface of the stopper-paste is slightly hollowed. The scratch can now be painted over as described earlier in this Section.

Repair of dents in the car's bodywork

When deep denting of the car's bodywork has taken place, the first task is to pull the dent out, until the affected bodywork almost attains its original shape. There is little point in trying to restore the original shape completely, as the metal in the damaged area will have stretched on impact and cannot be reshaped fully to its original contour. It is better to bring the level of the dent up to a point which is about $\frac{1}{8}$ in (3 mm) below the level of the surrounding bodywork. In cases where the dent is very shallow anyway, it is not worth trying to pull it out at all. If the underside of the dent is accessible, it can be hammered out gently from behind, using a mallet with a wooden or plastic head. Whilst doing this, hold a suitable block of wood firmly against the outside of the panel to absorb the impact from the hammer blows and thus prevent a large area of the bodywork from being 'belled-out'.

Should the dent be in a section of the bodywork which has double skin or some other factor making it inaccessible from behind, a different technique is called for. Drill several small holes through the metal inside the area – particularly in the deeper section. Then screw long self-tapping screws into the holes just sufficiently for them to gain a good purchase in the metal. Now the dent can be pulled out by pulling on the protruding heads of the screws with a pair of pliers.

The next stage of the repair is the removal of the paint from the damaged area, and from an inch or so of the surrounding 'sound' bodywork. This is accomplished most easily by using a wire brush or abrasive pad on a power drill, although it can be done just as effectively by hand using sheets of abrasive paper. To complete the preparation for filling, score the surface of the bare metal with a screwdriver or the tang of a file, or alternatively, drill small holes in the affected area. This will provide a really good 'key' for the filler paste.

To complete the repair see the Section on filling and respraying.

Repair of rust holes or gashes in the car's bodywork

Remove all paint from the affected area and from an inch or so of the surrounding 'sound' bodywork, using an abrasive pad or a wire brush on a power drill. If these are not available a few sheets of abrasive paper will do the job just as effectively. With the paint removed you will be able to gauge the severity of the corrosion and therefore decide whether to renew the whole panel (if this is possible) or to repair the affected area. New body panels are not as expensive as most people think and it is often quicker and more satisfactory to fit a new panel than to attempt to repair large areas of corrosion.

Remove all fittings from the affected area except those which will act as a guide to the original shape of the damaged bodywork (eg headlamp shells etc). Then, using tin snips or a hacksaw blade, remove all loose metal and any other metal badly affected by corrosion. Hammer the edges of the hole inwards in order to create a slight depression for the filler paste.

Wire brush the affected area to remove the powdery rust from the surface of the remaining metal. Paint the affected area with rust inhibiting paint; if the back of the rusted area is accessible treat this also.

Before filling can take place it will be necessary to block the hole in some way. This can be achieved by the use of zinc gauze or aluminium tape.

Zinc gauze is probably the best material to use for a large hole. Cut a piece to the approximate size and shape of the hole to be filled, then position it in the hole so that its edges are below the level of the surrounding bodywork. It can be retained in position by several blobs of filler paste around its periphery.

Aluminium tape should be used for small or very narrow holes. Pull a piece off the roll and trim it to the approximate size and shape required, then pull off the backing paper (if used) and stick the tape over the hole; it can be overlapped if the thickness of one piece is insufficient. Burnish down the edges of the tape with the handle of a screwdriver or similar, to ensure that the tape is securely attached to the metal underneath.

Bodywork repairs – filling and respraying

Before using this Section, see the Sections on dent, deep scratch, rust holes and gash repairs.

Many types of bodyfiller are available, but generally speaking those proprietary kits which contain a tin of filler paste and a tube of resin hardener are best for this type of repair. A wide, flexible plastic or nylon applicator will be found invaluable for imparting a smooth and well contoured finish to the surface of the filler.

Mix up a little filler on a clean piece of card or board – measure the hardener carefully (follow the maker's instructions on the pack) otherwise the filler will set too rapidly or too slowly.

Using the applicator apply the filler paste to the prepared area: draw the applicator across the surface of the filler to achieve the correct contour and to level the filler surface. As soon as a contour that approximates to the correct one is achieved, stop working the paste – if you carry on too long the paste will become sticky and begin to 'pick up' on the applicator. Continue to add thin layers of filler paste at twenty-minute intervals until the level of the filler is just proud of the surrounding bodywork.

Once the filler has hardened, excess can be removed using a metal plane or file. From then on, progressively finer grades of abrasive paper should be used, starting with a 40 grade production paper and finishing with 400 grade wet-and-dry paper. Always wrap the abrasive paper around a flat rubber, cork, or wooden block – otherwise the surface of the filler will not be completely flat. During the smoothing of the filler surface the wet-and-dry paper should be periodically rinsed in water. This will ensure that a very smooth finish is imparted to the filler at the final stage.

At this stage the 'dent' should be surrounded by a ring of bare metal, which in turn should be encircled by the finely 'feathered' edge of the good paintwork. Rinse the repair area with clean water, until all of the dust produced by the rubbing-down operation has gone. Spray the whole repair area with a light coat of primer – this will show up any imperfections in the surface of the filler. Repair these imperfections with fresh filler paste or bodystopper, and once more smooth the surface with abrasive paper. If bodystopper is used, it can be mixed with cellulose thinners to form a really thin paste which is ideal for filling small holes. Repeat this spray and repair procedure until you are satisfied that the surface of the filler, and the feathered edge of the paintwork are perfect. Clean the repair area with clean water and allow to dry fully.

The repair area is now ready for final spraying. Paint spraying must be carried out in a warm, dry, windless and dust free atmosphere. This condition can be created artificially if you have access to a large indoor working area, but if you are forced to work in the open, you will have to pick your day very carefully. If you are working indoors, dousing the floor in the work area with water will help settle the dust which would otherwise be in the atmosphere. If the repair area is confined to one body panel, mask off the surrounding panels; this will help to minimise the effects of a slight mis-match in paint colours. Bodywork fittings (eg chrome strips, door handles etc) will also need to be masked off. Use genuine masking tape and several thicknesses of newspaper for the masking operations.

Before commencing to spray, agitate the aerosol can thoroughly, then spray a test area (an old tin, or similar) until the technique is mastered. Cover the repair area with a thick coat of primer; the thickness should be built up using several thin layers of paint rather than one thick one. Using 400 grade wet-and-dry paper, rub down the surface of the primer until it is really smooth. While doing this, the work area should be thoroughly doused with water, and the wet-and-dry paper periodically rinsed in water. Allow to dry before spraying on more paint.

Spray on the top coat, again building up the thickness by using several thin layers of paint. Start spraying in the centre of the repair area and then, using a circular motion, work outwards until the whole repair area and about 2 inches of the surrounding original paintwork is covered. Remove all masking material 10 to 15 minutes after spraying on the final coat of paint.

Allow the new paint at least two weeks to harden, then, using a paintwork renovator or a very fine cutting paste, blend the edges of the paint into the existing paintwork. Finally, apply wax polish.

5 Major body damage – repair

1 Because the car is built without a separate chassis frame and the body is therefore integral with the underframe, major damage must be repaired by competent mechanics with the necessary welding and hydraulic straightening equipment.

2 If the damage has been serious it is vital that the body is checked for correct alignment as otherwise the handling of the car will suffer and many other faults such as excessive tyre wear and wear in the transmission and steering may occur.

3 There is a special body jig which most large body repair shops have, and to ensure that all is correct it is important that the jig be used for all major repair work.

6 Doors – tracing and silencing rattles

Having established that a rattle does come from the door(s) check first that it is not loose on its hinges and that the latch is holding it firmly closed. The hinges can be checked by rocking the door up and down when open to detect any play. If the hinges are worn at the pin the hinge pin and possibly the inner hinge will need renewal. When the door is closed the panel should be flush. If not then the hinges or latch striker plate need adjustment. The door hinges are welded or bolted to the doors and pillars. To adjust the setting of the door catch first slacken the screws holding the striker plate to the door pillar just enough so that it can be moved but will hold its position. Close the door, with the latch button pressed, and then release the latch. This is so that the striker plate position is not drastically disturbed on closing the door. Then set the door position by moving it without touching the catch, so that the panel is flush with the bodywork and the other door. This will set the striker plate in the proper place. Then carefully release the catch so as not to disturb the striker plate, open the door and tighten the screws. Rattles within the door will be due to loose fixtures or something having been dropped inside them. Do make sure that all sealing rubbers are effective and that the prop stay is not itself loose.

7 Front wing panels – removal and refitting

1 Fortunately the front wing panels, which are probably the most exposed of the body panels, are secured in position by bolts and can therefore easily be removed for repair or replacement. Before removing a wing panel obtain a sealer such as Glasticon Dum Dum putty which will be required for reassembly.

2 Commence by disconnecting the battery earth connection.

3 Remove the front bumper unit.

4 Detach and withdraw the headlight unit from the side to be removed and remove the front side/direction light unit. Refer to Chapter 9 if necessary.

5 Undo and remove the nine bolts retaining the wing panel which are located as shown in Fig. 11.2. Leave a couple of the top bolts until last and when these are out remove the old wing.

6 Before fitting the new wing hold it in position to make sure that it fits correctly. If not try to dress it judiciously so that it does align, but don't be too enthusiastic in this respect. It should be possible to adjust

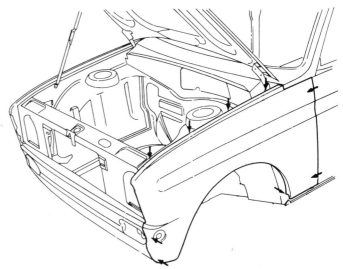

Fig. 11.2 The wing panel retaining bolt positions (arrowed) (Sec 7)

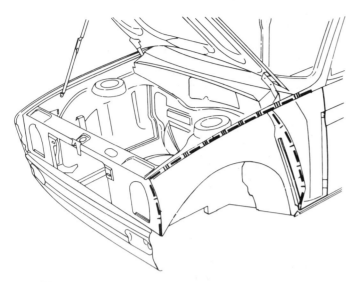

Fig. 11.3 Apply sealant to the areas indicated (Sec 7)

the position of the new wing so that any discrepancies are spread around evenly. Sealant must be applied around the periphery of the panel in the same position as the original but, before applying it, clean off all traces of grease, mud and oil sealant to ensure good adhesion of the new sealer.

7   Fit the new wing, checking that the sealant is applied thickly enough to fill the gaps that may exist between the new wing and the car body. Secure the new wing with bolts but, before tightening them, check the front door and bonnet clearances. On completion coat the underside of the new panel and all bolt heads with underseal or a suitable underbody protective finish.

8   Refit the bumper and lights, and check the headlamp alignment as explained in Chapter 9.

8 Bonnet – removal and refitting

1   Open the bonnet and have an assistant support it.
2   Mark around the hinges to show their correct location to facilitate reassembly and then unscrew the hinge retaining screws on each side and remove the bonnet. Protect the paintwork on the car with rags, felt or similar soft material and stow the bonnet in a safe place where it cannot get damaged whilst it is not fitted to the car.
3   Refit the bonnet in the reverse order and check it for alignment before fully tightening the retaining nuts.

9 Bonnet release cable – removal and refitting

1   Raise and support the bonnet. If the cable has broken, which is unlikely as it is a single strand steel wire, access to the release catch will have to be gained by removing one or both headlamps as described in Chapter 9. It might also help to support the front of the car on a ramp or axle stands and work upwards behind the radiator. In any case this will be an awkward job. A hooked tool made of steel rod will be helpful in releasing the latch.
2   Disconnect the cable from the release catch by bending the hook in the end of the cable and undoing the clamp bolt nut.
3   The inner cable can now be pulled out of the outer sheath by pulling on the release knob in the car (photo).
4   If it is intended to change the complete cable and sheath assembly, disconnect the inner cable as described. Then undo the locknut on the release knob assembly in the car. Free the outer sheath from the retaining clips in the engine compartment and withdraw the assembly by pulling from inside the car and feeding the sheath through the rubber grommets.
5   Refitting a new cable or assembly is the reverse of the removal procedure. Grease the inner cable with a general purpose grease before installation. After tightening the inner cable clamp bolt on the release catch, get an assistant to pull the release knob while you check that the catch opens fully.

10 Bonnet release catch – removal and refitting

1   Unfortunately the radiator prevents the removal of the catch and it must therefore be moved before the catch retaining bolts can be removed.
2   Refer to Chapter 2 and remove the radiator.
3   Disconnect the release cable from the catch as described in Section 9.
4   Undo the catch retaining bolts and remove the release catch (photo).
5   Refitting the catch is the reverse of the removal procedure. Lightly grease the moving parts with a general purpose grease. Have an assistant operate the release knob while you check that the catch opens fully and test the bonnet closed and release operations before refitting the radiator. Adjustment of the bonnet closed position is obtained by loosening the locknut on the bonnet pin and screwing the pin in or out to get the correct setting. Tighten the locknut on completion (photo).

11 Door trim – removal and refitting

1   To remove the inner trim panel from a door, first unscrew and remove the armrest.
2   Disconnect the window winder handle. Press the plastic moulding into the door trim and, using a thin screwdriver, remove the spring clip retaining the handle to its spindle (photo). The handle and plastic moulding can then be removed.
3   Insert a thin, flat bladed tool between the door trim and the door and carefully lever out the retaining fasteners. Work round the panel until it is free and can be removed (photo).
4   Refitting the panel is the reverse of the removal procedure. When refitting the window winder handle, position it on the spindle so that, with the window closed, the winder knob is out of the way of the driver's or passenger's knee.

12 Door fittings – removal and refitting

Lock remote control
1   Remove the door trim as described in Section 11.
2   Undo the two screws retaining the remote control lever assembly to the door and remove the assembly. The remote control rod merely pulls out to disconnect (photo).
3   Refitting is the reverse of the removal sequence. Lightly lubricate the lever assembly with oil on refitting and check its operation when completed.

Key cylinder
4   To change a key cylinder first remove the door trim as described in Section 11.
5   Slide the retaining plate out to release the key cylinder and withdraw the cylinder from outside the door.
6   Refitting is the reverse of the removal procedure. Make sure that the cylinder operating lever engages with the door lock before sliding the retaining plate into position (photos).

Door lock
7   Remove the door trim as described in Section 11.
8   Undo and remove the three special headed screws securing the lock to the door and remove the lock (photo).
9   Unclip the remote control rod from the internal mechanism and remove the mechanism through the door aperture.
10   Refitting the door lock is the reverse of the removal procedure.

13 Door window glass and winder mechanism – removal and refitting

1   Remove the door trim panel as described in Section 11. after opening the window two or three inches.
2   Undo the two nuts retaining the window winding mechanism to the door and, holding the glass panel to take the weight, move the mechanism to free the two studs and then disengage the mechanism

9.3 The bonnet release cable knob (arrowed)

10.4 Undoing the bonnet release catch retaining bolts

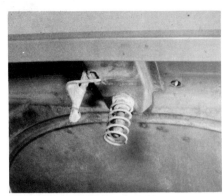

10.5 The bonnet pin is adjustable

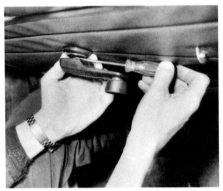

11.2 Remove the spring clip

11.3 Removing the door trim panel

12.2 Removing the door remote control

12.6a Inserting the key cylinder and ...

12.6b ... securing it with its retaining plate

12.8 Removing the door lock

from the window girder. Manoeuvre the mechanism out of an aperture in the door (photo).

3   Remove the window glass by lowering the front end first and then lifting the panel at an angle from the door recess (photo).

4   With the panel removed the weatherstrip can be renewed. Release the retaining clips with a screwdriver inserted in the window recess and then remove the weatherstrip (photos).

5   Refitting is the reverse of the removal procedure. Lightly grease the winder mechanism with a general purpose grease before refitting. Check the window winding operation before refitting the door trim panel.

14 Doors – removal and refitting

Front or rear doors

1   Both front and rear doors are removed by knocking out the hinge

pins. First open the door to be removed and support it underneath without actually lifting it.

2   A special tool is used by Peugeot to remove the hinge pins but with care these can be drifted out, after removing the plastic caps, using suitable drifts.

3   Drift out the roll pin from the check strap and remove the door.

4   Installation is a direct reversal of the removal procedure. Use new hinge pins if the old ones are worn and lubricate on assembly.

5   Close the door and check the lock function and door alignment. If necessary adjust the door lock striker plate.

Boot door

6   Disconnect the battery earth lead and then disconnect the electric cables feeding the rear number plate lamps. Remove the support strut lower attachment screw.

7   Undo the hinge bracket nuts and remove the boot door (photo).

8   Refitting is the reverse of the removal procedure. Lubricate the hinges and the latch mechanism on assembly. If necessary adjust the

13.2 The window winding mechanism removed from the door

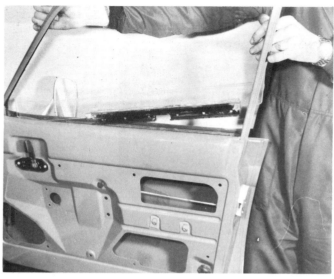

13.3 Removing the window glass from the door

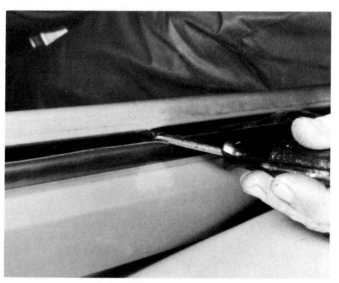

13.4a Disengage the spring clips ...

13.4b ... to remove the weatherstrip

14.7 One of the boot door hinges

14.9 The striker position is adjustable

14.11 A gas-filled strut balljoint on the tailgate. Note the electrical connector

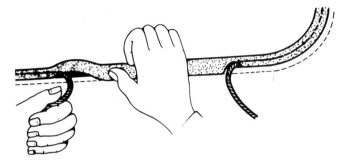

Fig. 11.4 Method of locating windscreen seal (Sec 15)

fit of the door by loosening the hinge bracket nuts slightly, repositioning the door, and then tightening the nuts.

9   The door lock striker has elongated bolt holes to permit adjustment if required to obtain correct fit on closing the door (photo).

Tailgate

10   Each of the two tailgate hinges is attached to the car body roof structure by two bolts in elongated holes. Unfortunately access to these bolts can only be gained by removing some of the roof lining. This is difficult to refit without leaving wrinkles so it is a job best done by someone with experience in fitting roof linings. Therefore, if your tailgate needs removal and refitting, see your Peugeot agent.

11   If the gas-filled struts need renewing, first open the tailgate and support it with a prop of wood to take the weight. The struts are attached by balljoints. To release a strut from its balljoints, lift the tabs on the strut. If a tab is stiff, gently lever it up with a small screwdriver. Disconnect the electrical connectors and remove the strut. It is better to remove and refit one strut before working on the other. Refitting is the reverse of the removal procedure (photo).

   Caution: Never attempt to repair or dismantle a gas-filled strut. Avoid scratching the piston rod as this will allow the gas to escape rendering the strut useless. Never pierce the cylinder as this could be dangerous. Any malfunction of a strut will necessitate renewal.

15   Windscreen – removal and refitting

1   If you are unlucky enough to have a windscreen shatter, or should you wish to renew your windscreen, fitting a replacement is one of the jobs which the average owner is advised to leave to a professional. For the owner who wishes to attempt the job himself the following instructions are given.

2   Cover the bonnet and front bodywork with a blanket to prevent damage and block the space between the top of the facia and the windscreen with rags to prevent chips entering the defrosting ducts. Remove the windscreen wiper blades and arms as described in Chapter 9.

3   If the screen is still in one piece, remove the metal insert in the rubber seal. Gently slide the clips which cover the joints at the bottom and top of the screen to one side, and carefully lift out the two halves of the insert taking care not to damage or distort them.

4   Put on a pair of lightweight shoes and get into a front seat. With a pad of soft, folded cloth between the soles of your shoes and the windscreen glass, put both feet on one corner of the screen and push firmly.

5   When the seal has freed itself from the body flange in that area work round the windscreen, leaving the bottom edge engaged. From outside the car remove the windscreen and seal together. Detach the seal from the old panel.

6   If the screen is shattered, knock out any remaining glass working from inside the car. Remove the metal insert from the seal as described in paragraph 3, and remove the seal from the body flange. Carefully clean out any glass fragments remaining in the seal.

7   If the screen had been leaking or if the seal is old, cracked or damaged, a new seal should be used on fitting the new screen. If the old seal is quite sound, make sure that no glass remains in it or this could lead to water leaks.

8   Fit the rubber seal to the new screen, making sure that it is well bedded down. Clean the body flange on the car ready for refitting the screen.

9   A length of smooth strong cord, about $\frac{1}{8}$ in (3 mm) thick is now required, long enough to wrap round the seal and overlap by at least a foot (300 mm). Fit the cord into the groove in the seal into which the body flange fits. Lubricate the body flange and its groove in the seal with, preferably, a rubber lubricant or a mixture of soap and water, don't use lubricating oil or grease which could affect the seal rubber.

10   With the help of an assistant, fit the lower edge of the glass and seal assembly onto the body flange and push it down so that it seats well home. Make sure that the glass is central and fit a bottom corner of the seal onto the body flange. Make sure that the ends of the cord are inside the car and, with an assistant pressing down firmly on the outside of the screen, pull on one end of the string to lift the seal progressively onto the body flange. Work round the screen until the seal is completely bedded on the body flange.

11   If required a layer of sealant should be applied between the seal and the body flange, inside and outside the car. Clean off any surplus before it hardens.

12   Refit the metal inserts in the rubber seal and position the clips to cover the joints. Clean the glass and refit the windscreen wiper blades and arms.

16   Tailgate window glass – removal and refitting

1   The procedure for renewing the window glass in the tailgate is broadly similar to that for renewing the windscreen as described in Section 15.

2   The principal difference concerns heated rear windows. Apart from the connections to the conductive struts it is most important to remember that the heater element bonded to the inside of the window is prone to damage. At all times great care must be observed to avoid damaging the element.

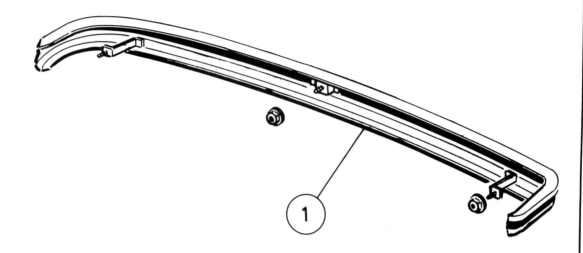

H11285

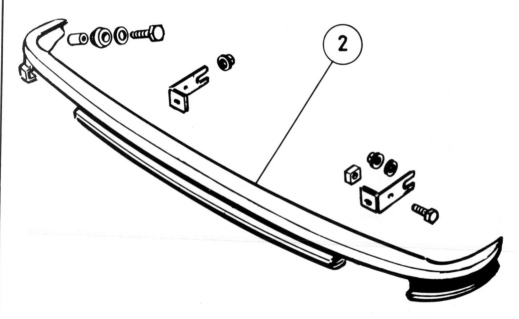

Fig. 11.5 The bumpers and attachment brackets

1   Rear bumper   2   Front bumper

Metric conversion tables

Inches	Decimals	Millimetres
1/64	0.015625	0.3969
1/32	0.03125	0.7937
3/64	0.046875	1.1906
1/16	0.0625	1.5875
5/64	0.078125	1.9844
3/32	0.09375	2.3812
7/64	0.109375	2.7781
1/8	0.125	3.1750
9/64	0.140625	3.5719
5/32	0.15625	3.9687
11/64	0.171875	4.3656
3/16	0.1875	4.7625
13/64	0.203125	5.1594
7/32	0.21875	5.5562
15/64	0.234375	5.9531
1/4	0.25	6.3500
17/64	0.265625	6.7469
9/32	0.28125	7.1437
19/64	0.296875	7.5406
5/16	0.3125	7.9375
21/64	0.328125	8.3344
11/32	0.34375	8.7312
23/64	0.359375	9.1281
3/8	0.375	9.5250
25/64	0.390625	9.9219
13/32	0.40625	10.3187
27/64	0.421875	10.7156
7/16	0.4375	11.1125
29/64	0.453125	11.5094
15/32	0.46875	11.9062
31/64	0.484375	12.3031
1/2	0.5	12.7000
33/64	0.515625	13.0969
17/32	0.53125	13.4937
35/64	0.546875	13.8906
9/16	0.5625	14.2875
37/64	0.578125	14.6844
19/32	0.59375	15.0812
39/64	0.609375	15.4781
5/8	0.625	15.8750
41/64	0.640625	16.2719
21/32	0.65625	16.6687
43/64	0.671875	17.0656
11/16	0.6875	17.4625
45/64	0.703125	17.8594
23/32	0.71875	18.2562
47/64	0.734375	18.6531
3/4	0.75	19.0500
49/64	0.765625	19.4469
25/32	0.78125	19.8437
51/64	0.796875	20.2406
13/16	0.8125	20.6375
53/64	0.828125	21.0344
27/32	0.84375	21.4312
55/64	0.859375	21.8281
7/8	0.875	22.2250
57/64	0.890625	22.6219
29/32	0.90625	23.0187
59/64	0.921875	23.4156
15/16	0.9375	23.8125
61/64	0.953125	24.2094
31/32	0.96875	24.6062
63/64	0.984375	25.0031

Millimetres to Inches

mm	Inches
0.01	0.00039
0.02	0.00079
0.03	0.00118
0.04	0.00157
0.05	0.00197
0.06	0.00236
0.07	0.00276
0.08	0.00315
0.09	0.00354
0.1	0.00394
0.2	0.00787
0.3	0.01181
0.4	0.01575
0.5	0.01969
0.6	0.02362
0.7	0.02756
0.8	0.03150
0.9	0.03543
1	0.03937
2	0.07874
3	0.11811
4	0.15748
5	0.19685
6	0.23622
7	0.27559
8	0.31496
9	0.35433
10	0.39370
11	0.43307
12	0.47244
13	0.51181
14	0.55118
15	0.59055
16	0.62992
17	0.66929
18	0.70866
19	0.74803
20	0.78740
21	0.82677
22	0.86614
23	0.09551
24	0.94488
25	0.98425
26	1.02362
27	1.06299
28	1.10236
29	1.14173
30	1.18110
31	1.22047
32	1.25984
33	1.29921
34	1.33858
35	1.37795
36	1.41732
37	1.4567
38	1.4961
39	1.5354
40	1.5748
41	1.6142
42	1.6535
43	1.6929
44	1.7323
45	1.7717

Inches to Millimetres

Inches	mm
0.001	0.0254
0.002	0.0508
0.003	0.0762
0.004	0.1016
0.005	0.1270
0.006	0.1524
0.007	0.1778
0.008	0.2032
0.009	0.2286
0.01	0.254
0.02	0.508
0.03	0.762
0.04	1.016
0.05	1.270
0.06	1.524
0.07	1.778
0.08	2.032
0.09	2.286
0.1	2.54
0.2	5.08
0.3	7.62
0.4	10.16
0.5	12.70
0.6	15.24
0.7	17.78
0.8	20.32
0.9	22.86
1	25.4
2	50.8
3	76.2
4	101.6
5	127.0
6	152.4
7	177.8
8	203.2
9	228.6
10	254.0
11	279.4
12	304.8
13	330.2
14	355.6
15	381.0
16	406.4
17	431.8
18	457.2
19	482.6
20	508.0
21	533.4
22	558.8
23	584.2
24	609.6
25	635.0
26	660.4
27	685.8
28	711.2
29	736.6
30	762.0
31	787.4
32	812.8
33	838.2
34	863.6
35	889.0
36	914.4

1   Imperial gallon = 8 Imp pints = 1.20 US gallons = 277.42 cu in = 4.54 litres

1   US gallon = 4 US quarts = 0.83 Imp gallon = 231 cu in = 3.78 litres

1   Litre = 0.21 Imp gallon = 0.26 US gallon = 61.02 cu in = 1000 cc

Miles to Kilometres		Kilometres to Miles	
1	1.61	1	0.62
2	3.22	2	1.24
3	4.83	3	1.86
4	6.44	4	2.49
5	8.05	5	3.11
6	9.66	6	3.73
7	11.27	7	4.35
8	12.88	8	4.97
9	14.48	9	5.59
10	16.09	10	6.21
20	32.19	20	12.43
30	48.28	30	18.64
40	64.37	40	24.85
50	80.47	50	31.07
60	96.56	60	37.28
70	112.65	70	43.50
80	128.75	80	49.71
90	144.84	90	55.92
100	160.93	100	62.14

lbf ft to kgf m		kgf m to lbf ft		lbf/in^2 to kgf/cm^2		kgf/cm^2 to lbf/in^2	
1	0.138	1	7.233	1	0.07	1	14.22
2	0.276	2	14.466	2	0.14	2	28.50
3	0.414	3	21.699	3	0.21	3	42.67
4	0.553	4	28.932	4	0.28	4	56.89
5	0.691	5	36.165	5	0.35	5	71.12
6	0.829	6	43.398	6	0.42	6	85.34
7	0.967	7	50.631	7	0.49	7	99.56
8	1.106	8	57.864	8	0.56	8	113.79
9	1.244	9	65.097	9	0.63	9	128.00
10	1.382	10	72.330	10	0.70	10	142.23
20	2.765	20	144.660	20	1.41	20	284.47
30	4.147	30	216.990	30	2.11	30	426.70

Index

Printed by
Haynes Publishing Group
Sparkford Yeovil Somerset
England